Isaac Gregory Smith

Faith and Philosoph

Essays

Isaac Gregory Smith

Faith and Philosoph
Essays

ISBN/EAN: 9783744652902

Printed in Europe, USA, Canada, Australia, Japan

Cover: Foto ©Thomas Meinert / pixelio.de

More available books at **www.hansebooks.com**

FAITH AND PHILOSOPHY.

ESSAYS ON SOME TENDENCIES OF THE DAY.

BY

THE REV. I. GREGORY SMITH, M.A.

RECTOR OF TEDSTONE DELAMERE
AND
LATE FELLOW OF BRASENOSE COLLEGE, OXFORD.

LONDON:

LONGMANS, GREEN, AND CO.

1867.

LONDON

PRINTED BY SPOTTISWOODE AND CO.

NEW-STREET SQUARE

PREFACE.

THESE ESSAYS will be found to bear more or less directly on questions which affect the present position and prospects of the Church of England very urgently. They are now revised and republished, having appeared in various forms during the last ten years, in the hope that they may contribute, however slightly, amid the peculiar dangers and difficulties of our day, to calm the fierceness of controversy, and to indicate a sure standing-ground for minds perplexed by the apparently, although not really, conflicting claims of Faith and Reason.

While these pages have been going through the press, the danger against which they are intended, so far as they can, to provide, has appeared more threateningly than before. The columns of the most influential of our daily papers, only too faithful a mirror generally of public opinion, have been filled lately with indiscriminate denunciations, not only of what is really 'un-English' in doctrine and ritual, but of things which are as thoroughly 'English' as our parliaments or our trial by jury. It is therefore more important than ever to draw the line plainly between what is indeed sanctioned by our English Prayer-book, and what is not; between, for instance, using private confession exceptionally, and requiring it ordinarily; between the ministerial and the judicial function in absolution; between the spiritual and the material presence in the sacraments. It is hoped that these pages may tend to establish this distinction; and to show that, notwithstanding the aberrations of scepticism on the one hand, and fanaticism on the other, there is a deep and essential harmony between the English Church and the English nation.

Tedstone Delamere:
Dec. 20, 1866.

CONTENTS.

FAITH AND PHILOSOPHY.

ON MODERN SCEPTICISM AND SOME OF ITS FALLACIES.

'THE truth of the Gospel is more widely doubted in Europe than at any time since the conversion of Constantine.' A statement like this claims attention, especially if it come, not from an avowed assailant, but from an apparently friendly quarter; it is a note of warning not to be disregarded by those whose post exposes them to the first shock of the assaults of infidelity. It is their duty patiently to take into account the obstacles which lie in the way of a right belief, and diligently to remove them by solving, to the best of their power, the perplexities of the age reasonably and with candour.

Nor is the statement devoid of truth. No one conversant even slightly with the present literature of England or of Europe can fail to be aware how largely it is imbued with a spirit of scepticism. The counter-statement is indeed equally true; or, rather, the half-truth requires to be complemented from

B

another point of view. Never since the days of
Constantine was the Christian faith held with a more
intelligent appreciation, with a more matured and deliberate conviction; for doubt is the probation of belief.
Still it remains unquestionable, that Christianity is
now undergoing a keener trial than any recorded in
its history, a strain on its powers of endurance far
more severe than ever it experienced from the perse-
cutions of Roman emperors, or even from the subtle
questionings of Eastern theosophics. The fact in itself
is nothing to excite surprise. Those who observe the
connection of cause and effect are prepared to see, as
the inevitable consequence of advancing civilisation,
less of ready acquiescence in received truths, more of
inquisitive research into the reasons for believing.
The change is in part intellectual, a result of the advance of inductive knowledge, by which a habit is
engendered of appealing from the decisions of the past
even in matters which are beyond the cognisance of
induction; in part moral (and in that respect a
change for the worse), a result of the self-indulgence
and self-confidence which are fostered by civilisation,
and which alike shrink from the stern denial of self
exacted by the doctrines of the Cross. Such a state
of things is accepted by the devout Christian as one
of the successive dispensations of Providence, slowly
sifting and perfecting the world for the coming of its
Lord; and he recognises the fulfilment of a Divine
promise in the intenser conflict between good and
evil which marks the close of the era.

The emphatic words which have been quoted on

the prevalence of scepticism occur in an Essay* which has attracted general notice, not only by its ability, but as indicating the tendencies of thought in this day. Certain difficulties are alleged in the received account of the origin of the three first Gospels; and an answer is imperatively demanded on behalf of the laity from those whose province is the study of theology. The object of these pages is, not so much to attempt an answer in detail to the objections which are raised as to show that, whether valid or not, they are not really of such moment as may appear at first sight. A complete investigation of these and similar points may well be left for more elaborate treatises. Meanwhile it may be of service to the cause of truth to show that even on the lowest ground, and after conceding for the sake of the argument far more than need fairly be conceded, the faith of the Christian Church stands unimpaired, unshaken, and unaffected by the controversy.

In these days every thinking person, whether among the laity or clergy, is irresistibly forced to ask himself, ' *Why* do I believe ? ' It is of the utmost importance that this question be answered rightly. Those who see clearly what the foundation of their Christian faith really is, and how indissolubly the whole superstructure, from base to pinnacle, coheres together, will be comparatively indifferent to controversies, whether about the Old or even the New Testament, which complicate the question, but are really

---

* Criticism and the Gospel Narrative; *Fraser's Magazine*, Jan. 1864.

extraneous to it. The prayer of Ajax for light which may dispel the rolling clouds of scepticism is felt, if not uttered, by many hearts. There would not be so many who believe in Christianity with only a timid, partial, dubious belief, or who, as Carlyle has expressed it, 'only believe that they believe'—not so many who are panic-stricken whenever a new theory of scepticism starts into existence, if the great essentials of the faith were grasped more firmly. There would be no need of new 'Declarations of Faith,' nor of new definitions of mysteries, if the ancient Creeds were appreciated as they ought to be. Those who are content to hold fast the truth as it comes from Christ and His Apostles, preserved in the formularies of the Church Catholic, not as fossil-remains in a state of petrifaction, but in all the freshness of vitality, need not be alarmed, though the waves of controversy surge high round them, for they stand on a rock, 'and that rock is Christ.' In the great fact of the Incarnation, involving as it does the other articles of the Creed, they have a sure foundation, which cannot be moved, under their feet, even though the ground on every side round them heave and quake with convulsive throes.

Before considering the objections which 'modern criticism' arrays against the received authorship of the synoptical Gospels, it is important to note the influence of ideas, now widely prevalent, which prejudice the mind against an impartial hearing of the case on its own merits. Faith and Reason are spoken of, not for the first time, as in direct if not violent opposition, as antagonistic to each other. They are opposed not only as abstract qualities, but practically, as respectively characterising separate classes of persons. By a broad and arbitrary line of demarcation some periods in history are distinguished as 'ages of faith;' while our own, it is implied, is, as the infidels of the last century called it, the ' age of reason.' Similarly, while persons of strong intellect are grouped together on the side of reason, weaker or less mature minds, as those of women and children, are relegated to that of faith. Accordingly, a presumption is raised that in this scientific age reason will demolish what faith has constructed in the past.

There is a great fallacy, and more than one, in such a mode of reasoning. Reason and faith are indeed distinct actions of the mind; but, far from being contradictory, they are invariably co-existent and inseparably connected. The act of assent, by which the mind embraces any statement proposed for its acceptance, is indeed posterior in time to the act of reasoning; but it necessarily presupposes the preliminary process to have been performed, more or less correctly. Belief, it matters not whether of spiritual mysteries or of the most trivial matters in daily life, there cannot be, except in consequence of reasons sufficient to approve themselves, whether rightly or not, to the judgment which pronounces on them. These reasons may be derived from many sources; from the senses, from intuition, from authority; or from more than one of these sources: the chain of argument which connects the first and last link in the process may be concise or lengthy, direct or tortuous, compactly welded or insecure and inconsecutive, logically sound or full of flaws; but some reasons for belief, and those of sufficient weight to turn the scale of judgment, there are and must be in every instance. In spiritual matters the faith of St. Paul or of Pascal is as truly belief as that of the child; it rests on a similar foundation, on reasonings deeper and wider, but not more conclusive to the person concerned. The belief of Faraday and of a ploughboy in anything which belongs to the material world is the same act of assent in both, and in both depends on a process of reasoning, although that process may be far more scientific in the one case than in the other. This co-operation of reason and faith is not only invariable, but incessant and continual: for belief is the attitude into which the mind falls naturally, the only position in which it can be at rest. Disbelief is in reality an act of belief; for it accepts the direct negative of the statement proposed. Even that apparent suspension of judgment which neither affirms nor denies, is a form of belief; for it accepts, as an intermediate proposition, the possibility of either affirming or denying. The infidel believes; for of two propositions he embraces that which asserts that certain doctrines are false. Even the Pyrrhonist believes; for he holds that nothing is credible. The opposition, therefore, is in reality not between belief and unbelief, but between belief and misbelief; not between faith and reason, but between those processes, whether true or false, of the reason, by which the mind makes its decision. Supposing the reasoning faculties to be sound, and to have all necessary information at command, they attain the truth with the regularity of a machine; unless, as happens too often, there be some extraneous hindrance, some interference from the emotive element in human nature, perverting the judgment. All error is the growth either of imperfect knowledge, of imperfect ratiocination, or of some obliquity in the moral nature. Belief will be right or wrong, just as the reasonings on which it depends are good or bad; but, plainly, far from being in any case incompatible with reason, it is, not the antithesis of reason, but its necessary sequence and result.

There is no force at all, therefore, in this imaginary distinction between an age of faith and an age of reason; nor in the consequent assumption that the progress of time is likely to reverse the judgment of former ages, unless it can be shown that time has brought an accession of knowledge bearing on the points in question, or has considerably improved the mental faculties, or has removed some moral hindrances which formerly perverted the judgment. When we speak of some persons as being more sceptical than others, we mean either that their reasoning faculties, being more developed, require naturally to be more fully enlightened before being convinced, or, as is only too often the case, that excessive self-confidence indisposing them to receive the testimony of others, or some other moral infirmity, revolting from the truth proposed, makes them unwilling to believe. In the same way, one century may be more credulous than another, either from its facilities for reasoning being more limited, or from a moral predisposition towards believing any particular doctrines; but not otherwise. When it is argued that the nineteenth century, because it is more scientific, is therefore likely to cancel and supersede the faith of the preceding eighteen centuries, it must be shown that in those days there was either an irrational eagerness to embrace the doctrines of Christianity or an inadequacy of information on the subject; for it cannot be seriously maintained that, apart from the action of these causes, there is any appreciable disparity in the reasoning powers of this and those generations.

Now it is inconceivable, that in any age there should be a proclivity or predilection, in opposition to the dictates of reason, towards doctrines so self-renouncing as those of Christianity. To affirm this of a religion the very essence of which is the complete and continual sacrifice of self, is too paradoxical to require an answer. Nor can it be said that the advance of scientific knowledge affects the question. For it is not *in pari materia*: it is chiefly if not solely in that department of knowledge which, though apt to arrogate to itself exclusively and most unwarrantably the name of 'science,' is bounded by the hard confines of the material world; it is only in knowledge which can be enlarged and corrected by induction, and in which consequently the widened observation and additional experience of a later century count for everything. But Christianity is no system of geology or of chemistry; its tenets are undisturbed by their

discoveries. In the regions of immaterial science—
in ethic, for instance, or metaphysic—it is not so evident that any real progress has been made, except
indeed such as may be indirectly traced to Christianity
itself. But what if there has been progress here also?
Christianity was not given as a philosophical theory
on the soul or on virtue, but for the practical guidance
of life. As the revelation of the true relations, in-
augurated by itself, between man and the Deity, it is
unaffected by the onward march of time. It is vain
to argue, that because certain mediæval superstitions
have crumbled into nothing at the touch of modern
science, therefore the work of destruction will be
carried further. Physical causes may be brought to
light, sufficient in themselves to account for this or
that circumstance which was reputed miraculous in
the Middle Ages; but this is not to prove an universal
negative on the subject of miracles. Nor can any
conceivable advance of science account for the transcendent truths of a moral and spiritual nature, which
are no excrescence to be pared away by a touch of
the knife, but the very life of Christianity. Let it be
granted, for the argument's sake, that modern geology, precarious, and fluctuating as are its guesses at
present, may some day disprove conclusively the
Mosaic account of creation; or, that minute researches into the Judaical history may detect undeniable inaccuracies there; or, that 'modern criticism'
applied to the Gospels may refute the traditionary
account of their authorship; or, that modern science,
by elucidating the apparently uniform action of the

laws which regulate the universe, may place miracles in a new light—for revelation does not vouchsafe any theory of the *modus operandi*—manifesting them to be in harmonious accordance with the laws* of the Divine economy, rather than an arbitrary violation of them; still, amid all these and other vicissitudes of thought, the articles of the Christian faith, based as they are on the Word and Person of Christ, as of one proved by His life and death to be the Son of God, would remain identically the same as before. The vaunted pretensions of progress, if closely scrutinised, dwindle into insignificance. They amount, in fact, to scarcely more than this, that, as time goes on, a few phenomena relating to the physical conditions, past and present, of man's being are rescued here and there from the vast surrounding darkness, as children snatch a few shells and stones from the wave as it recedes from the shore; while on the frail basis of these scanty phenomena new theories are reared, too often, like the sand castles of the little architects, only to be swept away by the next wave as it rushes in. At all events, if it is in the knowledge of the *material* universe that progress has been made, there is no reason in the assumption that Christianity is in danger of being confuted, or even modified, by the discoveries of modern science.

History abounds with illustrations of this great truth, often strangely overlooked, that progress of a

* Some confusion arises in the use of the terms 'natural' and 'material.' That which is a violation of a *material* law may be in perfect accordance with a law of nature in the true sense of that term.

moral and spiritual kind is not of necessity coordinate with progress in material knowledge, nor even with that enhanced subtlety of the intellect which accompanies material civilisation. Among the nations before the Christian era, Egypt, China, India, were eminent in the cultivation of material arts and sciences, but not proportionately in their ideas of God and morality. Their debasing superstitions show that in these they were far surpassed by the comparatively inartistic and unscientific tribes of the Hebrews. The Greeks of the day of Pericles were far more advanced than their ruder forefathers in material refinement and intellectual culture; but their gross and puerile mythology is a declension from that nobler faith, the grand outlines of which loom dimly, because fast fading away, through the tragedies of Æschylus. In the history of the world, as in the growth of each individual mind, progress is but another word for increased experience, and is therefore of necessity confined to those subjects our knowledge of which depends on our own experience or that of others.

The testimony, therefore, of Christendom during eighteen centuries, or in other words, of those nations which have proved themselves in moral qualities the foremost in the world during that period, cannot be set aside as of little value among the evidences of Christianity; for the inferiority of those centuries in the inductive sciences cannot invalidate their testimony on other and higher subjects. Their testimony is valuable also as showing, in point of fact, what are,

and what are not, the doctrines historically transmitted as the Christian faith.

But it is asserted, that the ' Anglican' Communion (as it is the somewhat pedantic fashion to call
it) cannot legitimately make use of this argument;
that, owing to the dissensions and disruptions of
Christendom, it does not, and cannot fairly, reason
from authority in calling on its members to believe.
Now it is true, of course, that the English Church
does not propound authority as the ultimate reason for
belief; it cannot say, as if claiming infallibility, that
this or that doctrine must be taken for granted
simply on the authority of the Church.   But beyond
this the assertion has no meaning.   So far as the
doctrines of the English Church are common to all
Christian communities—and in this point of view
the concurring testimony even of those communities
which have separated themselves from the Church
Catholic is of weight—this unanimous consent is a
valid argument.   So far as the doctrines are distinctively peculiar to itself, there is the appeal to the
earliest Christian centuries; and on no other ground
than this can answer be made adequately to those who
dissent from these doctrines on either side.   That
what is new, in spiritual matters, is not likely to be
true, and that the old ways are best, are as much
axioms of the English Church now as before the sixteenth century, and may be used now with more
consistency.   The very instance quoted* to the con-

---

* Criticism, &c. ; *Fraser's Magazine,* Jan. 1864.

trary is an instance to this effect. The doctrine of a material change in the consecrated elements is rejected, because it is believed to be an innovation on the faith transmitted from Apostolic times. This is invariably the test which the English Church applies to any doctrine, its guiding principle in accepting or disallowing it. The great characteristic of the English Prayer-book is, that it is essentially derived from the ancient symbols and formularies of the Church. There are other and deeper reasons for believing in Christianity, reasons which underlie this argument from authority, that is, from the testimony of former generations. But it is this argument which for all persons presents itself to the mind first in order of time; for the poor and unlearned this is the only argument within reach, except that greatest of all arguments which rises from the practical assent of the conscience presiding in every breast. As determining historically what the Christian faith really was in apostolic and sub-apostolic times, this argument is, so far as it can be ascertained, quite conclusive. In both senses, whether as historical evidence to prove what are really the doctrines of Christianity, or as one of the cumulative evidences for the truth, the Church of England, notwithstanding her isolated position, can fairly use it; for on the cardinal points of the faith the appeal is made to the consent of the Christian world, on points in dispute to that of Christian antiquity. In neither sense is the force of the argument from authority in danger of being weakened by modern discoveries.

It is characteristic of the exaggerated importance attached to the crude theorizings of modern scepticism, that the effect produced through Europe by M. Renan has been compared to the electric shock of Luther's writings in the sixteenth century. Certainly Luther's fellow-countrymen would not admit the comparison. The rationalists of Germany repudiate M. Renan's rhapsodies. Even in Paris, where the social atmosphere is such as to predispose men to welcome an attack on Christianity under the guise of a sentimental enthusiasm, and where a semblance of logical precision with symmetry of method and elegance of style go far to outweigh deeper considerations, even in Paris it may safely be predicted that his influence is only transient. His speculations are not likely to gain even a momentary ascendancy where, as in England, there is an instinctive repugnance to unreality in every shape.

Such theories as those of Strauss and Renan carry in themselves their own refutation. They contain an admission of all that the advocate of Christianity need require as the postulates of his belief. The conclusions at which the sceptic arrives are often strangely inconsistent with the premisses which he cannot altogether exclude from his scheme. There these admissions remain, an unacknowledged and unintentional evidence for the very truths against which he is contending. Thus when he allows, as M. Renan does, the authenticity, even in the barest and most general sense, of the narrative comprised in the Gospels, he encounters an insuperable difficulty. He

cannot explain that narrative in any intelligible manner—except on the supposition which is the basis of
the Christian faith—without either an absolute denial,
or a palpable distortion equivalent to denial, not of
particular details here and there, but of all which is
distinctive in the narrative, of that which pervades it
from beginning to end, of that which alone gives life
and coherence to its parts. 'L'Evangile selon Renan,'
as it has been termed, differs from the Gospel of the
New Testament, not in this or that particular, but
throughout, in substance, in character, in essence.
It is only necessary to place the two narratives side
by side: the unlikeness is self-evident.

For the Christ of this neology is not in any true
sense the Christ of the Gospels. It is a being different not in degree but in kind. The Christ of
these new evangelists is a man, gifted indeed in
greater or less measure with qualities that win affection and respect, but with more or less of alloy in
His composition; at the best only a man. The Christ
of the Gospels is presented to us as of more than
human excellence, as the incarnation of Deity. On
the theories of Strauss and Renan it is simply impossible to account for the idea of Christ which con-
fronts us in every page of the Gospels, as of a Person
divine though wearing the form and nature of men.
What has been often said as to the impossibility of
the character of Christ having been a mere invention
of any human imagination, is true of that character
as we find it in the Gospels, and as we do not find it
in these humanising versions of them. 'L'inventeur

en serait plus étonnant que le héros.' For the Christ pourtrayed in the Gospels is a sinless being without moral frailty or infirmity, holy and wise in a super-human degree. The difference between Christ so depicted and others, the best and wisest of the human race, is not the difference between persons more or less faulty, not between good men and one who is better, but between One who is without any the least moral blemish and others who are all more or less imperfect. For, though described in the Gospels as sharing in all the ordinary physical conditions of man's nature, Christ is there without taint or speck of moral evil. His teaching and His life both bear this impression of divinity. His teaching is marked by a sublimity of moral and spiritual wisdom which far transcends the highest attainments of the Jewish or Gentile world; by precepts and doctrines hitherto unexpressed, but recognised at once, when uttered, by their innate sovereignty over the conscience; by great truths, not dimly adumbrated as by the lips of Jewish seers, nor evolved to a hesitating and faltering conclusion by a laborious process of guesses and sur-mises as in the Platonic Dialogues, but enounced clearly and ' with authority,' in all the fulness of in-tuition, in a tone and with a manner which, while thrilling the depths of the heart, is yet majestically calm and composed, and perfectly free from superficial excitement. No wonder that those who heard Him said that ' He spake as never man spake.' And of whom else could it be said without reserve, ' He hath done *all* things well ?' What other life has ever been marked in its every aspect, in each word and deed, without even a momentary shadow of inconsistency, by that which is the principle of moral excellence, pure and unalloyed unselfishness, manifested in the unresting activity of its benevolence, in its entire re-signation under suffering, in its complete devotion of self in order to do good to others and to do the will of Heaven? What other life in respect of truth and purity will bear a close and microscopic inspection but this? What other is marked by a width of sympathy co-extensive with the whole human family, yet tenderly discriminating for each individual; by a simplicity and gracious dignity of demeanour (very unlike the undignified grotesqueness of the great moralist of Athens) never lost for a moment, by an unerring insight into the hearts of men, by the unva-rying manifestation of an unclouded conscience, and of the most intimate communion with His heavenly Father—in short, by qualities not one of which in anything like perfection can be descried even singly in the recorded life of any saint, hero, or philosopher, but which are all in their combined perfections to be seen in Him?* It cannot be disputed that this, and far more than this, is the representation of Christ in the Gospel; nor that the Christ of neologians is some-thing very far short of this. Such a development of human nature as this, and in the person of a poor Galilean of the age in which Christ lived, is super-human and divine.

* The argument for the divinity of Christ from His character is well enforced at length in 'The Christ of History,' by J. Young, LL.D. (Allan.)

Whence then has this conception of Christ, this image of perfect humanity, found its way into the Gospels, except from reality ? That the followers of Christ should have been led, even by the wildest fanaticism or by the most shameless audacity of imposture, to assign divine attributes at all to such a person as He was according to the *Vie de Jésus,* is highly improbable. But it is simply impossible that they should have been able to imagine or invent a character so ineffably worthy of love and reverence, so far transcending the highest examples to be found in history or fiction. The result of all these futile and abortive attempts to eliminate the divine element from the person of Christ is to leave, on the one hand, as historical, a narrative inconsistent with itself, unmeaning, and palpably unreal; and, on the other hand, a faultless character—which appeals to all that is good in man's nature more persuasively and commandingly than the noblest utterances of Greek philosophy—as the invention either of the Evangelists, whose names the Gospels bear, or of others in a literary point of view as obscure as they. These neological theories confute themselves. It is inexplicable that one, who lived and died a Galilean peasant, should have been even what they allow Him to have been, unless He were indeed something far greater. It is inexplicable, again, that the divine features, which they expunge from His life, should ever have been imputed to any one, and, most of all, to one in those circumstances, unless they actually existed. The evangelic narrative, with the whole superstructure of the Christian faith, rests on the foundation of truth, purity, and love; or, in other words, on the perfect wisdom and goodness embodied in the person of Jesus Christ.

Inadequately as they may have been expressed, these considerations may serve to show that the pretensions of scepticism are self-confuted, and that the believer in Christianity, descending from the vantage-ground of his high position, may meet and repel the adversaries of his faith even on the open plain. If only the veracity of the gospel-narrative is allowed in the roughest and most general sense, the great central truth of the incarnation, with all its momentous corollaries, follows as a consequence which cannot be denied. Christianity rests on foundations so deep and wide, so firmly laid in human nature, that it cannot be shaken by the passing gusts of controversy and criticism. Objections therefore, whether good or bad, against the reputed authorship of the Gospels, are comparatively of slight importance.

These objections, in the form under which they are now presented,* may be stated in few words. It is argued, both on external and internal grounds, that the three synoptic Gospels—for the authorship of St. John's Gospel is not contested—instead of being independent narratives by the writers whose names they bear, were compilations made from one source. The idea of anything like collusion or cooperation on the part of the Evangelists is discarded as untenable, as disproved not only by the amount of difference

* Criticism, &c.; *Fraser's Magazine,* Jan. 1864.

in their respective narratives, but also by the absence of any reference in one to another, and by the unquestionable proofs of their sincerity and good faith. It is suggested, that the source from which the main portion of each Gospel is taken was a narrative drawn up by the Apostles, immediately after the commencement of their mission; while, whatever is peculiar to any one of the three Gospels was added subsequently by other persons. Clearly there is nothing here, whatever may be the tendency of other theories on the subject, that militates against the historic accuracy of the evangelic narrative, even in its details. For, as is not unreasonably urged, if the several narratives can be traced substantially to those who were the immediate followers of Christ, the force of that testimony, as ' the collective view of the Apostles,' is in some respects stronger than it would be otherwise. That portion of the narratives which would be referred on this supposition to the Apostles themselves would, together with St. John's Gospel, be more than enough to establish the main points in the life of the Saviour. Nor can the existence of those other passages, which would not be comprised under this head, be reasonably explained on this theory, except as originating from traditions oral or written in the Church. When it is borne in mind how watchfully the Church of those days treasured the deposit of the faith, and how admirably the preservation and transmission of its records, written or unwritten, was secured by the compact organisation of its framework in the midst of an alien world, and by the continual intercommunication of its members, this in itself obviously forms a strong guarantee of truth. On the whole it may fairly be assumed, *in limine*, that there is nothing in such a theory as this, whether plausible or not, which of necessity conflicts with the credibility of the Gospels. It may be worth while, however, while leaving it to receive a more thorough examination elsewhere, to consider now, as briefly as possible, some of the most salient points in the arguments which are brought in support of it.

What, then, are the arguments from internal evidence ? ' The resemblance,' we are told, of the three Gospels, ' is too peculiar to be the work of accident, and impossible to reconcile with the fact that the writers were independent of each other.' This is a strong statement. How far is it warranted by facts? That the same events, for the most part, even out of the eventful abundance of the life of Christ, should be selected by three independent writers, is not extraordinary. Obviously, the most remarkable incidents would be selected by all alike, unless when the interference of some special purpose led the writer to make his selection on some other principle. More stress is laid on the same words being used. But the fact itself is questionable. It would be more correct to say, that while there are some undeniable coincidences, there are at the same time delicate variations of expression and shades of discrepancy in the wording, precisely such as would be expected in independent narratives of the same thing. Take, for example, the incident of the Rich young man, contained in all the synoptic Gospels. Neither in its attendant circumstances nor in the words narrated is there anything that approaches to exact verbal coincidence. On the contrary, the traces of difference in the language, though minute, are perceptible in almost every verse. They are enough to stamp the narratives, however striking their similarity may be, as by no means identical. An amount of similarity which does not exceed these limits is certainly not irreconcileable with the independence of the several writers.

The illustrations which are used to show the improbability of verbal uniformity are very fallacious. The cases are not really parallel. The correspondents of a newspaper, when describing a battle in America, are engaged on a subject of a very complex kind, presenting many sides to the observer, and by its breadth and variety affording scope for almost endless diversity of treatment. It would indeed be marvellous if several persons describing it should exhibit a close coincidence in their language. But in the description of a few remarkable incidents, not like a battle covering a wide extent of ground, but each naturally compressed into a few words, the marvel would be if we did not find this coincidence. Where the actors in the scene, as well as the points of the incident, are few, there is less room for divergence from that one type of narration which naturally occurs as ready at hand to all the writers alike. There is, for instance, far less resemblance between two canvases representing the same battle-field than between two statues of the same person; less resemblance between two histories of the same nation than between two biographies of the same individual.

There may appear at first sight a more insurmountable difficulty in these coincidences, when they are found in the recital of the parables and discourses. How, it is asked, can words spoken originally in Syriac have fallen, under the hands of independent translators, into modes of expression which are so nearly the same? Would this be likely to happen if several reporters were translating into English the speeches of a Prussian general? But here, again, the very fact on which the argument turns cannot pass unquestioned. A close and critical inspection of the discourses recorded by the several Evangelists brings into light faint traces of difference, to a careless eye imperceptible, and yet not without significance. But there is, besides, a broad fallacy underlying the argument throughout, which betrays itself conspicuously in this illustration borrowed from modern usages. The cases, again, are not parallel. In that of the Evangelists causes were at work, naturally leading to uniformity of language, which are absent in the other instance. Writings of the age and country to which the Gospels belong cannot be measured by a standard so disproportionate as that of modern Europe. For a nation which is without the many facilities, mechanical and other, of modern literature for multiplying the modifications of language, a nation which naturally and habitually regards things simply and objectively as matters of fact, and without all the intricacies of thought which attend their subjective aspect, a nation which transmits its information for the most part by memory, is very apt to repeat and reproduce, like a child, set forms of speech.   Eastern nations are peculiarly retentive of whatever is customary and conventional.   It must be remembered also that Jews, translating from the language of their country into one with which they were less familiar, would not be likely to have at their disposal, nor to use if they had, much variety in their choice of phrases.   Nor would the sayings which they had to translate, couched as these were in an unrivalled simplicity of diction, require, nor suggest, nor even admit of any such amplification.   When everything has been taken into account, the verbal coincidences, even in the discourses, might well have been closer than they are, without being incompatible with the independence of the several Gospels.

An argument for the authorship of the third Gospel has usually been drawn from the apparent identity of the writer of St. Luke's Gospel and the writer of the Acts of the Apostles.   In reply to this it is objected, that probably only the latter part of the Acts was written by the companion of St. Paul, and that consequently the link is wanting which connects St. Luke, the companion of the Apostle's journeyings, with the writer who in the beginning of the Acts makes reference to his previously written Gospel, and addresses himself, as before, to Theophilus.   But what are the evidences to support this theory ?   What reasons are there for supposing that the latter part of the Acts was not written by the same person as the earlier chapters? True, that the book is in some degree episodical in its composition—that the first mention of the writer as actually accompanying St. Paul is abruptly introduced and without comment; but can any certain, or even probable, conclusion be drawn from such premisses as these? The record, or 'memoir,' as it has been aptly termed, of the chief events in the fortunes of the early Church, could hardly be other than episodical, by the very exigencies of the case. As to the manner in which the presence of the writer, as accompanying the Apostle, is indicated for the first time, the sweeping assertion cannot easily be substantiated ' that no other instance in literature occurs of a change in person introduced abruptly without explanation.' Even in the letters and journals of modern days instances might be found of the writer passing from scenes in which he took no part to those in which he was actually present, without any formal introduction of himself, especially if he had no wish to thrust himself prominently into the foreground of his story. But it is a still more hasty assumption to apply such a canon, dogmatically and peremptorily, to the Acts, without regard to the difference between that and more formal and elaborate narratives. And what if Theophilus has not been mentioned in the extant Epistles of St. Paul? It cannot seriously be maintained that every one known to St. Luke, or even that every person of note among his acquaintance, must have been mentioned by name in the Apostolic greetings. Stronger reasonings than these are needed to overthrow the traditionary argument of the identity of St. Luke, the companion of St. Paul, with the writer both of the Acts and of the third Gospel.

Nor is the reasoning from external evidences more convincing. That the citations extant in the Apostolic Fathers are not in the very words of any one Gospel in particular, and that we find words of Christ quoted by them (as by St. Paul) which are not in any of the Gospels, can only show, not of necessity that they quoted from any archetypal Gospel, but, more probably, that they quoted from recollection of several narratives which were not precisely the same; and that the sayings of Christ were, as we know, far more than could be included in any narrative. Nor, even if it be granted that we have not any extant reference to the four Gospels by name* before the close of the second century, would that be enough to prove that there are no such references in writings of an older date now lost, still less that the four Gospels were not previously in existence, though not cited specifically and by name. At most it is but a presumption, and not a very cogent one. On the other hand, the advocates of this theory have to explain the disappearance of their ' original Gospel,' a document which, if ever existent, would have been highly valued in the Church, and guarded accordingly.

Above all, it must be remembered that the 'burden of proving' lies on those who dispute the received and traditionary account of the authorship of the

---

* But see Westcott ('Canon of New Testament,' pp. 79, 80, 238), who quotes earlier references.

Gospels. A tradition which, to say the least, can be traced to a date within a century of the death of the last of the Apostles, and which, as it cannot fairly be regarded as a mere figment of that date, may claim a higher antiquity—such a tradition, transmitted under circumstances peculiarly favourable to its integrity, is not lightly to be cast aside. Not that other evidences are wanting. The distinctive character which stands out in each Gospel, and naturally connects it with what is known of its reputed author, as well as the great though not insuperable difficulty in harmonising the several narratives, in which, if they were different versions of one original, a general uniformity of outline might be anticipated, are arguments for the independence of the Gospels which cannot easily be controverted. The dreams and chimeras of modern theorisers fade into nothing when confronted with fact.

But the object of these pages is not to attempt an adequate examination of this or any other theory of modern criticism, but rather to show that the faith of the Christian Church is in no danger of being compromised by them. When the clergy of the Church of England are challenged to answer such objections, it is a sufficient answer, for those who have not the opportunity of investigating them fully, that they do not affect the moral certainty of a single article in the Creeds. Were this theory, which has been cursorily noticed as a sample of the many such products of a perverted and fruitless ingenuity which spring up every day on the other side of the German Ocean,

—this theory of the three first Gospels being in part copies from one original, in part the work of the second century, demonstrated to a certainty instead of being a not very plausible suggestion, it could make no difference in the view which a sensible and impartial mind would still take of the Gospels, even in their minuter details. For, as has been shown, there would be, on that hypothesis, the authority of the Apostles themselves for all the more fundamental parts, while the other parts would rest on the authority of the Church in its earliest days as a guarantee of their historical accuracy.

A similar answer may and must be made to other more destructive theories which, hydra-like, rear their heads against the faith. If there is any force in what has been urged as to the moral evidences of Christianity, the Creeds of the Church are not imperilled by any possible result of modern criticism, because they rest on a foundation which is beyond the reach of such speculations. In the essay to which reference has already been made it is well said, 'that the sources of Christianity, as the roots of almost all living things'—certainly of all that is greatest and most enduring—'are buried in obscurity.' Nor is it hard to see how wisely it is ordained that this absence of demonstrative certainty should attend researches into the origin of the oldest documents of the Church. Where mathematical certainty can be attained, there is no room for the proper exercise of faith. By this absence of certainty the mind, providentially deterred from idolatry of the written Word, is led to seek through and beyond the medium of the writings in which it is pourtrayed for that which is the very keystone of the arch, as well as the sole object of adoration, the Person of the Incarnate Deity. There is too often a propensity to look for an elaborate and categorical exposition of revelation in the sacred Scriptures, such as we have no warrant to expect vouchsafed to us there; in forgetfulness of the fact, that the books of which the holy volume is composed were originally addressed, not to an unenlightened and heathen world, but to persons trained in the faith by the instruction of living teachers; in forgetfulness of the fact, that the words and works of Him who is the truth, communicated through His Apostles to the Church, and thus transmitted by the agency of the Holy Spirit, not in one mode only, but in many, to latest generations, are the true groundwork of revelation.

The same absence of demonstrable certainty in the spiritual world meets the inquirer in every direction. The vain craving for an infallibility which can never be attained, and which, if attainable, would destroy the very conditions under which alone faith can grow to its full stature, has been the occasion again and again, even in highly-gifted minds, as our own age can lamentably testify, of prostrate superstition or of reckless infidelity. Men are apt to forget that the evidences of the Christian faith are cumulative and mutually corroboratory, rather than singly and separately conclusive. When arguments are drawn from the actual results of Christianity in the world for the

divine nature of its doctrines, and, again, from the
sublimity of its doctrines to show that its mission was
of a kind to elevate and purify, this is no arguing in
a circle; for either premiss is evident in itself, not
based upon the other, though acquiring a corrobora-
tive force from it.   When once the credibility of
Christianity is ascertained, so far as can be in the
region of undemonstrable truth, from that moment
whatever is mysterious in its tenets is accepted on
that authority, and cannot be subjected to the inqui-
sition of the understanding, because it transcends the
processes of that faculty.   In the days of the Schoolmen the danger lay in the undue application of the
deductive process; in our day it lies rather in the
improper use of the inductive process in matters
beyond its cognizance.   The ultimate foundation on
which Christianity rests is, it must be repeated, its
exquisite harmony with the moral sense and the perfect satisfaction, elsewhere impossible, which the
highest aspirations of human nature find in the Person of the Incarnate Deity, in that 'beauty of holiness' without blemish which wins their homage irresistibly.   Christian faith is the entire surrender of the
soul to that one object which can claim its devotion
worthily.   Thus faith and obedience are one.   And
in this belief in the Person of Christ are involved all
other articles of the Christian faith, since we have the
historic testimony of the Church that through His
Apostles they emanate from Him.

    To question the authority of this moral sense by
pointing to the different estimates in different

countries of what is morally good, is simply to say that moral truth is not mathematical. With those exceptional minds who raise such a cavil there is an end of argument, for no arguments can supply them with that community of feeling, not with the Christian world only, but with the most enlightened heathens, in which they own themselves deficient. They may make their counter-appeal to the savages of Africa, to the unchristianised hordes of Asia, or even to communities in a material sense more civilised than these, and boast that there is a preponderance of numbers against the moral standard of Christianity. But others will be satisfied by the practical argu- ments, that those nations which have proved themselves superior in intelligence and earnestness have agreed in recognising the code of Christian morality, when presented to them; that all other systems of morality, notwithstanding the advantage which they may have in long pre-occupation of the ground, recede and disappear before it if once fairly exhibited; and, above all, that its dictates are enforced in the heart by a voice which, though silenced perhaps for a time, inevitably asserts its awful supremacy in those mo- ments of crisis which sooner or later in every life test the sincerity of a man's convictions. That there is a practical uniformity on questions of morality, based not indeed on universal consent, but, as the greatest of moral philosophers taught long ago, on the consent of those who prove themselves most qualified to judge, is a truth as convincing in its way as any mathematical axiom, and one which a reasonable man accepts as more than sufficient for his guidance among the otherwise endless uncertainties of a responsible existence. Those who desiderate a more absolute certainty than this, forget that without Christianity they are encompassed by far graver uncertainties; that here alone is comparative certainty, because here alone is a possible clue through the labyrinth, a not inadequate solution of the mysteries of their being. Too often, by a strange infatuation, men seem willing to believe anything, however inexplicable, except that without which life is an incomprehensible and meaningless unreality. The moral certainty on which Christianity stands is no fiction of the imagination, it is the only certainty worthy of the name in a world of doubt.

This, then, appears to be the ultimate foundation of the Christian faith—for beyond this, argument fails; a foundation sure and solid enough for all practical purposes. The acceptance, therefore, or rejection of its truths, if indeed the moral element is so vital a constituent in its nature, must rightly be regarded as dependent on moral far more than on intellectual causes. It is this which practically equalises, or rather proportionates the probation of all classes, rich and poor, old and young, learned or unlearned, more or less advanced in civilisation. The Gospel applies the very same touchstone to all whom it addresses in every age and clime; the same to an Englishman now as to a native of Jerusalem in the earthly lifetime of its Founder. That which constituted the guilt of the men of Jerusalem was that when Divine Holiness Incarnate was manifested to them, they rejected it through the antipathy which blinded them to its true nature:—

' Virtutem videant, intabescantque relictâ.'

The practical allegiance of the conscience is that which Christianity strives to gain, that on which its claims ultimately rest for confirmation. Questions of criticism, in comparison with this, are of secondary importance. Englishmen are sometimes reproached with being behind the continental schools of theology in their researches. They may rest content under the accusation, while they see one ingenious theory after another starting up to displace its predecessor, all alike vitiated by the hopeless fallacy of arguing from incomplete data with a preposterous assumption of omniscience; they may well confess themselves indifferent to the results of modern criticism, in comparison with those more practical considerations which are really effective in determining their course amid the perplexities of life. Instead of flimsy assertion and showy paradox, instead of a maze of speculations, circulating in endless confusion, like the tangled dance of gnats on a sultry evening, they require something more solid and real, and which will not elude the grasp in that hour when things of earth fade away from the glazing eyes.

FALLACIES ON PROGRESS, OR SKETCHES OF
THE EARLY CHURCH.

IN these days we hear much of progress. Probably no preceding period ever was so conscious of its own superiority. Certainly none ever had so much to say in justification of this complacency. But in the notions that are current on the subject, there is, as usual, a mixture of truth and error; sometimes in very unequal measure. Pascal's famous paradox, for instance, that ancient times are really the childhood of the world, modern times its old age, is triumphantly reiterated by superficial philosophers like Whately, very often in a sense which it will not bear. When the din of the trumpet with which they herald their grand discovery is stilled for a moment, the lurking fallacy is detected. While professing to correct one vulgar error they commit themselves to another. The saying which they misquote till it is threadbare is true in one sense only. A man living 2,000 years ago stands to a man of this century in the relation of a child to an old man, as being, of necessity, without the benefit of that experience which he lives too soon to enjoy. On the other hand, whatever of custom or opinion comes down to posterity from early times, comes in all the hoariness of age, tried and tested by length of years, venerable because of its antiquity. The invention of to-day—whether good or bad, remains to be proved—is, at all events, of recent birth, in its babyhood at present, and therefore devoid of any prescriptive title to acceptance or respect. Like a person with no hereditary honours, it has to start entirely on its own merits. It must approve itself to the world, and establish its own position there, simply by what it is, without the adventitious aid of a recommendation from the past.

But there is another very important distinction too often disregarded. Without question, this vaunted progress is a fact, within certain limitations. The grown man, unless he is a downright fool, is continually advancing in every kind of knowledge which depends on *experience.* So in the history of mankind each succeeding generation can turn to account, if it will, the gathered results of previous experiments. It learns a lesson even from the mistakes and failures of its predecessors as well as from their good guessings. It is for ever ascending on ' the stepping-stone of its dead self' to a yet higher vantage-ground. But —and let this be noted carefully as a fundamental law—progress is only in those matters where experience is our guide. The neglect of this essential limitation leads to an almost hopeless confusion in our ideas about progress.

In mechanics, in chemistry, in geology, and briefly, in all that appertains to the material world, the nine-

teenth century must be vastly in advance of its forefathers, or there must be a fault somewhere.   Again,
in that border-territory, which partly at least owns
the dominion of experience, time· can hardly fail to
involve progress and improvement.   In the science,
for example, of political economy, experience has no
mean part to play, in adjusting and reconciling principles as old as the first groupings of men round the
paternal hearth to the new complications of material
circumstance, which act upon social life, and are,
again, reacted upon by it.   Accordingly we find progress here also.   But when we come to those more
abstract departments of knowledge which treat of
things immaterial, to pure mathematics, for instance,
and mental philosophy, we no longer meet with corresponding signs of progress.   Nor is it to be expected.   A certain degree of material civilisation
indeed these sciences may require for their development, and for existing at all ; but they do not necessarily keep pace with its strides, as it marches onwards.
Euclid and Aristotle have not yet been supplanted
and superseded by later discoverers ; nor are they
likely to be.   So in the domain of the imagination,
in the arts which clothe and adorn the ungraceful
nakedness of man's terrestrial life.   Homer and Dante,
Shakspeare and Milton, still sit in undisturbed majesty
on their thrones.   So, too, in what may be called ma-
terialised poetry.   The chisel and the brush are
evidently more dependent than the poet's unfettered
fancies on the material circumstances around them.
Yet even here the mind reverts instinctively to the

past. The statuary of ancient Greece, the paintings of mediæval Italy, are still the acknowledged types of beauty and power to an age that is far more highly civilised. Lastly, in the science of Ethics, though time, or rather civilisation, may develop a more enlightened regard to self-interest—a poor and feeble restraint, at best, on man's rebellious passions—it cannot do more. Thus far it may attain, but no farther. It cannot lift itself unaided to the level of pure unselfishness, of a disinterested sense of the obligations of duty. There is a line drawn, like that which marks the highest inroad of the tides, beyond which it cannot pass. If it succeed in exorcising some forms of vice, it brings others, an evil compensation, in its train. Thus a wide and careful survey shows that the boast of progress can only be substantiated with considerable qualification. The vague illusive idea shrinks into smaller dimensions when we grasp it. Progress in some respects there is positively none. In others, it is found, on a closer inspection, to be very like what the Irishman called 'a progress backward.' At most and at best it is but the ramification of certain unchanging first principles within a prescribed sphere.

There is, however, a yet further distinction, and one of paramount importance, if we wish to understand clearly what progress is, and what it is not. Yet this also is too often repudiated practically, if not in so many words. When our knowledge is of a kind which cannot be acquired by mere experience, because it transcends our faculties; when it comes to us, not

in any degree through the gradual workings of experiment, but by direct communication from a source
extraneous and superior to man, then it is given once
for all. By its very nature it is stationary, not progressive, until, at least, it shall be reversed or re-
modelled by a new revelation. Thus, though the
precepts of Christianity may appear to be modified
by contact with the outer world, by the conditions to
which they are subjected at any given moment, they
are not really changed. They may encourage the
monastic life as an indispensable refuge amid the tur-
bulence of a rude and violent age, or the community
of goods as a bond of union appropriate to a Church
consisting of a few persecuted members. But the
principle remains the same, though it may seem to
vary; it is simply the primary obligation of love to
God, of love to man. There is nothing of change or
progress in the precepts of Christianity. Still less
can there be any change or progress in its doctrines.
Its morality indeed, though infinitely purified and
elevated, because it partakes of His divine nature
who brought it into the world, is yet in a rudimen-
tary form the common property of mankind. Its
doctrines are essentially what reason could never
have known without revelation. Without that, these
heavenly truths would have remained hidden from
men to this day. There is no occasion now to reca-
pitulate the credentials of Him * by whose lips they
were revealed. It suffices for the present argument
to say, once for all, that in a revealed religion, if the

* Vide supra, pp. 14-18.

fact of the revelation be once admitted, progress, in the proper sense of the word, whether as regards doctrine or precept, is out of the question, until a new revelation shall be given.

Yet there are not a few nowadays who loudly and arrogantly proclaim a progress of this kind. They are fond of citing, in a sense which its author never intended, Bacon's quaint apophthegm, that a dwarf standing on a giant's shoulders can see further than the giant. But the illustration itself confutes them admirably. For the question is not here of seeing, but of hearing. The knowledge in question is not that which the mental vision gains for itself, but that which is imparted as by a voice breathing its utterances into the ear. Who will say, that Apostles and men of sub-apostolic times had not an advantage in this way in their proximity to the great Author of Christianity, which no acuteness of modern criticism can countervail, however far-sighted it may be, and though it may stand on a commanding eminence, armed with all its appliances for gazing back into the past? Without taking into account whatever of especial guidance may have been vouchsafed to some of them, the mere fact that the faith of the Christian Church is transmitted by an authenticated tradition from those who were nearest to the source whence it flowed, ought to silence all who take upon themselves to refashion and rehabilitate it with their 'free-handling.'

The assailant of the Christian Faith, it is remarked often, has changed his mode of onset. Christianity is no longer impugned as false, utterly false from its beginning. But we are told, that it has already undergone great changes in its onward progress, and that it must and will undergo many more. For this reason, whatever tends to elucidate the history of the early Church is peculiarly valuable now. Mr. Westcott, among others, and beyond others, has done good service to the truth in this way. In his learned and suggestive ' History of the Canon of the New Testament,' * which he has lately abridged, with some additions on the Old Testament, in ' The Bible in the Church,' we have a contribution, which can hardly be overrated, towards a solution of the great question of our day. By enabling us to realise the condition of the primitive Church, of its doctrines and discipline, he enables us to answer, fairly and truly as it deserves, the momentous question, whether the faith has indeed been in a perpetual state of flux and change, as is pretended, since its commencement, inconstant and variable as the sand in its shifting phases, or whether we may safely trust our hopes to its rock-like stability, leaning on it fearlessly, as on that which has once for all been deposited with the saints in its absolute integrity.

It is rare to find laboriousness in research combined with the power of viewing a subject comprehensively and of drawing profound conclusions; rare, too, to find a tone of judicial calmness and sobriety in one

* ' A General Survey of the History of the Canon of the New Testament during the First Four Centuries.' By Brooke Foss Westcott, M.A., late Fellow of Trinity College, Cambridge. (Macmillan.)

whose sympathies are heartily enlisted. This is what makes a man at once historian and philosopher. Nor is there perhaps any subject which demands more imperatively all this patience, candour, and intuition than the early history of the Church. There the investigator has no common difficulties against him. There is so much to provoke prejudice and partialities, and the supply of accessible materials is scanty. Cautious, exact, and deliberate, Mr. Westcott amasses his materials with the minute diligence of a German professor, while he uses them with a practical common sense, and an eye to proportion, in which German professors are often lamentably deficient. He is too dispassionate to allow the advocate to intrude into the seat of judgment. He guards himself scrupulously from all those hasty plausible assumptions which detract so much from the value of recent writings on the subject, more highly coloured than his, but made of less solid stuff, and less deserving of reliance. There is nothing rhetorical in his pages, nothing of frothy declamation. They form a worthy continuation to the labours of Bull, Pearson, and Waterland. Probably they would be more attractive, generally, if he were less sparing of embellishment. Many readers who might profit largely by his teaching may probably be deterred by a style that is dry and 'closely-twisted together.' For their sake, if for no other reason, it may be worth while to reproduce as briefly and clearly as may be some of the impressions suggested by his book, with some legitimate inferences from it.

His main object is to trace the Canon of the New Testament from its origin: in other words, to ascertain from the evidence of history how the several books, which constitute the New Testament as we have it, came to be regarded as canonical, that is, of special authority in the Church. The result of his inquiries—and it is one which an unbiassed mind can hardly hesitate to accept—is, that with some few exceptions, the books of the New Testament in its present form were recognised universally among Christians, orthodox and heretic alike, from the very first, as genuine* and authoritative. Though not formally expressed by the collective voice of the Church till the fourth century, this recognition is inferred, if not with certainty yet with strong appearance of probability, from references extant in early writers, as a fact coeval with Christianity. At first, indeed, it was implicit and unavowed, because unquestioned. Gradually it became explicit, pronounced in set terms. The outlines of the Canon were shaped more and more precisely, as controversies arose, which had to be determined, on the subject. As to the 'disputed' books, the evidence is less unanimous, the verdict less decisive. Clearly we have here, in this traditionary acceptance of the same sacred Scriptures, a strong argument, so far as it goes, for the fixity of the faith from the beginning. The Canon grew; but its growth was that of a plant retaining its original elements and structure—of a flower which, after all,

---

* It is strange that a writer so learned and accurate as Mr. Westcott should use 'authentic' for 'genuine.' See his 'Canon,' &c. *passim.*

is only the bud expanded. Or we may find a closer analogy in what takes place, when the eye, by looking more attentively, discovers features in the landscape which were there all the time, but unnoticed before. The whole question of canonicity was ignored at first, because a canon was unnecessary for the contemporaries of the Apostles. It remained dormant afterwards, so long as the Christian world was agreed on the subject. Only under the pressure of controversy it became necessary to draw the line of demarcation sharply and definitely between canonical books and uncanonical. Then the hitherto floating particles settled into permanent cohesion.

But in establishing this point, other collateral points of yet greater moment are brought to the surface. This very fact of the absence for some time of any authorised definition of Scripture testifies to the existence of another stream parallel to that of Scripture, distinct but never divergent, ruling the doctrine and practice of the Church, the living stream of custom and tradition. A Canon was not wanted while the Apostolic teaching was fresh in the recollection of the faithful. Appeal could be made, and was made, to the testimony of men still living, who had sat at the feet of the personal followers of the Lord. The truth was transmitted from the lips of saint to saint, of confessor to confessor. It was enshrined everywhere in the public liturgies of the Church. The very air was saturated with the tradition. The early writers are in the habit of quoting the sense rather than the very words of Scripture, because they quoted from memory, like a man preaching without a written sermon, not like the same man at his desk with his books at hand. Justin Martyr, for instance, refers in a general way to the ' Memoirs of the Apostles '—τὰ ʼΑπομνημονεύματα τῶν ʼΑποστόλων—that is, as abundant passages show, to records* received from the Apostles and their immediate followers—he does not give the reference to any particular Gospel or Epistle. The teaching of Christ and his Apostles was too deeply stereotyped on the mind of the Church for men to wrangle about texts. Faith rested securely then on that foundation on which the Church is built, the word communicated by Him to His Apostles, and through them to the world at large.

We are apt not to realise adequately the closeness and living efficacy of the ties which bound the members of the Church into one body in those days. Its organisation was compact though extensive. Christians were scattered far and wide, sundered by differences of race and climate, yet united, not by any mere sentiment, but by real, actual communion. No doubt the gigantic network of iron which the Roman Empire had flung over its dependencies, compressing and welding them into one massive system, though it could not fuse into thorough assimilation elements so heterogeneous, served by the wisdom of Providence to make this intercommunion more practicable than it could have been otherwise. We, Englishmen

---

* Other parts of the New Testament are perhaps included in this very vague designation; but it is usually understood of the Gospels only.

of the nineteenth century, are so insulated from
active sympathy with our fellow-Christians of the
East and of the West, that we cannot easily understand the feeling of fellowship which pervaded the
Church then.   Not all the many facilities which
science furnishes for intercourse and correspondence
avail to bridge over this estrangement for us.   We
have resources, which the second century had not, in
our press, our postal machinery, our means of transit,
our electric wires flashing intelligence through the apparently impassable barriers of mountain and sea.
But we have not that essential unity of doctrine and
habitude which they had.   It flowed from causes
quite irrespective of things like these.

The framework of ecclesiastical discipline, though
elaborated more and more as time went on, existed
in outline from the first.   Church-Government was
the same in outline then as now.   The Church in
each place might indeed wear some distinctive characteristics.   But these were as nothing in comparison of the broad identifying stamp of Catholicity
which was everywhere.   Each community might
cherish with especial reverence some portion, addressed in the first instance to itself, of the Sacred
Writings.   Each particular Version might assert its
nationality by some minute traits.   There might be
a tendency towards this or that direction in schools,
as of Antioch and Alexandria.   But inter-commu-
nion connected and amalgamated all these idiosyncrasies.   The Epistle treasured as in a sense the
private property of one city was read aloud in the

public services of other places also. A Christian
changing his home, or dwelling for a time among
strangers, carried letters of commendation from one
bishop to another. The 'brethren'—and how vividly
does that word pourtray the relation of Christians to
one another then—were frequently sending alms and
greetings to others far away, who were in need. The
inevitable danger of error insinuating itself through
the personal bias of one teacher, or of one school, was
checked by the counter-tendencies of another. The
part was sound because of the healthy action of the
organic whole. The due relative proportion of the
Articles of the faith, which private predilections un-
restrained tend to destroy, was preserved by that
conflict of opposing forces which results in the harmony of all. Hence the spirit, not of rigid uniformity, but of essential unity, which animates the
ancient Creeds.

But we are sometimes told that the early Church
was divided into two great sections or parties, headed
respectively by S. Peter and S. Paul. These are represented as widely severed, and strongly opposed;
each party holding only a fragment of the truth, and
insisting on that exclusively with a narrow intolerance. Thus the doctrine of the early Church is
spoken of as the result of a compromise gradually
effected between them. Such a state of things is
graphically and picturesquely depicted, and made the
basis of grave inferences. But there is more of imagination than of fact in it. A closer attention to the
early writers shows, that this struggle between the

Jewish and Gentile schools is very much exaggerated, and that the Judaizers of whom we hear so much were, in fact, in the position of persons half-converted, rather than truly within the pale. When we turn to ' the first Greek Epistle which can be regarded as authentic.' * we meet at once with proofs of harmony and agreement. S. Clement was, if we may trust history, a follower of S. Peter. But his epistle bears palpable traces of the influence of S. Paul, not in its line of thought only, but in its very turns of expression. A more remarkable instance could hardly be desired of the great truth, that Christianity is not the result of a long series of contests, and compromises, and oscillations, but a code of doctrine and practice complete in the main from the very first. Particular persons then, as now, and as always, are apt to seize with avidity, and to dilate into a false prominence, one or another article of the faith. One great teacher was led by temperament or external associations to regard the faith chiefly from one point of view; another contemplated it in a different aspect. But are we, therefore, to assume that either of them denies all that he does not affirm, or that both aspects were not duly appreciated by the collective mind of the Church in their day? Even the heresies of earliest date seem to leap forth into the world, like Pallas from the head of Zeus, full-grown in stature and equipped for the fight. By the mere fact of their presence on the field of battle they imply that there was a definite system there already, which they

* Westcott's 'General Survey,' &c., p. 29.

would not acquiesce in. The more closely we look, the more plainly we see that the faith of the Christian Church is not the progressive growth of long years of controversy, but a thing given to men in all its fulness, and once for all, by a heavenly Teacher, to be expanded, indeed, and developed in its application to the outer world, but not to be re-shaped and re-modelled by man's ingenuity, as if it were his own invention. The first centuries of the Christian era are sometimes called the infancy of the Church. So in one sense they are. In another they are its maturity. For the older covenant was the discipline preparatory for manhood. Christ came 'in the fulness of time;' and what He came to communicate He gave without stint, without imperfection, without need of further 'progress.'

There is indeed a progress which ecclesiastical history unfolds in page after page. Each nation and each century in turn is made subservient to the workings of Providence. The Jew, stern and stubborn, and with a moral sense disciplined for the work, is the first to receive the new teaching, that through his retentive nature it may lay a hold on the world, which shall never be shaken off. Next, the supple Greek lends all his multifarious resources of thought and language to express, interpret, illustrate it; that its 'sound may go into all lands.' Then the Roman, the conqueror of the world, unconsciously obeys the behest of a higher power while ministering to the Church those excellences in which he is pre-eminent, of orderly obedience to law, of systematic policy and organisation; that 'the ends of the world' may be subjugated to its 'word.' The sturdy Teuton, again, brings with him the intense consciousness of individual responsibility. Here is progress. But it is the growth of a huge primæval tree, branching out freely on every side, while it is too firmly rooted in the earth to swerve from its centre. That legitimate development which keeps the analogies of the faith is gradual and insensible. Error betrays itself by announcing itself to the world as something new. Athanasius and Augustine advance with one hand firmly grasping the past. Simon Magus publishes to the world his 'Great Announcement,' as if himself a new Avatar, or, at least, a prophet, if not something more.

But the early fathers, we hear it said, were not critical. That depends on what is meant by the word. In its specific sense it means the analysis, as from without, of a language, which lives only in the past. In this sense the early fathers were decidedly uncritical. But they had no need of this kind of criticism for their purpose. The subject with which they had to do was not enwrapt like a mummy in the cerecloths of a dead language. It was embodied in a form yet warm with the breath of life, instinct with motion and vitality. A man can dispense with the help of the microscope in things with which he is practically conversant and familiar by daily, hourly use. In this sense, it may be conceded at once that the early fathers, till the Alexandrine school, were not critical. The word has, however, a wider signification. The

E

critical faculty in man is that which tries and verifies for itself what is presented to it by the senses or the understanding. A critical mind is one which can thus adjudicate clearly and well. Now, notwithstanding much that is said plausibly, but fallaciously, on this point, one age can be more critical than another only in those matters of which it has fuller and more accurate information. For those differences in moral character which make one man more precipitate and inconsiderate than another, or which otherwise pervert and distort the judgment, are lost in the comparison of age with age. In this respect the average is much the same generally. If a man has his reasoning faculties in their normal state, and if these are uninterrupted in their working by moral hindrances, there is nothing more wanted than a competent knowledge of the facts to enable him to judge rightly and well. For the process of reasoning is the same in every person—in the peasant and in the philosopher—a mere form of syllogising, consciously or not—quicker or slower, according to constitution and training, but correct as a machine always, unless interfered with either by ignorance or by some bias thwarting its proper action. Now, their most prejudiced opponent will hardly say that the early fathers, unless blinded by the grossest fanaticism (which is easily disproved), were biassed by any sort of self-seeking towards doctrines which exposed them to so much persecution. Clearly, therefore, the difference in power of judging between them and the men of our self-styled more critical age must be, if anywhere, in point of know-

ledge—in knowledge, that is, of the particular subject
under consideration. For it has been shown already
that progress in physical science, and in its cognates,
cannot affect the question. If, indeed, it engenders a
habit of doubting, where doubts are unreasonable and
out of place, so far it is prejudicial. It only remains,
therefore, to ask, whether the Christians of the earliest centuries were sufficiently acquainted with the
facts of their religion. They may have been very
credulous, because they were very ignorant, on the
subject of the Phœnix, or in their notions of geology
or cosmogony. But what then? Our own Elizabethan writers appear ridiculous, if they are quoted on
a subject about which the world in which they lived
knew nothing. But, for all that, the men of that era,
not only the exceptional men, like Bacon and Shakespeare, but the men of average ability, were as truly
critical within the range of their experience, as just
and wise, so far, in their conclusions, as the wisest of
their posterity. So with the early fathers. Let it
only be granted, as of course it must, that they had
the ordinary power of reasoning from their premises,
and that they were unbiassed, and it follows that they
were as discriminating in the matters under their
cognizance, as a modern professor in his sphere of
geology or electricity. · In questions of religion they
speak of what they knew better than those who are
farther removed from the epoch of its revelation.
Uncritical about other things, they were not uncritical nor incompetent in speaking of Christ
and Christianity. There they speak as being eye-

witnesses themselves, or as having learnt from those who were.

The great point to be borne in mind by those who appeal to the early Church, and defer to its decisions, is that the appeal must be made, not to any one writer, however eminent, not to any one Council, however nearly Œcumenical, but to the general consent of all. The terms that cancel each other are fairly eliminated from the equation. Just as in attempting to recover the correct text, we cannot trust unreservedly to any one manuscript or version as infallible, so, in questions of doctrine, we look to a collation of evidence from various sources. The faith of the Church is not to be extracted from the pages of any one of its Doctors, however saintly or wise, nor from chapter and verse in the sacred books. Nor was it the result of any one great controversy. It is the accumulation of the treasures committed to the safe keeping of the Church; it is the solemn utterance of the voices of Christendom in its purest age, blended and harmonised together by the Holy Spirit, like the richly swelling chords of a stupendous organ. The Lirinensian rule is a good one: *quod semper, quod ubique, quod ab omnibus.* Only it must be taken with the qualification which common sense requires. Literally taken, it stultifies and destroys itself. The infallibility which would be implied by an unanimous sentence of all Christians in all places, and throughout all time, is beyond the reach of man, and inconsistent with the probation of a being, who must prove his faith by trying all things and holding fast that which is good, and who has to contend, not solely against wrong-doing, but against errors in belief, which sooner or later end in what is practically wrong. Absolute infallibility is not to be had on this side the grave. But each ancient writer in turn contributes weighty testimony—and that testimony is more or less weighty according to his nearness to the Apostolic age—to some part of the truth. Each Council discharges its appointed task by affirming, more explicitly than before, some one of its many aspects. A sound judgment knows how to attach proportionate weight to the evidence which history brings before it. In studying the canon of Scripture, a sensible man is in no haste either to accept or reject dogmatically such portions as have been 'disputed,' though not expunged, by the ages most competent to decide. In controversies of doctrine he cannot but feel less assured on those points where an apparent collision of authorities calls upon him to pause and suspend his judgment. But as he does not expect either from the lips of Popes, or from the votes of Councils, or from the too confident promptings of his own conscience, an infallibility for which he has no right to crave, so he is content to remain in suspense, even on much that he would fain know for a certainty, till the time shall come; content if only light enough be shed on his way to guide him step by step onwards to the end.

Never was it more needful than at the present time to bear in mind this great truth, that 'As it was in the beginning,' is the motto of Catholic

Christianity, the watchword of the English Church. When questioned of our faith, our answer is this : ' We believe that which has been believed from the beginning.' Tried by this test, the pretensions of a spurious catholicity are detected and exposed. The word Catholic has become popular ; it is bandied to and fro till it is in danger of degenerating into a mere sound and nothing more ; it is even paraded, ' a strange device,' on the banners of transcendental neology, in a sense diametrically opposite to its real meaning.   Yet the idea, which the word represents, remains deeply, broadly true for ever.   It is the consent, as the greatest sage of heathendom * has taught us, not of the many, but of those most competent, most qualified to judge.   Apply this principle to the questions belonging to the Christian faith.   The consent, however general—nay, though only not universal—of any subsequent period, is simply valueless, unless it includes the consent of the Church in the apostolic and sub-apostolic age : for, as we have been endeavouring to show, the belief of the Church then is, on these points, the one thing most worthy of attention, most weighty in turning the scale.   In the days of Athanasius, the many even within the Church were against, not with the truth.   So it may be at any time, if once we relax our hold on the tradition of the Church from the beginning.   The discordant echoes of controversy are only stilled and reconciled by an appeal to what has been.   The

* οἱ ἱκανῶς πεπαιδευμένοι. Aristot. Nichom. Ethic.

imperious claims of Rome on the one hand, and on the other the preposterous assumptions of scepticism, can only be met thus. When once the divine mission of the Founder of Christianity has been established, then whatever article of belief can be traced, through the continuous testimony of the Church, up to that source, commands assent irresistibly. If this great principle of adherence to antiquity were more clearly recognised as the vital principle of the English Church, the strength of her position would be appreciated more generally.

At the present time many, who have hitherto been leaning unreasoningly on an arbitrary theory of mechanical inspiration, finding their confidence rudely shaken, and the prop on which they leaned failing them under a weight and a pressure which it was never intended to bear, are asking in utter bewilderment for support and guidance. They hear a Babel of voices round them, the din of controversies, and ask in alarm, How are English Churchmen to know what to believe, in the uncertainty which the late judgments of the Privy Council* appear to them to create and sanction? But these feelings of uncertainty and alarm cannot touch those whose standard of belief is not ' the Bible and the Bible alone,' but the historic teaching of the Church from the beginning. They, at all events, know what they believe, and why. Their faith ought to be proof against speculations and surmises which cannot reach it. Such

* Williams *v.* Bp. of Salisbury. Wilson *v.* Fendall. 1864.

questions, for instance, as were raised in the notorious
' Essays and Reviews ' cannot disturb the mind of
one whose belief is built up on that rock, which the
divine Ruler of the Church in His infinite wisdom
deposited in depths unfathomed by the plummet of
man's intellect, and unvexed by the storms of controversy which rage on the surface, as its sure foundation.
Take the last of the seven essays ; the most dangerous
of the number, because, in its tendency, the most
profoundly subversive of the very principles of
revelation. Such a theory as is there propounded on
the interpretation of the Scriptures, obviously ignores,
from beginning to end, the existence of an historic
tradition of the truth, external to these books : it
proceeds on the assumption that every Christian is to
take his Bible and find out for himself his religion
from it. However plausible in one aspect it may be,
this is simply like working a sum with less than half
of its figures. It is a curious instance of the extent
to which the leaven of Puritanism, with its abhorrence
of authority and its presumptuous assertion of the
individual conscience, has penetrated the English
nation, that the panic occasioned by ' Essays and
Reviews ' should have been so general even in quarters
where it was least to be expected. Believers in
Christianity would not have been so terrified, if they
had known how inexpugnable is their position when
they appeal to primitive tradition, not to the Bible,
not to the Conscience alone.

Hæc certamina tanta
Pulveris exigui jacta compressa quiescunt.

Certainly the importance of the recent controversies which have been so recklessly provoked by Dr. Colenso and the seven essayists is very much diminished, as soon as we appeal from the letter of the Scriptures to the concurrent testimony of the Church Catholic in its purest age.

This great principle for which we are contending—that what the English Church has to do now, is to hold fast her existing formularies, as being the embodiment of primitive orthodoxy—is in danger of being overlooked in the excitement of the moment, and in the outcry which is raised for a new court of ecclesiastical appeal. We are not saying that the alarm is groundless. It is justified in some measure; not, indeed, by the mere fact of heretical notions being promulgated, for that is no new thing, but by the fact of their being promulgated by clergymen. Still, the alarm is disproportionate to the occasion. We are not defending the recent decisions. But those who are panic-stricken by it, seem to forget that it was a natural consequence of the slippery and evasive nature of the statements delated: and that writings which are so cautious as not to jeopardise this responsibility of the writer even while stirring up the gravest doubts and perplexities in others, could not easily have been made amenable to law in any court of justice. At all events, a bad decision, or even more than one bad decision, is not enough to condemn a tribunal, or to settle a question which ought to be entertained calmly and dispassionately on its own merits. Those who could not object to the same court, presided over by a Roundell Palmer or a Page Wood, must not be immoderate in their denunciations of it because there happens to be a Bethell on the woolsack. No possible or conceivable court could be guaranteed from fallibility. We are not defending the constitution of the present court as perfect. The presence in it of a removable and political and partisan judge, such as the Lord Chancellor must be, is its greatest defect. We only urge, that whatever court is most likely to keep closely to the Formularies as they are, is best. Probably no sort of court is less in danger of being swayed, by gusts of temporary excitement, to any deviation in one direction or another from the letter of the Formularies, than a court composed of English judges. They need the assistance of theologians to explain the force of theological terms, just as ' experts ' are needed in certain cases, or interpreters are needed in any lawsuit which concerns foreigners; but the ultimate decision is perhaps as safe in their hands as anywhere else. They may be predisposed, by the habits and instincts of English jurisprudence, to take the restrictions imposed by the Formularies in the widest sense permissible, and to give the accused the benefit of every doubt. But they are not likely, as a rule, to strain the Formularies to meet a particular case, nor to pervert their meaning under the bias of party-feeling. A court composed solely of ecclesiastics would be more likely to read the Formularies not as they are, but as, in its opinion, they ought to be, and as its members would wish to have them. If we look to other countries, we may see enough to make us pause before insisting on a change. Would the English clergy be willing to exchange their present position, with all its safeguards of law, for that of a Presbyterian minister, subject to the variable impulses of a General Assembly, or of a French priest, liable to be removed from his post at any moment by the irresponsible act of his bishop? Would the English laity be satisfied with any Court of Appeal which acted on any other principle than that of simply taking the Formularies as they are, or which, avowedly or unconsciously, followed its own theories of orthodoxy, instead of keeping closely and strictly to the letter of the law? A purely spiritual Court of Appeal would be the first step towards a new Prayer-Book, and towards the disruption of Church and State in England. It is only those who regard the Christian faith as a thing to be recast every year who need desire it. To reform the present Court of Appeal is one thing—to extemporise a new Court of Appeal is quite another.

But the cry is raised of ' Erastianism.' It would be Erastian to allow the civil power to make doctrine for the Church. But it is the business of the Court of Appeal not to make doctrine, but to take it as it finds it. The State has established the Church in England as holding and teaching a certain definite belief, expressed in certain Formularies, which have been framed by the spiritual and accepted by the temporal party to the compact. On these conditions the Church retains her national position; a vantage-ground for inculcating the truth, not to be surrendered

lightly, nor without overwhelming necessity. Both
parties, therefore, have an interest and a voice in de-
ciding whether or not those conditions have been vio-
lated in any instance, and whatever machinery is
best adapted for ensuring a strict observance of these
conditions without regard to anything else is the best
Court of Appeal.

The English Church may well be thankful to hold
fast the inheritance which has providentially been
transmitted to our day in our existing Formularies.
We cannot be too watchful against whatever threatens
their stability. We enjoy in them the fruit of the
labours of our forefathers in the Church Catholic.
They have laboured, and we enter into their labours.
Here is a vast difference between our age and that of
Athanasius and Augustine. By the dispensation of
Providence, we of these latter days receive ready to
our use, shaped and fashioned under many a fiery
trial into its present clearness of definition, but essentially and substantially the same always, the time-
honoured symbols of the ancient faith. The same
Providence which watched over and matured the
labours of our predecessors in the Christian Church,
while they formed creed and liturgy, bids us to retain
and preserve what we have received. 'We have
heard with our ears, and our fathers have declared
unto us the noble works that God did in their days
and in the old time before them.' Our place in the
history of the world, and of the Church, marks out
our work for us. Even the heresies that we have to
contend with are but the old errors disinterred and re-

suscitated; even against them our strength is in the past, without resource to novelties. The recent dogma of the Roman Church on the Immaculate Conception is a warning against change in the disguise of development. But it is no obstructive and unprogressive conservatism that we advocate. The Church of Christ is no petrifaction, no fossil exhumed from by-gone strata, and alien to our world : it is the tree, whose branches are ever spreading themselves more and more widely over the future, because its roots are deep in the past.

Quantum vertice ad auras
Ætherias, tantum radice in Tartara tendit.

There is much to be done in the adaptation of what is old to new requirements in presenting ancient doctrine in the form most intelligible, most persuasive to modern habits of thought; in applying immutable precepts to the ever-varying conditions of humanity; in conforming the traditionary frame-work of ecclesiastical organisation to the needs of our rapidly increasing population at home and in our colonies; in reclaiming the separatists who by causes of one kind or another have been estranged from the one true fold ; in restoring the intercommunion, too long unhappily suspended, of the several churches of the East and of the West, in order that all may unite against the aggressions of infidelity. Here is work enough, and more than enough, to be done ; and here rather than in adding supererogatory Articles to our Creed, in attempting to define what has providentially been left undefined, we may trust that the Great

Head of the Church, now as ever, will bless our exertions with the guidance of the Holy Spirit. But our first care must be, not to lose what has been so hardly won for us. In our Convocation, in our ruridecanal synods, in our several spheres of personal influence, let English churchmen unite uncompromisingly to preserve their Prayer-Book intact, in church and in school. Without claiming for that book an impeccability which cannot be found on this side of the grave, it is not too much to say, that it providentially enshrines the teaching of the primitive Church, in terms which assert the truth firmly and clearly in all its essentials, and which, at the same time, allow a wise and legitimate latitude for those inevitable diversities of thought and sentiment which distinguish one man from another, and mark each as having an individual and responsible existence. So long as we keep our Prayer-Book intact, there is no cause, we will not say for despondency, but even for anxiety, as to the future of the Church of England.

THE REVISION OF THE PRAYER-BOOK.

THE revision of the Prayer-Book—is it, or is it not, desirable?—is a question in itself most momentous, and, at the present time, of pressing importance. The maintenance of the Christian faith in its purity and completeness depends essentially on the authorised formularies of the Church. Therein are contained, expressly or implicitly, the great doctrinal truths of our religion. Thence is derived the practical and devotional character which is the growth and consequence of a real belief. Above all, if we keep in mind that the mode and manner of approaching the Divine Majesty in solemn worship is the question under consideration, we cannot but feel its paramount importance. At the present moment, owing to a concurrence of causes, the proposal of revision occupies no small amount of attention, not among the clergy only, but among the laity also. In Parliament as well as in Convocation, though in very different senses, it has been gravely entertained. The time is come for those who desire the welfare of the Church in England to form an intelligent opinion, and to take a decided part for or against revision.

If it is always necessary in any discussion to define clearly and exactly the meaning of the terms that are used, it is especially so in regard to such a phrase as the revision of the Prayer-Book. The words are familiar to our ears. They are tossed to and fro in casual conversation, in the columns of newspapers, in sketchy and superficial pamphlets; but their force and significance is lost in vague uncertainty. Many persons advocate revision without knowing what they mean and what they want. Not only is there the widest possible difference of opinion on the kind and measure of change desired by different persons, who may seem at first to make common cause, but also and equally on the no less difficult question of the proper way of effecting it. On both points a dangerous confusion of ideas exists even among educated persons. The great distinctive truths embodied in the Prayer-Book are, it must be owned, so insufficiently appreciated, and the proper position and office of the Christian Church have been so ignored and misapprehended, that much ignorance and many prejudices must be removed before the subject can be treated fairly. It will be the aim and endeavour of the following remarks to clear the subject, so far as may be possible, of the manifold perplexities by which, in the minds of many persons, it is encumbered and embarrassed, and to consider a question so momentous calmly and dispassionately, without the bias of partisanship; regarding it in all its various bearings, and endeavouring to weigh justly the reasons which incline the scale to one side or the other.

Of course it must be admitted, on all hands, that the idea of revision, in the abstract, is not unreasonable. It would be an unwarrantable and indefensible assumption to maintain that the Prayer-Book cannot, by any possibility, be amended. However excellent already, still, like everything else of human origin, it may be conceived more perfect than it is. The wise and holy men who compiled it were not infallible. Besides, as change is the law of all things earthly, it may need that sort of alteration which is meant by adaptation, in order to be translated, as it were, so as to suit the requirements of a new generation. All this may fairly be granted *in limine.* The idea of revision cannot be tabooed as preposterous. It may claim a hearing. But from this point begin the difficulties, as soon as the question is moved from the abstract to the actual—from what might be to what is. Are there really any serious faults of omission or commission in the book? Are they such as to justify incurring the risks always involved in change? Lastly, even if desirable *per se,* are these supposed amendments practicable at the present time?

There are three courses proposed. There is a doctrinal revision, desired, if not by Lord Ebury himself, at all events by some of his clients. There is the revision of a very different kind, which has been recommended by some of the most eminent members of both Houses of Convocation: a revision which would preserve the Prayer-Book as it is, while supplementing it with an Appendix of Services, composed in part by re-arrangement of those already existing. Lastly, there are persons, of no less weight and authority, who deem it, on the whole, the safest course to keep the Prayer-Book exactly as it is, and to rest content with what they have, rather than to risk the dangers of any change.

The idea of any such revision of the Prayer-Book as would alter its doctrinal character may be dismissed very summarily. It is simply an impossibility. The small section of clergymen whose petition is adopted and patronised by Lord Ebury, are strangely mistaken if they suppose that any change such as they desire would be tolerated by the English Church at large. There are others who would wish to see the alteration, if any, made in a diametrically opposite direction; who would like to see the services of the English Church, if in any way altered, not brought nearer to the Genevan type, but to that of the Greek and Roman Communions. But there is no likelihood of either change. A great overwhelming mass of the clergy and laity are unequivocally opposed to any such change at all. It is morally certain, that in the event of the Prayer-Book being remodelled after the manner desired by Lord Ebury's petitioners, an immense majority of the clergy would simply adhere to their present Prayer-Book, and refuse to recognise the new one, in spite of any penal consequences. But, in fact, it is inconceivable that any Parliament, even one reformed on Mr. Bright's principles, could be so infatuated as to face such a national disruption as would ensue. However deplorable the misunderstandings existing on ecclesiastical matters may be in too many professing churchmen among the laity, any aggression so tyrannical as the attempt to enforce a new Prayer-Book on an unwilling majority at the request of a minority unimportant as in numbers so in 'calibre' and position, would be too reckless a violation of the rights of conscience. If ever a trial so severe should be allowed by the inscrutable wisdom of Providence to befall the English Church, men will not be wanting in thousands among the clergy to endure loss and suffering for the truth's sake. But those who agitate for a doctrinal revision ought to reflect on the consequences of what they are trying to do. In the vain and hopeless attempt to conciliate the Dissenters—vain and hopeless, for it is the animus of Dissent which puts and keeps men in that position, not this or that passage in the Prayer-Book—they are taking the likeliest way to precipitate a schism in the English Church, and in all probability an abrupt severance of the ties which hold Church and State together. But there is no danger, provided that all those who are opposed to a doctrinal revision will take the trouble to make their sentiments known. Petitions ought to be presented from every rural deanery, signed by clergy and laity alike, against it. The almost universal conviction 'that any such attempt, at the present time, would be fraught with great danger to the peace and unity of the Church,' ought to make itself heard at once. If the almost universal feeling in favour of preserving the Prayer-Book shall once make itself understood, the impending evil will, in all likelihood, be averted.

It is unnecessary here to enter into a vindication of the doctrines of the Prayer-Book as it stands. That has been done, and done thoroughly, over and over again already. Received and transmitted from the earliest ages of the Christian Church, these have been assailed by some fresh cavil or objection in each succeeding age, and in each age they have been illustrated and enforced by the wisest, most learned, and holiest theologians. Suffice it to say now, in reply to the proposal for a new Prayer-Book, that the Church of England is decided in its conviction that such a thing *cannot be.*

But it may be answered that Lord Ebury disclaims any alteration of doctrines. That amiable and well-meaning nobleman is no doubt sincere in the disclaimer. But probably he is hardly aware where changes of doctrine begin. The Prayer-Book is so penetrated by the spirit of primitive Christianity; even in its minuter arrangements, it is framed and compacted so carefully on the type of older rituals; so often a great and cardinal principle is involved, if not expressed, by some traditionary phrase, or some apparently trifling piece of ritual—that no ordinary learning and tact would be required to touch the Prayer-Book at all without provoking a theological controversy. But, whatever may be Lord Ebury's intentions, it is easy to see in the pamphlets which echo the cry for revision, how delicate and dangerous an undertaking it would be to operate on the Prayer-Book. Mr. Davis* and his friends rush in where wiser persons would fear to tread. He steps boldly and complacently among the smouldering fires of controversy. His pamphlet is an example of the popular confusion of ideas on the subject. He gravely proposes, almost in the same breath, first, ' to revise the Prayer-Book, without altering any doctrine in any direction,' and then, ' to alter those few points on which unhappy differences have arisen, according to the standard of the Thirty-nine Articles.' In this vague and hazy way men speak and think on a subject requiring such careful deliberation, such clearness of intellect, such learning, such profound spiritual wisdom, as the alteration of the Prayer-Book. Mr. Davis seems happily unconscious of his inconsistency. Perhaps he would excuse himself on the ground that he asks not for the doctrines to which he takes objection to be directly negatived, but that they should be ' generalised,' and left open to be taken in either sense—either as affirmed or denied. But what is this but to expunge them ? So expressed, or rather so denuded of all expression, the truth in question becomes lost by silence. '*De non apparentibus et non existentibus eadem est ratio.*' When you have subjected the Prayer-Book to a process of this kind, eviscerating it of all its distinctive

---

* ' Liturgical Revision.' By Rev. C. H. Davis. With an Introduction by Lord Ebury. (Seeley & Co.) The very title is obviously inexact; for the thing meant is revision, not of the ' Liturgy,' but of the Prayer-Book generally.

principles, erasing at the arbitrary dictation of each little clique of sectaries, the peculiar doctrine, however precious to the hearts of others, which does not approve itself to their predilections,—what remains but a lifeless, inorganic residuum, void of form and colour, strangely unlike the clear and majestic outlines of Christian Truth which we have received as a precious legacy from our forefathers in the faith?

For the same reason, the idea of leaving all the passages, to which exception can be taken, optional, to be used or not at each clergyman's private discretion, is equally inadmissible. Any such course would be simply tantamount to making two Prayer-Books— one for those who adhere to the ancient Formularies, one for dissentients. Two Books of Common Prayer in real, if not avowed, antagonism:—the one by implication, and in effect, if not in express words, a contradiction of the other! No. Any generalisation of the controverted passages so as to leave the doctrine which they convey no longer there, or any permission to substitute other forms in their stead, must be firmly and strenuously resisted, as equivalent in reality to a new Prayer-Book, and equally certain to disquiet and disunite the Church.

It is simply chimerical to fancy that the Dissenters can be restored to the Church by tampering with the Prayer-Book in this manner. No amount of concession to their prejudices, no mutilation of the Prayer-Book, however ruthless, would satisfy the insatiable self-will which is the animating principle of Dissent.

If each sect had free liberty to pare away those parts of the Prayer-Book to which it feels repugnance, the residuum would be almost nothing. If, besides, they were allowed, as they would not unnaturally expect, to introduce their own peculiar tenets, the result would be an incongruous and unintelligible patchwork. But in neither case would they be content. So long as ignorance and misconception prevail, so long as men's minds are swayed by self-will and self-conceit instead of by reverence and humility, there will still be Dissenters. No doubt there are always a certain number of Dissenters not by deliberate choice, but by accident—not by fault of their own, but owing to external causes. At the present time in this country a large proportion of Dissent is of this kind, not responsible for its own existence, the result of past neglect and of an overpowering increase of population. Dissenters of this kind may and will, with the Divine blessing, be restored to the fold, as the Church more and more zealously fulfils its mission. But they must come to the truth: it cannot be cut and fashioned to suit their fancy. The Christian faith is a sacred deposit committed to the Church, to be preserved whole and entire for all ages. The Church has no right to compromise it in any way by suppression of any part in order to please human preconceptions. The suppression of the truth is the same thing as the promulgation of error. The Church is bound by fidelity to our Divine Lord and Master to keep his truth unchanged as it is in its own transcendent nature unchangeable, till the end. But it is needless to insist on what must be evident to any thoughtful mind unwarped by party spirit. The utter futility of any such comprehension of Dissenters as we have been speaking of is plain even from the admissions of its most eager advocates. Mr. Davis, after enumerating the various and important alterations of doctrine which he recommends, is constrained to confess a misgiving, not only 'how far agreement could be secured to such alterations,' but 'whether or not they would satisfy, provided they could be obtained.' Dr. Robinson * appears more sanguine as to the success of his scheme for the restoration of unity; but it is truly an extraordinary one. He proposes, with the utmost *naïveté*, that 'each denomination should prepare a service for themselves out of the Book of Common Prayer, omitting such prayers and canticles as they object to,' and then that all this motley group of Prayer-Books should be sanctioned for the respective congregations by the Bishops of the Church! Dr. Robinson has certainly discovered a new way of promoting unity. If this be all which can be said in favour of the comprehension of Dissenters by altering the Prayer-Book, the scheme will not gain many adherents. We repeat that dissentients must alter themselves to the Truth, it cannot be altered to them. The more clearly and unfalteringly the Church proclaims her heavenly message, the more distinctly she announces the spiritual blessings which she alone is commissioned

---

* 'Church Questions.' By Rev. C. Robinson, LL.D. (Hatchard & Co. 1859.)

to convey to mankind, the more likely it is that the wanderers may be recalled to her fold. It is mainly because men have become blind to the great truth, that there is one divinely appointed way of salvation —one channel for diffusing throughout the world the blessings which flow from the Cross—that so many have turned from the living waters to hew out shallow and soon-exhausted cisterns for themselves. Real unity among Christians is a priceless treasure; but the hollow delusion of professed union, without real unity, is not worth purchasing at any price— most certainly not at the cost of any sacrifice of the truth. First, and above all things, truth; secondarily, peace, ought to be the desire of every Christian.

The pamphlets which have been already referred to are only valuable as indicating, with more precision than usual, the chief alterations in the Prayer-Book which are demanded by those whom the authors may be supposed to represent. Dr. Robinson's fitness to pronounce an opinion on liturgical questions may be estimated not only from his extraordinary panacea for dissent, which we have already mentioned, but from other passages in his pamphlet. In proposing to substitute a Collect from the Commination Service for the present Absolution, he prefixes to it a Rubric, directing the clergyman to 'stand up and pronounce this absolution.' There may be conceivable reasons why the priest should stand, as is customary in some other instances, while offering up this prayer; but how can saying a prayer by any possibility be called pronouncing an absolution? Mistakes like this show a fatal ignorance of the very simplest principles of divine worship. Again, in criticising the Ordination Service, he betrays a strange confusion in his mind even on so fundamental a part of the Christian faith as the office and operations of the Holy Ghost. He objects to the words, ' Receive ye the Holy Ghost,' that they are out of place, inasmuch as the candidate for the priesthood has already professed his belief that he is inwardly moved by the Holy Ghost; as if the grace by which every good desire is stirred and fostered within the heart, and which is common to all Christians, were the same thing as that gift of spiritual power to exercise an holy office which is communicated by the laying on of hands in ordination. All this shows with what insufficient knowledge and indistinctness of ideas men venture to pronounce an opinion on the highest and most awful questions. In the same unconsciousness of what he is doing, he thinks that by ' leaving out some twenty-five words' here, and ' some thirty-five words' there (without considering how much would be involved by the omission of those few short sentences), the Prayer-Book might be improved so as to give general satisfaction! Mr. Davis's theological knowledge and reasoning are of the same order. In endeavouring to import a more ' Protestant*istic*' character, as he calls it, into the Prayer-Book, he quotes largely from such sources as a Presbyterian Free Church Review, and other similar periodicals. He lays a great stress on the fact of the Prayer-Book having been revised more than once already; as if that were not a *raison de plus* for expecting that it does not require to be revised again. His argument throughout is of a not very solid texture, and will hardly succeed in convincing any but those who are beforehand determined to agree with him. There is no need to waste further time on brochures so crude and inconclusive as these. May the Prayer-Book be saved from such manipulation as it would experience, if every one, qualified only by his own opinion of his own competency, is to lay rash hands upon it!

It is no new thing in the history of the English Church, this eager craving for change, combined with a slight and superficial theology. There has always been a section within the Church, more considerable for zeal than for learning and discretion, not heartily sympathising with the traditional teaching of the Church, and more or less disposed to fraternise with the seceders from it. Not seldom in the last century men of high purpose and earnest devotion were inclined in this direction partly from the apathy and indifference of many about them. But now, in the re-awakening energy of the Church, the case is changed. Every year gradually and insensibly draws men of this character, though born and bred amid the associations of Dissent or semi-Dissent, nearer and nearer to those who hold fast the received belief of the early Church. As time goes on, and as men of opposite parties come mutually to a better understanding, and learn to meet on common ground, it may be hoped that old suspicions and prejudices will be dissipated, and that the English Church will present a more compact and united front against the heathenism and immorality that we have to contend with. The Formularies, as they are now, afford a bond of union which, without too closely circumscribing or compressing the instinctive tendencies of either party, holds both parties together, and facilitates their arriving in time at more perfect agreement. But this gradual approximation of high and low churchmen would be rudely stopped, and a yawning chasm would open itself between the two parties, if these Formularies were to be changed. Instead of blindly and restlessly grasping at a change which could only satisfy the one party by extruding the other, it were better to acquiesce in the providential dispensation which has given us a framework which, with a strict regard to general orthodoxy of belief, admits nevertheless some diversity of opinion on controverted points. At any rate, a time like the present is peculiarly ill-suited for revision.

The objections made to certain parts of the Prayer-Book are often based on a misconception. Many persons form a distorted idea of the doctrine which they fancy intended, and waste their strength in fighting a shadow. It may be worth while to consider very briefly the chief points in controversy, in order to show how much nearer would be the unity of the Church, not if the passages in question were altered, but if they were more clearly and duly understood.

It is a trite remark that the English Church allows a certain amount of latitude on controverted questions.

But we must be careful as to the sense in which this remark is true. The latitude is not in regard to the objective truth in its own essential nature, but subjectively as to the precise manner of expressing it. Invariably the mystery is enunciated, so plainly as to preclude mistake, in its great eternal outlines; but no attempt is made—hopelessly impossible as it always must be—to define rigorously, and in set terms, that which always remains after all beyond the reach of the human understanding. Let us take in order the chief points in dispute, and we shall see how much room there is for those differences of opinion which result necessarily from the diversities of human idiosyncrasies, without losing for a moment our firm grasp on the great substantial verities of Revelation. The interminable dispute on Predesti- nation is left by our Formularies logically undecided, without any attempt to solve what is insoluble, and to reconcile within the narrow limits of the human intellect the two apparently irreconcilable principles each in itself practically true, of the Divine fore- knowledge overruling all things on the one hand, and of man's perfect free agency on the other. So again on the doctrine of Sacramental grace. It is clearly stated, in terms of which men have been unable though desirous to evade the force, that in the one Sacrament the child is born again; and, in the other, that a Real Divine Presence consecrates the elements of bread and wine; but how this won- drous spiritual change is effected, and to what precise degree—in what way and how far the sinful nature

is changed by the Baptismal waters, and fresh communication of life divine imparted in the Holy Eucharist—is left for the revelations of that time when we
shall 'know as we are known.'   In both cases the English Church recites the formula of Holy Writ, without
presuming to dogmatise more exactly on its significance.   A new birth in Baptism is indeed affirmed,
as in Holy Scripture, so by the English Church; but
men are not required to assent to any definition how
far the original nature of mankind is abolished, or
how far it still remains to thwart and hinder the new
life in the soul.   Very often persons may be found
objecting to Baptismal Regeneration, as if by the
term was intended a belief that the soul is from the
moment of Baptism actually rather than potentially
sanctified.   Similarly, objection is made to the doctrine
of the Real Presence, and to the spiritual sacrifice in
the Holy Communion, as if assent were demanded to
some logically impossible statement.   But invariably
the Church simply repeats the words of Him who is the
Truth, and delivers them to the faithful believer un-
restricted by the subtle refinements of a too dogmatic
phraseology.   There is no attempt to adapt to human
reason what is of necessity above, though not contrary
to reason.   So again in the Ordination Service, it is
a not uncommon mistake, as we have already seen,
to suppose that the words, 'Receive ye the Holy
Ghost,' imply—not, as they really do, the gift of the
Holy Spirit for official ministrations in the Church
—but the gift of some superior personal holiness.   If
men would but realise distinctly the independence of

the office and the person who holds it; if they would open their eyes to the fact, that the messengers of Christ are merely messengers, not acting with inherent authority, but simply as ministers even in the most solemn exercise of their deputed powers; and that the message of blessing and pardon is entirely provisional and conditional on the state of the heart in the eyes of the only all-seeing Judge; then they would cease to be scandalised, as they sometimes are now, at the doctrine of Absolution. Again, no subject has occasioned more acrimonious controversy than Private Confession. Here again the Church of England leaves a certain discretion as to the use of the ordinance. The principle is plainly sanctioned; the practical application of it is left, as in reason it ought, to be determined by circumstances. The popular outcry against Confession would not have been roused, if it had been clearly understood that Confession to a priest is not required in the Prayer-Book as necessary in order to receive his message of forgiveness. For receiving advice and direction common sense shows that private confession is necessary; but for Absolution, repentance alone is requisite, which may evidently exist even where there is no confession.*

In the same uncompromising, yet tolerant spirit, the Prayer-Book speaks of Fasts and Feast-days, without imposing any minute regulations of diet. A

---

* We are not speaking here of the extraordinary cases for which a special Absolution is provided in the Prayer-Book, but of the ordinary ministrations of forgiveness in the Public Services of the Church. Both the public Absolutions, though differing in form, alike convey pardon to the penitent.

wise liberty is allowed in the application of the principle to the cases of individuals. The scruples that are felt by some persons on both these points arise, as usual, from a misconception. Their scruples about so plainly scriptural a practice as Fasting would cease, if they would only look through what they choose to regard as a mere outward formality to the deep evangelical principle of self-denial which underlies it; nor would they object to the observance of Saints' Days, if they were brought to see that the honour paid in such observances is not paid primarily to the faithful servants of Christ, but to Him from whom alone all their graces are derived.

Lastly, the scruples which some persons feel against the use of the Athanasian Creed would be removed, if they would but understand that what they erroneously call the damnatory clauses are really and truly minatory: a warning such as Christian charity requires to be uttered, not a sentence of condemnation; and that even in this point of view an intentional, so to speak, not a formal or literal or actual assent, is implied by the words, ' which except a man believe faithfully, he cannot be saved.'

Another point in the Prayer-Book, though of far less importance, to which exception is taken, is the custom of requiring the sponsors to answer in the name of the child. Here again the difficulty is more imaginary than real; the fancied confusion of responsibility, on which the objection is grounded, exists rather in the mind of the objector than in the ordinance itself. Nor can much weight be fairly attached to the repugnance which Mr. Davis and others manifest to some parts of the Marriage Service. Who will say that, with the present low tone of morality both in town and country, the solemn warnings against impurity are not needed? Granting that the language of the admonition is plainer and more outspoken than accords with modern usage, still that is no valid reason for altering it. The outward and superficial delicacy of speech, which is part of our modern civilisation, is no certain warrant for real inward purity. On fitting occasions it is most salutary to break through the reserves of social conventionality in order to touch the hidden springs of thought and feeling. The solemn celebration of holy matrimony is, without question, such an occasion, justifying the seeming violation of social propriety, which would otherwise be inexpedient and wrong. Language which would be out of place and unbecoming among lighter and less reverend associations, falls with a chastened sound on the heart at such a moment, when the mysterious bond of union for life and for death is being sealed between man and wife in the presence of the Most High. But we need not dwell on this point. The too fastidious scruples, which used not long ago to lead to the mutilation of the Marriage Service, are very infrequent now. There is a more general feeling of the necessity for speaking plainly, if at all, in the way of exhortation; and the deepening sense of the awfulness of holy places and holy rites counteract the morbid fear of apparent indelicacy which we have been speaking of. These scruples, we repeat, are not now of wide prevalence; and, like many others of the kind, vanish before a little reflection.

We have another imaginary difficulty, though of a still more minute kind, in the objection to the words 'most religious' as applied to the reigning sovereign. Of course there is no real difficulty at all. They are applied, like the title 'Defender of the Faith,' to the office, not to the person. Good King George III., whom Mr. Davis quotes, showed his humility rather than his common sense in saying that instead of 'Most religious King,' it ought to be 'the most miserable sinner.' Some other of the many alterations proposed are too trivial to deserve much notice; for example, the substitution of 'Morning' and 'Evening' Prayer for 'Matins' and 'Evensong,' 'Festival' for 'Feast,' and 'day by day' for 'this day' in the Lord's Prayer. Certainly there is such a thing as a *cacoethes emendandi*.

But there is one point of real importance which ought not to be overlooked. A tendency may be discerned in some quarters, as in these pamphlets, to wish to alter what are called the 'obsolete phrases' in the Prayer-Book, such as are found, for example, in the Marriage Service. But where is the necessity? From having been used continually and generally, such phrases can never really become obsolete. They are no real difficulty even to the uneducated persons who fail to understand their exact meaning. Evidently, on merely literary considerations, it would be a great mistake to obliterate these racy and idiomatic relics of our old English tongue. But they are venerable from their age, and familiar by long usage; they form a link between the successive generations who have knelt in the same holy places, and joined in the same holy services. The loss in this respect would far outweigh the trifling advantage of making the service rather more generally intelligible. It would be a fatal error to abandon the time-honoured diction of the Prayer-Book, by modernising and simplifying it, for the sake of attaining what is really unattainable and most undesirable—a form of Prayer lowered to the level of every one's comprehension.

But it is in the attempt to shorten and re-arrange the services that popular reformers of the Prayer-Book betray their incompetency most egregiously. What shall we say of the celebration of the Holy Communion *in the evening,* in disregard of the prescriptive custom of the Catholic Church, and in apparent ignorance of the important considerations on which that custom is grounded? We mention this as one instance among many others. Both the writers before us try their hands at this work of 'revision' as if it were the easiest thing in the world. It is in vain to look for any regulating principles of reconstruction in these pamphlets. There is no reference either to the great standard treatise of our old divines on the Prayer-Book, or to the no less valuable works of living authors, such as Jebb, Freeman, Palmer, &c. The one writer would curtail a few verses from most of the Canticles, as if the sense would remain unimpaired. The other would omit, strange to say, the *Second* Lesson from

one of the services.   Both seem agreed, if not in other
details of their plans, in demurring to the repetition of
the Lord's Prayer, as if all repetitions were alike included under the censure pronounced against 'vain
repetitions;' as if there were no precedent in the
garden of Gethsemane for repeating the same words
of fervent prayer more than once, and as if that divine
prayer did not occur with fresh significancy and appropriateness, however often it may be used in the
service.   It is wearying to hear this continual outcry
against any prayer, but especially this prayer, being
recited more than once in the same service.   The
writers in question seem perfectly unaware that the
various services, which of late years have been strung
together into one long Morning Service on Sunday, may
be used separately, as seems to have been originally
intended.   Crude and ill-advised suggestions, such as
those which have been mentioned, framed on no guiding
principles, unauthorised by liturgical precedents, the
result of hasty and inconclusive reasonings, cannot be
too earnestly deprecated.   It is like a child pulling
a watch to pieces, and vainly trying to re-adjust in
proper order its exquisite and intricate mechanism.
These two pamphlets are not in themselves in any
way remarkable, but they are samples of the rash
and mischievous innovation which threatens the
Prayer-Book at this time.   If anything really must be
done in the way of forming new services, it must be
done in a very different way.

It is a relief to turn from the incoherent and unpractical projects of these self-constituted reformers

to the Reports of Convocation. There we find the same subject, the revision of the Prayer-Book, brought forward more than once in the last few years. Both Houses have pronounced—the Upper with perfect unanimity, and the Lower with only one or two faintly dissentient voices—that the ' Prayer-Book ought to be preserved entire and unaltered.' But on the further question of introducing supplementary services, we find some difference of opinion. Certainly, if Convocation has done nothing else, it has afforded a good opportunity for the ventilation of important questions, not only by eliciting the opinions of the most eminent of the clergy in both Houses in the course of discussion, but also by the Reports resulting from the more silent labours of the Committees. Whatever may be the defects in its present constitution, it represents and gives utterance as nothing else does to the sentiments of the Church of England. It is worth while to trace its proceedings on this subject.

In 1854 a Joint Committee of both Houses reported in favour of dividing the services, and of adding some new occasional services, ' to be formed from the Prayer-Book.' In February 1855, a debate ensued in both Houses on this Report. After considerable discussion, certain resolutions proposed by the Bishop of Oxford were finally carried in the Upper House, to the effect that some modification in regard to the services is desirable, but only so far as concerns the Rubric, the division of the services, the Psalter, and the Table of Lessons. It was agreed that these resolutions should be embodied in any address that might be presented to the Crown. A very similar resolution was passed by the Lower House; with this difference, that they insisted on restricting the alteration of the Rubric, Psalter, and Lessons by the following limitation: 'only so far as may be necessary for the division of the old and formation of new services.' Most of our readers, we think, will concur with the Lower House in wishing to narrow, as far as possible, the alterations required. Waiving for the present the question, which is no easy one, of the legal possibility of altering the Rubric without an Act of Parliament (a question which seems to affect any alteration of the Calendar as well as of the Rubric), there is an important distinction in another point of view to be drawn: any project for altering the Rubric would be the beginning of endless controversy.

But to return to Convocation. The subject was resumed, after a considerable interval, in February 1859. The Bishop of Oxford, with all the persuasiveness of his earnest eloquence and commanding intellect, urged the expediency of appending six or seven occasional services to the Prayer-Book, and thought that this could be done by license from the Crown, without any recourse to Parliament. But the Bishops were divided in opinion; some feared the danger of stirring the question of revision at all; others doubted this licensing power alleged to reside in the Queen's prerogative. The motion was lost, but only by the casting vote of the President. Meantime a resolution of similar tendency had been agreed to in the Lower House.

In the cautiousness and deliberation of this movement, there is nothing to cause surprise or regret. Many and serious are the considerations involved. Granting, for the moment, that there is much to be desired—that shorter and more diversified services would be a great gain, especially in the present state of our population; allowing all due weight to the argument that a wise and moderate reform is the best preventive of revolution; still one great difficulty stops the way. How can such alterations be made, in the face of the Act of Uniformity, without permission of Parliament—a Parliament no longer consisting of even nominal Churchmen, but influenced in no slight degree by interests hostile to the Church, and singularly unqualified by temperament and constitution to act as a tribunal in such a matter as the revision of the Prayer-Book? It arises, we conceive, from a sense of this danger—a danger which indeed can hardly be overrated, that we find some of those who usually sympathise with Bishop Wilberforce hesitating to commit themselves to unreserved agreement with his proposal.

But we must be clear on this point. We are not disputing for one moment that Parliament has a voice in the matter. The two Houses of Parliament, together with the Crown, represent the nation, and as such are one of the two parties to the compact between Church and State. This compact rests on the principle that the Formularies once approved and ratified cannot be altered without consent of both parties. The State has clearly the right of with-holding the legal sanction of its authority to any alteration which it disapproves. Otherwise the State might find itself continuing to support and uphold a religion changed in doctrine and practice from the first intention. It may refuse its assent; and if the alteration be persisted in, it may even withdraw the temporal privileges which it has conferred. There is no grievance or injustice so far. All this is plainly involved in the very idea of an Established Church. But this is all. The State may accept or reject alterations proposed by the Church; and might even proceed, in case of the Prayer-Book being altered without its consent, though this would be an extreme measure, to refuse to observe any longer a contract, which, it might contend, had been broken; but it has no right to enact any alterations of its own motion; no right even to take this or that part of the scheme proposed by the Church, so devising in fact a scheme of its own. It must accept or reject *in toto*. Now the danger is, that this important distinction would at the present time be disregarded. It is extremely unlikely that Parliament would consent to pass an enabling Act to authorise the Church to make new Formularies; that such a permission would be granted, implying, as it would, an assent by anticipa-tion, seems out of the question. Nor in all probability would Parliament be content simply to say ' Yes ' or ' No ' to any plan of alteration laid before it. Probably the plan would be discussed in detail; the most inconsiderate suggestions would be proffered, and perhaps adopted; and questions which ought to be calmly and deliberately considered by a conclave of Churchmen only, would be rudely handled by a miscellaneous assembly composed not entirely even of nominal Christians.

Clearly the Prayer-Book cannot be altered without a new Act of Uniformity, to repeal the force of the 36th Canon as it now stands. Equally certain is it, that there are reasons which make an appeal to Parliament for this purpose a most dangerous step at this time. When the Church of England becomes, as we may reasonably hope it will in time, more united in itself, more adequately represented by synods; when the various questions of the connection between Church and State shall be no longer, as they are now, in process of solution, but decided one way or the other, then the Church will be in a position to make whatever alterations may be really necessary; and to claim for them, with more authority than at present, the ratification of the State; or, if the course of events should be overruled by Providence, to the gradual separation of Church and State, to proceed without the intervention of Parliament at all. Looking to either contingency, it seems the wisest course to wait.

But something can be done, it is said, and with apparent reason, without Parliament. The Bishop of Oxford, though guarding himself from being supposed to speak positively, has referred to legal authorities as supporting his view of the practicability of legalising new services without the help of Parliament. The same argument has been urged by Mr. Massingberd, a very competent authority, in an interesting letter which appears in the 'Journal of Convocation,' vol. I. He there cites several precedents from the reign of Elizabeth downwards, tending to show that the Crown has continually possessed and exercised this 'dispensing power' of authorising special services, drawn up by the Church, to be used without any violation of the Act of Uniformity. The special services of Thanksgiving and Humiliation, which emanate so frequently from the same source, and are generally received without question, as well as the custom of Parliament attending services ordered only by the Crown, go to prove the same thing. The scope of these precedents can hardly be extended so as to cover any infringement on the Prayer-Book as it stands, even in its Calendar of Lessons, but they appear to warrant the addition of new services to be used as occasion requires.

But supposing this mode of proceeding to be practicable, what are the particular points to which a Royal Commission of Bishops and other divines ought to direct their attention? Several new services have been suggested. A service of Thanksgiving for any especial public blessings, not for harvest-time only, but such as might be suitable on other similar occasions, is perhaps one of the chief desiderata. For, ever since the Reformation, a tone less jubilant and more penitential than in former times has pervaded our services. A Form of Humiliation and Deprecation, in times of pestilence, or of any other public calamity, is less urgently needed; we have one already in the Litany, and for extraordinary occasions in the Commination Service.* Another service, the want of which is sometimes felt, is one for the restoration to the Communion of the Church of those who have fallen away from it. A form of prayer for a blessing on the Missions of the Church has been spoken of, but this want is not a very pressing one. Still less has any case been made out for a Children's Service — an innovation of a most objectionable kind. The adoption of any such service, in the preposterous though popular idea of making all things plain to their understanding, would be virtually a debarring of the younger members of the Church from their share in common prayer. Dr. Jebb, in a thoughtful and interesting letter, in the ' Journal of Convocation,' vol. I., has demonstrated most convincingly the absurdity of such a scheme; ' public prayer for classes,' for the young, for example, as distinct from the old, being, as he remarks, ' a feature not to be found in any Liturgy.' Perhaps an exception to this ought to be made in the case of Prison Services. A congregation of criminals seems really to require a special form of prayer, not one intended for persons in full enjoyment of their spiritual privileges. A short, simple, fervent service for the sake of the neglected and almost heathenish masses to be found in our great towns, to be used in church after an open-air service

---

* The notion of having a fixed day every year set apart for national thanksgiving or humiliation, which some members of the Lower House seemed to entertain, is not very intelligible.

in the vicinity, would perhaps be a gain; but the Litany would suffice almost as well as any new service for the purpose. Anything like a form of prayer to be used in school-rooms, or any other unconsecrated building, ought not to be thought of. We are too apt in these days to forget that the house of God is the especial place where his presence dwells, and where, most of all, He may be sought and found. A form of Prayer for Consecration of Churches and Churchyards is wanted. The opportunity might be taken while framing and authorising these new services, to revise and improve the service for the Accession Day, and to give the formal assent of Convocation to it. These appear to be the new services that are required. They might be ordered to be used at the discretion of each Bishop in his own diocese. In cases of national rejoicing or humiliation, there would be a consensus of the Episcopal Bench generally.

Anything more than such occasional services as these which have been mentioned, however much to be desired, seems scarcely to be attained by the exercise of the Crown's prerogative. But, to some extent, a remedy is near at hand, without even this extraneous assistance. The long service on Sunday morning is, or rather was, a grievance of this kind; we say a grievance, for the Sunday Morning Service is cer-

---

* Convocation, even with its present imperfect organisation, still as representing ' de facto' the Church of England, seems quite competent to address the Queen for a Royal Commission to frame such additions to the Prayer-Book. The results of that Commission might be submitted, if necessary, to representatives of the Northern Province as well as to the Convocation of Canterbury.

tainly too long for most persons to enjoy it as they ought; besides, the symmetry and significance of the several parts are marred by the combination. It is now an established fact, that its component services may be used separately wherever it may be desirable. Many town churches have already taken advantage of this permission, which comes now supported not only by the dictates of common sense, but by the express approval of the Bishops. Plainly there is nothing in the Prayer-Book to forbid or discountenance this division of services. The more closely the history of the Prayer-Book is investigated, the more incontestable it seems that the modern custom of combining the several services into one rests on no real authority. Mr. Massingberd, whose opinion carries weight, not only from his learning but from his well-known candour and fairness, has contributed some useful facts bearing on this point. In his letter, published in the ' Journal of Convocation,' after citing Bishop Sparrow's opinion, he lays especial stress on the fact, that the Bishops in the Savoy Conference spoke of the services as distinct. Other proofs may be gathered from the immemorial custom of cathedrals and from history. But they are superfluous now. What we have to follow in the interpretation of our Formularies is not the intention of those who framed them, but primarily the plain literal and grammatical meaning, in the form providentially delivered to us. We repeat, for it is a point of the utmost importance, that it is difficult, if not impossible, to prove from the Prayer-Book that any one of the ordinary services contained in it may not be used separately at any time by permission of the Bishop. The town congregations are likely more and more to wish to avail themselves of this elasticity. In country parishes, where people come from a distance, and by habit and temper are less impatient of a long service, but, on the contrary, rather like it, there is less need to separate the services. Sometimes the service is rendered tedious less by its own length than by an elaborate and pompous way of 'preaching the prayers.' This is a defect that may be cured without a Royal Commission. That our services may be used separately, wherever expedient, is a fact now generally admitted, and one leading to most advantageous results.

A third service for Sunday evening has been proposed, but seems unnecessary with this division of services. The Litany, with catechising, is often used in the afternoon, and the Evening Service later in the day. Perhaps it is not against rule to read the First Lessons for the day in lieu of those for the Sunday afternoon, where the Afternoon Service is simply repeated in the evening. A discretionary power in the Diocesan to order Lessons would be of advantage, but seems incompatible with the law at present.

A short form of daily prayer would be useful. In this respect a hint may be taken even from such a source as the Irvingite Prayer-Book—a Prayer-Book not without great merits. It provides, unless we mistake, a longer and a shorter form for daily use. The omission of the introductory part, or of any other part of our Daily Service—a practice here and there ventured upon—is, of course, quite indefensible, and of most dangerous tendency. While the Daily Prayer remains as it is, it must be used in its integrity. Or why not sometimes substitute the Litany? If it be objected that many persons are deterred by the length of the service from attending it, the evil must be met in another way. Surely it would be far better for persons of scanty leisure to come for *part* of the service on week-days than not at all. Until this practice becomes more familiar to the English nation, the churches will remain almost empty from Sunday to Sunday. Another habit that ought to be encouraged, is that of resorting at spare moments to church for private prayer. It is because we realise so faintly the great truth that a Divine Presence resides in the house of God, there accessible to all who approach it rightly, that we are apt to think more of the congregation than of Him whom they come to worship; otherwise we should not so often hear the want of a large congregation alleged as a reason for not having week-day services. Our Daily Prayer may not be adapted, in its present form, for general use. Still this ought not to deter those who cannot attend during the whole of it, from being present at least during a part, or, if not then, at some other time of the day. It is much to be wished that the daily lives of Englishmen were sanctified by the hallowing custom, in these days strangely alien to our habits, of repairing to the house of God for a blessing on their work or their recreation. Even those very persons, who feel most strongly the holiness of one day in every week, often most inconsistently appear unable to perceive the corresponding sanctity of particular places.

The second exhortation in the Communion Service, that addressed to the communicants, has sometimes been objected to in Convocation. It has been said that this is calculated to raise disquieting scruples at a time when the hearers are fully prepared to draw near with faith and a quiet mind. The force of this objection is undeniable. But it is reasonably doubted whether that exhortation is not intended only for those occasions where notice of communion is given. In this view it is equivalent to the Presbyterian custom of 'fencing the tables,' and ought not to be addressed to the communicants: that is, it is not part of the Liturgy, strictly so called.

Only two difficulties, both of considerable importance, remain, which ought not to be unnoticed. The repugnance to some of the Apocryphal Lessons is not peculiar to the so-called Evangelical party. But we cannot see any legal way of substituting Lessons of a more edifying character than that of Bel and the Dragon. The only remedy seems to be to take opportunities of explaining the true position which the Apocrypha holds according to the Church of England. It is impossible not to wish that our Table of Lessons could be improved. Shorter and more select lections from Holy Scripture would be a great improvement. But it is one which we must be content to wait for, till a fitter time for alteration shall arrive.

The other difficulty is one still more generally felt,

and though often overstated, still one that cannot be denied. Almost every day, in one parish or another, proves how ill-adapted the Burial Service is for indiscriminate use. But it is not the service that ought to be altered; it is the indiscriminate use of it. The 4,000 Clergy who remonstrated against this evil have been misrepresented as asking for alteration in the service; but this unquestionably, so far from being the general desire, would be deeply regretted. The restoration of primitive discipline is one remedy proposed; but this is a course more easy to propose than to follow in the present relations of Church and State. Indeed, it seems as if it were providentially ordered that the Church in its maturity should gradually be deprived of those external restraints which were a support in an earlier phase of Christianity. Anyhow the present age is one which cannot be constrained by force in spiritual matters. The practical difficulty of enforcing ecclesiastical censures is insurmountable. What, then, can be done? The present service is evidently adapted, in its tone of joyful confidence, for those who die in full communion. A service less expressive of hope and joy is wanted for such persons as are not communicants. Clearly it cannot and ought not to be left to the Clergy individually to pronounce on the state of the deceased, whatever may be the appearances. But a broad line might be drawn between communicants and others. If such a service can be classed in the category of occasional services, it would be a great boon from a Royal Commission. Meantime it ought to be generally understood that the expressions of hope and thankfulness, properly belonging only to the faithful, are not withheld even from others, *simply because no clergyman has the right, by his own unassisted judgment, to assume that they ought not to be used in any particular case,* whatever misgivings he may be forced to feel as to their being inapplicable.[*]

It is time to conclude these remarks, very inadequate as they are to the importance and extensiveness of the subject. No doubt the Prayer-Book might be improved. But while admitting this, let us be heartily thankful for what we have already. We have a Prayer-Book not only instinct with heavenly beauty, breathing the wise and holy spirit of ancient times, but dear and precious, in spite of all detraction, to the hearts of the people. Their instinctive affection for it needs to be developed into a more intelligent reverence. The pulpit, by clearly enunciated, but not drily didactic, exposition of the doctrines of the Church, must defend the Prayer-Book. For such improvements as cannot safely be attempted now, let us wait hopefully. It would be a great improvement if we had more variety of colour, so to speak, instead of a sort of neutral tint, in our services for different seasons; a more special appropriateness, for example, in the Psalms and Lessons for days of joy and sorrow: the Catechism also

---

[*] A false analogy is sometimes drawn between these expressions of hope and the thanksgiving for regeneration in the Baptismal Service. But the cases are by no means parallel. In the infant there can have been no barrier to the divine grace : in the other case there may have been an unholy life frustrating it.

seems to want the insertion of some additional instruction on the nature and office of the ministry:
but for these and other such improvements, weighing
the preponderating risks attendant on the mode of
proceeding, we shall be wise to wait. But till when?
We answer, till the Church of England shall feel itself more prepared by matured convictions to undertake the critical task of revision; till parties shall
have become, as they are becoming, more fused into
agreement on cardinal truths, more willing to disagree
amicably on minor points; till the laity shall be more
sensible of their duties and privileges as members
of the Church. The tide of progress is advancing
steadily in this direction. What may be the ultimate
result of the now unsettled relations between Church
and State need be no cause for alarm. If there be
life and strength and unity within the Church, we
may feel easy about external appliances. Of course,
we ought to preserve them as long as we can; but
about the issue we need not fear. There are many
encouraging signs. Ruridecanal meetings of clergy
and laity, now becoming common, are a great step
towards lay co-operation, and synodical action on a
larger scale. The theological colleges are training
the clergy in a deeper and more accurate knowledge
of theology. The numerous schools for the Middle
Classes, now rising everywhere, of the same kind as
the great school at Hurstpierpoint, and, among other
things, the invaluable practice of public catechising,
are indoctrinating the laity. Everything indicates
that a clearer and stronger conviction of the objective

truths of religion is extending itself gradually through the Church, even in the face of many hindrances. We may reasonably hope, that in the course of some years the Church will be in a position to enter synodically on the consideration of those further improvements, which seem beyond the scope of the only legislative process at present safely open to us. Let us be content for a time to guard the Prayer-Book as it is, making only such additions to it as seem urgently needed, and are attainable without disunion in the Church, or an appeal to Parliament.

THE ROMAN QUESTION, OR CHURCH AND STATE.

'ROME is the only city in the world where one has never seen everything.' So speaks M. About, a caustic and unenthusiastic Frenchman; and so will every one allow who has ever been there. *Vedi Roma e mori.* As the traveller along the Via Appia crosses the arid plain, spanned at broken intervals by the colossal stride of the gaunt aqueduct of Appius Claudius, and catches his first sight of the huge dome of St. Peter's, rising clear and full against the brilliant sky, he begins already to feel the strange fascination which Rome exercises over all who approach her. This feeling is one which grows upon him every day. In exploring the piazzas and narrow tortuous streets, he lights at every turn on some fountain or obelisk, the relic of classical or mediæval times. Again and again he revisits the 'finest Christian temple in the world,' and while treading its imperishable Mosaic floor, and breathing its soft fragrant atmosphere, feels himself each time more and more impressed with the sense of its vastness and magnificence. When he gazes from the Pincian Hill, or the Pope's Terrace, to take a last look at the innumerable cupolas and obelisks bathed in the soft violet hues of an Italian evening, he feels how hard it is to leave such a city, and how impossible to break the many ties which bind him to it.

In these days a journey to Rome is no longer a difficult matter. Rome is now within a very few days of London. The eternal city is still the bourne of pilgrimages to multitudes even of those who are unactuated by any feeling of reverence for the Papal chair. At Rome are still to be met, as in ages past, the representatives of every country, and of every section of society. A crowd of sightseers in Rome presents a panorama of the varied phases of human existence. Among the dense masses that are compressed into St. Peter's on some grand occasion, to witness, either in curiosity or devotion, the performance of some gorgeous ceremony, it is interesting to look round on the strangely miscellaneous character of the crowd; to see the fair, bright complexion of travellers from the British Isles, side by side with the sallow cheeks of the natives of Southern Europe, or the duskier skin of some Oriental race; to hear the whispered compliment, or the ordinary phrases of conversation quickly succeeding the attention demanded by the celebration of some solemn rite; to think how for one cause or another, by inducements so widely different, the individuals composing that motley assemblage are drawn from their distant homes to one peculiar spot of earth ; and to remember that in almost every period of European history, this one and the same city, under many changing forms, the city of Scipios, Cæsars, Pontiffs, has retained an irresistible hold on the destinies of the world.

It is worth while to analyse more closely the various aspects of Rome, which render the place so attractive to travellers of so many different sorts. Some of course, and not a very few, are chiefly allured by the brightness of the Roman climate, and the gaieties of a Roman winter. The daily drive or promenade on the Pincian or along the Corso; the flirtations of balls and conversaziones; all this is only life in London or Paris, with the novelty of fresh accompaniments: it is the same picture in a new frame. Sojourners in Rome of this description might as well be anywhere else all the time. Artists and lovers of art are attracted by the rich treasures of the galleries and museums; the student of history, by the associations of its palaces and columns; the classical scholar by its rare manuscripts and inexhaustible antiquities. But there is one aspect of Rome which gathers to itself, irrespectively of personal or professional bias, the attention of every thoughtful mind; its religious aspect; its churches and catacombs. If, in the present unhappily divided state of Christendom, the former cannot but be regarded with very mixed feelings of sympathy and repugnance by those who do not belong to the Roman part of the Church Catholic, at any rate all Christian sympathies of every communion may meet unreservedly in the catacombs. There, in the memorials of martyrs and confessors, we may investigate and cherish the traces of the Christian faith, as it was in earliest and holiest days;

before the streams that issue from one common source had become less pure by contact with the earth, and before they had tracked for themselves diverging and, in some degree, antagonistic courses.

These and similar causes may account in part for the great number of foreigners that resort every year to Rome. But the interest of Rome does not reside only in works of art, or in monuments of the past; there is a living interest as well. The dark flowing robes of the ecclesiastics, and the picturesque capes and cloaks of the religious orders, which arrest the notice of the most careless sightseer by their continued recurrence, sometimes in long procession, sometimes in scattered groups of two and three, in the streets of Rome, are phenomena not simply curious to the eye, but suggestive of grave consideration : they are indications of life and power; of life it may be, not now in its full vigour, and of power ebbing away; still of a real living agency at work, the presence and operation of which cannot be denied. Rome is the centre of the world to all the myriads who believe in the Papal supremacy. From Rome her emissaries issue to every region of the world to extend and consolidate the limits of the Roman obedience; to bring mankind, as they conceive, within the pale of salvation. To Rome they repair from time to time, to render their account of the responsibilities of the commission which she has entrusted to them. It is not intended now to discuss the great doctrinal question of the Pope's supremacy, which lies at the root of the separation between the Roman and other branches of the Church, nor any of the other points of difference in doctrine and practice. But there is another question, which may appear at first sight closely connected with the theological one, which is, in fact, essentially independent of it, though accidentally affecting it in no slight degree — the ' Roman Question,' as M. About* styles it; the question of the Pope's temporal power, of his dominion over the States of the Church; a question which, in the present conjuncture of European affairs, calls urgently for a solution. In attempting to arrive at a conclusion on this point, some assistance may be gained from the books above mentioned, by comparing the conflicting testimony of those who defend and those who impugn the present state of things in Rome and the Legations.

It is difficult to classify Cardinal Wiseman's fat nondescript book.† It is 'not a history,' as he admits in his preface; 'not a series of biographies;' 'not a journal;' not what are called 'memoirs.' But it is not difficult, even before reading, to anticipate its character. The readers of ' Fabiola ' are prepared for a style wordy, turgid, and ungraceful, yet not deficient in power of an unwieldy sort; for trite quotations not always happily applied, and for a good deal of not unamiable egotism. Indeed, the impression of the Cardinal, which anyone would derive from his literary works, is very unlike the ideal of a Bonner or Hildebrand, such as impassioned declaimers against

* ' La Question Romaine.' Par E. About. Bruxelles. 1859.
† ' Recollections of the Last Four Popes, and of Rome in their Time.' By H. E. Cardinal Wiseman. (Hurst and Blackett.) 1858.

the Papal aggression have represented him. On the contrary, it is that of a good-natured easy-going man, with more application than genius, well satisfied with his own part in the performance, and disposed to make the best of things around him; one of those who have the knack of rising in the world. He looks back sympathisingly on 'the Carnival in the good old times,' before its feasting and sports had been curtailed by authority; and the task of '*collating* MSS.' calls up in his mind the more pleasing idea of a '*collation*' of a more refreshing and satisfying kind. His book abounds in anecdotes, but they are generally deficient in point; and in many cases serve only as an excuse for introducing the mention of his own acquaintance with some person of rank. But those who expect racy and highly flavoured gossip from his *personal* recollections of the four popes, must be disappointed. He is too discreet and complaisant a narrator to reveal much of their inner life. Nor, on the other hand, does he give much information on social or political subjects. What there is of private or public matters in his pages, is tinted by a pervading *couleur de rose*. Each Pope in his turn, of course, is honoured with a proper share of compliments; but even persons of far lower degree, or standing in a less friendly relation to the writer, have their share too in the general panegyric. From Queen Victoria and the French Emperor, from Consalvi and Pacca, down even to the 'active Sampietrini,' and 'the splendid noble guard' of the Pope, and the 'bearers of the canopy,' walking symmetrically and unflinchingly under their heavy burden, to every one is portioned out, and with a liberal hand, his respective eulogy. In a word, one might fancy oneself all the time perusing the columns of the *Morning Post*, or the *Court Circular*. There is the same profusion of common-place compliments; the same tone of indiscriminating deference for all great personages. In one instance this complaisance betrays the author into an amusing dilemma. In speaking of the first Napoleon's quarrel with Pio VII., he seems at a loss how to hold the balance between the colliding claims on his respect of two such men ; the one the head of his Church and his own earliest patron; the other the maker and deposer of kings; and, which is of more moment just now, the uncle and predecessor of one who has great power of serving the cause which the Cardinal maintains, and who has hitherto shown himself not unwilling to exercise his power for that purpose.

We have already spoken of Wiseman's style as awkward and grandiloquent. Without doubt some allowance must be made for a writer, so much of whose time is engaged in other occupations, and has been passed among un-English associations. Still, it would not be right to overlook such flagrant blemishes of style, and, it must be added, downright violations of the English language, as occur in his pages. Some of the sentences are not merely long-winded and involved, but, to say the least, barely grammatical. When a writer in the eminent position of Dr. Wiseman uses such phrases as a ' stark and

strong Providence,' and ' the personal fit of a sepul-
chre ' (to select only a few of many similar solecisms),
and applies to a boat under water the words 'toppled
over and clean dissolved,' it is necessary to protest
against such breaches of good taste, especially at a
time when a ' spasmodic ' style of writing and un-
gainly affectation of originality in the use (or rather
the abuse) of words, threaten to corrupt the simplicity and purity of the English tongue.

Still, in spite of these drawbacks, those who are
interested in Rome may pass some hours pleasantly
enough among Dr. Wiseman's Recollections, which
may serve, at the very least, to recall to mind their
own recollections of sunny days of travelling in Italy.
As an authority on the ' Roman Question,' his book
cannot have much weight, except with such readers
as have already prejudged the case, and only seek
arguments for a foregone conclusion. We are not
accusing him of intentional misrepresentation; on the
contrary, even his unscrupulous assailant, the notorious Gavazzi,* in his intemperate and scurrilous
parody on ' The Four Popes,' fails in convicting him
of any important misstatement. But, in truth, there
are very few facts of any importance in Wiseman's
book; and the tone throughout is that of a plausible
advocate trying to make the best of a slender case.
He claims the credit due to an eyewitness; but what
he has to relate in favour of his own view amounts to
almost nothing; and the violent bias of partisanship

---

* ' My Recollections of the Four Last Popes, and of Rome in their Times.'
An Answer to Dr. Wiseman. By Alessandro Gavazzi. (Partridge & Co.)

precludes the evidence of even an eyewitness from
being received except with considerable abatement.
Under the unruffled complacency with which he evidently wishes to regard the existing state of things,
may be detected at times a latent uneasy consciousness of the *régime* which he defends being hollow
and unsound at the core; even from his own lips
escape some ugly admissions in favour of his opponents. He is compelled to allow the existence
of discontent and revolutionary tendencies (p. 98).
Again, in trying to excuse the disgraceful system, as
it may be called, of brigandage in some parts of the
Papal territories, he is necessitated to resort to special
pleading of the most transparent kind. It is idle to
explain away an evil so monstrous, and yet, as was
proved during the French occupation, one not ineradi-
cable by a strong government, as the result of the
influences of mountainous scenery, or the excitable
temperament of the inhabitants. Again, in his
account of the manner in which the election of a
Pope is conducted, it is apparent how tenderly and
warily he treads on ground so dangerous, as if unable
to disguise even from himself the secular intrigues
and low selfish motives by which the conclave is
swayed—now by the jealousies of the great Roman
Catholic powers—now by the well-known preference
of the electors, as in the case of Leo XII., whom
Wiseman describes as almost '*moribund*' at the time,
for the one of their number who seems least likely to
stand long in the way of their own respective pretensions.

But the strongest points in the book against its author's case are the very instances which he brings forward for especial commendation of good effected by the Government. Let us see what they amount to. We are gravely told, for example, that Leo XII. distinguished his pontificate by an ordinance forbidding the osterias to retail their vino di paese 'to be drunk on the premises;' and by a still more momentous edict effecting a new arrangement of the ladies' 'seats in the Sistine chapel.' We are told, with the same ludicrously impressive solemnity, that Gregory XVI. established an insurance company, and made several highly laudable additions to the galleries of art. It is like Swift's 'Memoirs of a Parish Clerk,' or the beadle in 'Oliver Twist' recounting his achievements, or the 'vacuis ædilis Ulubris' in Juvenal, with his very limited jurisdiction over pots and pans, and weights and measures. Surely a strong and judicious government would have a better answer to make to its challengers than this. It is not the fault of the men, but of the system. 'The Four last Popes,' if we may trust Dr. Wiseman, were, to say the least, good average specimens of their order, attentive to business, sensible of the responsibilities of their power. If they had not the abilities of a Julius or a Leo, they were at all events, unless we give any credence to the railings of a writer like Gavazzi, innocent of the gross luxury and profligacy of some of their mediæval predecessors—kindly, well-intentioned, decorous, respectable men. They would have been more in place as heads of colleges than as rulers of the State. One would have been a learned canonist, another a benign and estimable professor, another a diligent curator of museums. Even Dr. Wiseman himself cannot say much for the results of their administration. It is obvious that the daily training, and other antecedents of a Pope, as we gather them from his ' Recollections of the Four Last,' are not such as are likely to produce good rulers in temporal affairs. We can easily believe what we are so often told by him, of their gracious urbanity in his interviews with them, and venerable deportment during the performance of their ' functions,' but something else is requisite for the adequate discharge of their responsibilities as heads of the State. Nor is it any answer to this, that the Government is really administered by the Cardinal Secretary for the time being. He is trained in the same school, and affected by the same influences as the Pope himself. The system is one of Clerical Government, and as such it must stand or fall.

On the whole, the impression left on a candid and impartial mind by Dr. Wiseman's descriptions is one of dull stagnation, of inertness and inefficiency ; of antiquated prejudices, of short-sighted and narrow-minded policy; in short, of senile imbecility and obstinacy in the Government of Rome. We look in vain for any indications of life and progress. Even literature and science seem stifled in the heavy atmosphere of repression and ' surveillance.' Mai and Mezzofanti are names illustrious in their respective specialties; but they stand alone, nor can even they be regarded as exceptions to the general rule. For

Mai's ingenious and laborious discoveries of palim-
psest MSS., and Mezzofanti's extraordinary gift of conversing in many languages, are no proofs of intellectual progress.   The study of theology, and that of the
dead languages of Greece and Rome, are those which
might be expected to flourish at Rome, even in the
dearth of other studies; but even these seem, by their
stunted and twisted growth, to betray the depressing
influence of the place.   The theology is still merely that
of the schoolmen ; the classical scholarship is of the old
contracted and pedantic sort.   We read of elaborate
' theses ' and ' disputations,' after the manner of the
schoolmen, on subjects more recondite than interesting ; of Cardinals versed in lapidary inscriptions, and
skilful in ' devolving a rounded period,' or in pointing
an epigrammatic antithesis in Ciceronian Latin; of
one Cancellieri, who wrote learned treatises ' on the
head physicians of the Popes,' ' on the country-houses
of the Popes,' ' on the bite of the tarantula,' &c. ; but
we find no sympathy with the profound and comprehensive philology which in other countries lends its
aid to the researches of history and philosophy.   We
shall have occasion presently to remark on the utter
impotency of all this coercion and restriction to
exclude the knowledge of evil.   At present it is
enough to observe that Dr. Wiseman fails to leave
a favourable impression even of the state of literature
in Rome.   In every point of view, intellectually as
well as socially and politically, Rome appears, on his
own showing, to be far behind other European States
under its present *régime*, and without the likelihood
of progress or development.

If this be the impression left by a writer so zealous for his cause as Dr. Wiseman, we may expect to find our suspicions realised by the writers on the other side. But we need not waste much time on a book like Gavazzi's. It is unworthy of consideration. Most persons are familiar enough with his name and reputation to know how much value can be attached to his testimony on this subject. Those, to whom his name is not so familiar, will be satisfied by reading a very few pages of his book without caring to read more. From beginning to end it is, as might be anticipated, a violent and sweeping invective; a long, confused, rambling tirade against the Papal system. He declares loudly against the ' Satraps of the Vatican,' as if the (generally speaking) inoffensive old men who wear the red hat of the Cardinalate were nothing less than monsters in the shape of men; and rails at their pomp and luxury, as if the tawdry lumbering carriages in which they drive about were marks of wealth, instead of being, as they are, handed down from one generation to another, rickety and battered like the Government to which they belong. He delights in the coarse insinuation of charges, which, if made at all, ought to be substantiated by solid proof, not paraded in a tone of revolting buffoonery. His bitter animosity against Wiseman and the Popes, and in particular against Gregory XVI., towards whom his deadly resentment can only be accounted for on personal grounds, breathes its venom into every line; and the thoroughgoing unfairness into which it leads him may be estimated from the fact, that he will not allow to these recent Popes even the merit, which belongs to them, of having attended well to the preservation and improvement of the museums. The style of the book corresponds with its contents. It is simply what is usually called 'Billingsgate oratory,' and that of a very tedious kind. Let us pass on to a writer whose remarks deserve far more consideration.

If it be objected to what has been said, that Wiseman's book refers to a bygone state of things, subsequently reformed by Pio IX., M. About supplies the answer. He declares explicitly that the celebrated Rescript of Pio IX. has been nugatory; and that the clerical *régime* still remains intact, with the exception of a few laymen being now admitted to clerkships and other offices of a subordinate kind; and he maintains, not unreasonably, that it cannot be otherwise so long as a Pope remains at the head of affairs. He speaks as one entitled to a hearing, both from his intimate acquaintance with Rome, and from his unquestionable acuteness and ability. Certainly some caution is necessary in accepting the dicta of a writer, who commences his book by a formal bow of the most distant civility to the faith in which he professes himself a believer; whose tone is that of a freethinker, not on Roman politics only, but on holier things also; and who sneers politely at the notion of wedded happiness and domestic purity. His style of writing, too, so smart, so pointed and epigrammatic, is one peculiarly exposed, especially in a Frenchman, to the temptation of brilliant fallacies. His pungent sayings and terse racy anecdotes—nay, even his keen and

trenchant logic—are just what too often betray a
writer into inaccuracy and exaggeration. For example, he calls the Roman priesthood 'a caste;' the
very thing which it is not, and cannot be by the
nature of things so long as the vow of celibacy prevails. But M. About knows well, that the 'mot'
will find favour with the multitude; it serves to give
point and spirit to his argument; it is too good a hit
to be thrown away. Many, if not most of his objections to the Papal Government, are not new; they
are merely old objections expressed with a clearness
and cogency which give them an air of novelty. Still,
with due allowance for these provisos, he well deserves
a hearing. Let us listen to the opinion of an observer
so penetrating and clear-headed, and so thoroughly
a man of the world as well as a man of letters.

M. About adds his testimony to that of many
other travellers, or rather of all excepting a very few
bigoted Roman Catholics, to the effect that the
Roman States are miserably misgoverned; and he
insists on the fact that those parts which lie nearest
to the seat of government are in the worst condition
of all. The taxes are very heavy, not if compared in
actual amount with those of wealthy countries like
England and France, but, which is the real criterion, in
proportion to the wretched resources of the tax-payers.
By the arbitrary disbursements of the revenue, a
door is opened to every form of waste and peculation.
Of course agriculture and trade cannot thrive under
the pressure of such taxation, and obstructed as they
are by monopolies and other vexatious hindrances.
The life is crushed out of them. In spite of having

two such advantageous ports as Ancona and Civita Vecchia, commerce can hardly be said to exist at all; and the natural fertility of the soil avails nothing, while the farmer has to contend with every kind of heavy discouragement both from his landlord and the State. The wines, for instance, of modern Italy, hardly seem worthy of bearing the names so highly praised in the days of Horace. The Campagna, once so fertile, is now by long neglect unproductive and pestilential. The malaria from it is gradually extending its deadly sway more and more widely every year. But it may be urged, that the happiness of a people cannot be measured by material prosperity; that moral and physical well-being may coexist with impoverished finances; that peace and contentment, tranquillity and order, are far better than any abundance of railways and manufactures. But we find none of these blessings to compensate for the want of modern civilisation in the Roman States. On the contrary, we find dissaffection and lawlessness, crimes of violence and sensuality. Their social condition is deplorable. The nobles and gentry M. About describes as idle and illiterate. What else can be hoped for of them, subjected in youth to a narrow and cramping education, and debarred in manhood from the responsibilities and distinctions of public life? Any one who has ever seen the pale students of the Roman colleges walking two and two in the streets of Rome, and has contrasted their effeminate and mummy-like appearance with the manly bearing of the young men at the great English Universities, will be disposed to agree with M. About on this point.

The middle classes, the 'mezzo ceto,' instead of forming a connecting link between those above them and those below, are dissociated by an impassable barrier from all sympathy with their superiors. The peasantry, numbers of whom may be seen flocking to the towns on great festivals, half-clad in their squalid goatskins, are, according to his account, poor, ignorant, brutish. The same class in the towns are either disaffected to the Government or only bribed into acquiescence by the old largess of 'Panem et Circenses;' by the same shallow and shortsighted policy which encourages them to rely on the alms of charitable persons, or a 'lucky' ticket in the Pontifical lottery, rather than in their own exertions and honest industry. Justice is so feebly administered, as to be a laughing-stock instead of a terror to evildoers. The army is so disparaged and discountenanced, as to offer no inducement, except to the refuse of society, to enter its ranks. On the whole, it is scarcely possible to conceive any European country in the nineteenth century in so truly forlorn and degraded a condition, both morally and materially, as M. About, and with only too much appearance of truth, describes that of the Roman States to be at the present time.

The Papal Government cannot even plead against this grave indictment, that it does succeed in effecting the one result, which it deems of paramount importance. In the attempt to secure orthodoxy and morality, and to exclude from its dominions the taint of heresy and infidelity, it fails egregiously. It has always been so, wherever coercion over the

conscience has been tried; and so it must be while
the world lasts; but Popes and Cardinals are slow to
learn even from experience.

It is impossible to force men to believe.   A belief
so created is not belief.   No amount of legislative
prohibition, no system however inquisitorial of
' douanes ' and 'espionage,' can impede the free growth
and interchange of thought and opinion, or stop the
way against the subtle entrance of even the most per-
nicious errors.   The evil is impalpable and ubiqui-
tous as the air that we breathe.   It cannot be so
dealt with.   It can never be counteracted by a process
which aims not at assimilating to itself but at de-
stroying every element of life.   Such a policy is like
that of the ancient conquerors, of whom it was said,
' solitudinem faciunt pacem appellant. '   It may
deaden the faculties into an unnatural lethargy; it
may succeed in checking for a time the expression of
opinion; but the stream flows on all the deeper and
stronger beneath the smooth treacherous surface, and
some day the pent-up volume of waters will burst its
barriers and sweep all things headlong before it.
The gradual decay of faith and reverence in Rome is a
fact patent even to the passing traveller. The must cursory glance at the crowds on the steps of the Ara Cœli
and in the piazza below, to see the exhibition of the San
Bambino, may observe year after year more of curiosity
for the spectacle and less of reverence for the sacred
meaning of what they see. Persons really conversant with the different grades of Roman society agree
with M. About that a spirit of scepticism is spread-

ing more and more among high and low. If it were true that the Papal States present a bright example, though not of material greatness yet of morality and religion, then a great argument would be established for the anomaly of government by ecclesiastics. But the Roman States under this government are a scandal and a blot on the map of Europe. The thousands who dwell within their pale are of course the chief sufferers. The evil is reflected from them over the other countries of Europe. It is no exaggeration to say that the see of S. Peter and S. Paul is a hotbed of infidelity, and that its misgovernment gives an occasion of triumph to the enemies of the Christian faith all over the world.

But there still remains one plea, in defence of the present state of things, to be considered. The interests of the small territory under Papal rule are quite secondary, it is argued by Roman Catholics, to those of the Church at large. It is indispensable at any cost that the head of the Church should be independent of extraneous influences. It would never do for him to be the subject of any temporal power. In order to be perfectly free, he must have a territory of his own. Thus they argue. It might be objected to such a train of reasoning, that the conclusion tends strongly to invalidate the premises. If the existence of one supreme head of the Church cannot be maintained except by such misgovernment as that of which the Roman States are the victims, then, on this consideration alone, and apart from other difficulties, we may well hesitate before accepting the Papal supremacy as of Divine ordinance. But the argument fails in another respect. Those who so argue seem to overlook the fact that the very object for which they consent to sacrifice the welfare of a population by no means inconsiderable is simply frustrated by any such arrangement. Real independence, as M. About well says, would be something very different from the Pope's present position. It is not independence, but a most uncomfortable posture of abject depend- ence, to be 'sitting on French bayonets.' It is not independence to be compelled, as has so often happened in the history of the Popes, to resort to the intrigues and manœuvres of diplomacy in order to play off one 'protecting' power against another, at one time by coquetting with Austria, at another time with France or Spain. It is not independ- ence to be trammelled and encumbered by the cares of government, by the expediencies of State-craft, it may chance even by the necessity of waging war. Real independence is to have little or nothing to gain or lose through others. The spiritual power and grandeur of the Papal See are compromised by its temporal relations. As a great spiritual poten- tate, the Pope may be independent of all earthly powers; as a petty temporal prince, his position is and must be degrading and ridiculous.

M. About's remedy, so far as he prescribes one, would be to curtail the Pope's dominions, by taking away the Adriatic provinces. There is a well-known story of the Papal Legate at Bologna, saying, with an

Italian shrug, in reply to some question about the
popularity of the Government which he represented,
' No one likes it except the Vice-Legate, and I am
not ' sure of him;' and recent events have shown how
gladly the Bolognese would welcome a change.   So
far it is easy enough to accept M. About's prescrip-
tion.   But why does he stop there?   Why, after
demonstrating so convincingly that the Papal Government is hardly worthy of being called a Government
at all, is he content with only narrowing the limits of
it, instead of eradicating so incurable an evil?   Probably the imperial influences which guide his pen
have not yet sanctioned or encouraged so bold a
proposal as the utter abolition of the Pope's temporal
power.   The profound and astute prince, in whose
hands the destiny of Italy now mainly lies, may see
other impediments in the way, besides the obvious
danger of alarming and exasperating the ' 40,000
emissaries of Rome,' who are at work within his
empire, and to whom M. About significantly alludes
in one passage, and of provoking them to sound the
' drum ecclesiastic,' hitherto so obsequious in its tone,
to notes of ' angry defiance.'   For some such reason,
most probably, M. About forbears to follow his argument to its legitimate conclusion.   But those who
regard the ' Roman Question,' not merely from a
Napoleonic point of view, but with reference to the
prospects of the whole of Christendom, may well ask,
whether something more than mere partition is not
required by the exigency of the evils resulting from
Papal misrule.   If these evils could be supposed to be

only accidental to, and not radically inherent in the
system; if there were any chance of improvement
without a thorough change ; then we might hesitate
to assent to an idea so open, at first sight, to the
accusation of being 'revolutionary,' forced upon the
mind though it be by all our foregoing considerations.
But the experience of history corroborates what
reason divines, that the confusion of temporal and
spiritual authority, at any rate in the present advanced state of European civilisation, is as injurious
in its consequences to both, as it is contrary to the
analogies of Providence.

M. About rightly styles an ecclesiastical despotism
' the worst despotism in the world.' It is fatal alike
to the rulers and to those who are ruled. For the
former it is a distraction and a degradation, a situation
full of peril, to have to turn from the duties of their
high and holy calling to meddle with the administration of the affairs of this world ; for the latter, the
consequences are still worse; they are placed in a
totally false position towards their spiritual guides.
They fear and suspect the spiritual fathers whom they
ought to reverence and love. They reject with impatience, when enforced by the strong hand of power,
the dictates to which they would eagerly give attention, as the utterances of a voice from heaven. They
resent the interference, and mistrust the motives, and
harden themselves against the influence of an authority which endeavours to constrain instead of persuading, and to convince by force not by reason.
The natural results are worldliness, ambition, luxury,

and a forgetfulness of their celestial office among the
clergy, thus exalted on the dizzy pinnacle of earthly
greatness; and among their subjects, either the blind
and slavish prostration of men, whose moral and spiritual life is paralysed and torpid, or a spirit of restless rebellion against all ties and all authority, either
human or divine.

Such a form of government may be, as Dr. Wiseman calls it, 'patriarchal,' or it may, though with less
exactness, be compared to the Mosaic dispensation;
but it would not be so easy to reconcile either the
theory or the practice of it with the larger and more
catholic spirit of Christianity. The startling disparity between the fishermen of Galilee and a modern
Pontiff is often commented on by controversialists;
and sometimes, it must be confessed, with undue emphasis. For it stands to reason, that as time goes on,
and circumstances assume new forms and combinations, a corresponding development is to be expected
in the outward appearance of the Church. For example, the Catacombs and the 'Upper Chamber' grow
into stately fabrics; the wandering habits of a missionary bishop are changed in converted countries for a
more settled and regular routine of work; the
Church, in short, acquires a fixed and recognised
position, and expands her organisation more and more
elaborately, and assumes the garb and attitude suited
to her rank, as 'in, but not of,' the kingdoms of the
world. All this may fairly be conceded. But these
are developments not of principle but of details; they
are modifications, not of the inner, but only of the

outward and visible, life of the Church.   To arrogate
power and jurisdiction in mundane affairs is a novel
principle, and at variance with the tenor of apostolic
traditions.   While Rome and the Roman States remain as they are, their state is repugnant to and incompatible with the words of Him, who made answer
to one asking for his interposition as an arbitrator of
earthly things, ' Who made me a judge or divider
among you?' and, who taught his disciples on another
occasion, ' My kingdom is not of this world.'

In England the principle for which we are contending has become almost a truism.   If not as yet universally admitted, it is at all events gaining ground
every day, and extorting an assent even from those
who are most reluctant.   The theory of Church and
State being identical has disproved itself.   It may
take the form of the grossest Erastianism in some
minds.   Theorists of the late Dr. Arnold's school
may conceive an Utopian state in which is merged
the distinct life and action of the Church.   On the
other hand, with the admirers of Laud, the State is
degraded to be the mere creature and servant of the
Church, tamely executing her mandates, and enforcing them, when necessary, with a strong arm.   In
either case the confusion is complete.   It may be
said that very few persons, if any, among those who
are capable of forming an opinion on such subjects,
could be found now holding either of these theories
in its integrity.   But a dangerous tendency in the
former direction still exists, and may be observed
continually in practice among men of politics.   By a

strong reaction from the mediæval system, which we have described as prevailing in most exaggerated form at Rome in the present day, they are apt to regard the Church as merely an instrument in the hands of the State; as dependent on the State even for its very existence. That the life and functions of the Church on the one hand, and the State on the other, are essentially distinct, is a point which needs to be plainly asserted at the present time. The political consociation of men, which we call the State, in all its manifold arrangements, in its laws and usages, its sanctions and prohibitions and conventional requirements, is properly engaged about their temporal affairs, and directs its aim at their temporal convenience and prosperity. The Church proposes to itself a still higher purpose; human happiness not in time only, but for eternity. The two objects to be attained are, as experience shows, really inseparable. These two great institutions, ordained by the wisdom of Providence, each for its own especial end, are evidently intended to work together and assist each other, and so they do in a healthy state of things. Their respective spheres of action, though each rounded and symmetrical in itself, intersect each other. Good morals, for example, are their common ground. Honesty, temperance, orderly and decent behaviour, are inculcated and enforced by both alike; by religion, as a part of duty, by policy as calculated to promote the welfare of a nation; but even here we may see a difference. The State deals mainly with overt acts, religion mainly with motives and intentions. Again, it is plain that no man can be a good citizen, except so far as he shapes his course according to the teaching of religion, which is the real groundwork of all morality. Nor can anyone be a faithful member of the Church who neglects his duty to his family or his country, or who in any of the various transactions of life, from the greatest to the least, forgets his obligations to society. Still, for all this, Church and State are really separate as soul and body, though like soul and body connected by the closest bonds of mutual dependence. As we have already seen how in Rome the Church is forsaking her appointed mission while claiming to wield temporal powers, so in this country there is often danger lest the civil Government transgress its proper limits by presuming to regulate questions affecting the conscience and belief of the Church. If unhappily the Church in England has so far alienated from herself, by neglect and owing to other causes, the hearts of the people, that she can no longer be rightly called national, then, in the course of the next half-century, one of two results may be looked for: either the people will return in large and gradually increasing numbers within her fold—a possibility not altogether hopeless to her quickened energies—or the few remaining ties between her and the State will one by one be severed, and she must then resign the privileges and the vantage-ground which naturally belonged to her in her ages past, when Church and State were working in harmony actuated by one spirit, and numbering the same persons in their respective pales. Whenever the latter result shall arrive, the great gain of free

and untrammelled action will be a compensation, we
do not say whether adequate or not, for whatever
facilities accrue to her from her present position as
national and established.

But it is time to return from thoughts of this
favoured island to the less hopeful prospects of Italy.
Of that lovely and unfortunate country, the prey of
foreign aggression, enfeebled and exhausted by the
still more fatal evils of internal degradation, who can
prognosticate the future? *   Whether Italy be des-
tined to lie prostrate under the ' iron heel ' of
Austria, or under the less galling but not less real
domination of French ' ideas; ' whether the outlying
kingdom of Sardinia will be able, like Macedon of old,
to make Italy a mere appendage to Turin, or united
Italy to assert her own nationality from sea to sea, the
most far-seeing of European statesmen would be presumptuous to predict.   The most enthusiastic friends
of Italy cannot but feel how much is wanting, before
she can be pronounced ready for self-government.
Ingenious, versatile, quick-witted, and accomplished
as Italians are, in all that pertains to art—nay, keen
and profound as the Italian intellect proves itself to
be, and enterprising their spirit, in affairs of State—
still men look doubtingly and distrustfully for evidences of the moral solidity, the uprightness and self-
control, the deliberate and enduring energy, by which
alone success can be achieved among nations as
among individuals.   The modern Italians have been
called a nation of actors; their character has been
described as *'having no backbone.'*   One thing may

* In 1859.

safely be asserted. Whatever changes may be in store for Italy, it is impossible for Rome to remain much longer as it is. Nor will the removal of the unpopular Antonelli, nor the introduction of the Code Napoleon suffice, so long as the Government retains its priestly character. As there are scarcely laymen in Rome at present of sufficient experience to undertake the Government, the change requires time. Rome, like the rest of Italy, has to learn the lesson of self-government. But sooner or later the great change which we have been contemplating must come. Many signs on the political horizon foreshow it. We have already given reasons for expecting it with hope, rather than with regrets or fears. It is not only, or even chiefly, for the sake of the Pope's wasted territory and misgoverned subjects, that we desire to see him relieved of his temporalities, but for still greater reasons. Whenever this shall happen, then one great obstacle will be removed to the reformation of the Roman Catholic Church, and a great step made towards the consequent reunion of Christendom. The obstinate persistence of that branch of the Church in those corruptions of the primitive faith, which cause division and estrangement between it and the reformed branches, is closely connected, as we have already remarked, with the condition of the Roman See. Rome is the centre of the Roman Catholic world: Rome is, as it were, the heart, the pulsations of which are felt in every throb through every limb of her gigantic system; from Rome a tone and a character is given to the half of Christendom. There is a passage in Dr. Wiseman's book strongly bearing on this point. He dwells on the fact, that what is called 'Ultramontanism' is encouraged and strengthened by the personal recollections which bind so many of the Roman Catholic clergy, even in foreign countries, to the city of Rome, and the occupant of the Papal chair. It is easy to understand this; and to see how the spirit which perpetuates the errors and abuses of that Church has been engendered and fostered by the appetite for power and dominion of a secular kind. The compulsory vow of celibacy, demarcating the clergy from the laity, in order to bind them by new and closer ties to their own order; the compulsory exaction of private confession, subjecting the laity to the 'direction' of their priests; the narrow and jejune education which Rome enjoins, reducing the mind to submission by a process of exhaustion and exinanition, these are the natural results of that ambitious and self-aggrandising spirit, which we find, though now in its decrepitude, in its coarsest embodiment under the shadow of the dome of S. Peter's. The Pope's secular power is the keystone in the arch; it rivets the structure of Romanistic innovations; if it were removed, they would be more likely to fall. Of course there would be many other difficulties to be surmounted before the great work of reformation could be feasible. But there would be some hope, to say the least, of the enormous pretensions of the Papal See to supremacy and infallibility being relinquished, when the bishop of Rome shall no longer be raised above the level of the other bishops of the Church by

the accidents of temporal sovereignty; some chance
of the restoration of primitive simplicity both of doctrine and practice throughout the many channels of
the Roman communion, when the mass of corruption
shall have been cleared away from the fountain-head.
Rome itself, the city of Rome, the beautiful, the
eternal city, would still retain its proud pre-eminence
in the world, as the city of historical recollections, of
æsthetical wonders; as the city of galleries, museums,
libraries; of paintings and sculptures; of fountains,
obelisks, and ruins; of basilicas and catacombs, of
cloudless skies and buoyant atmosphere.   Rome
might be, not all this only, but a metropolis also of
literature and philosophy.   Rome would be all the
more worthy of admiration and love, if disenthralled
from the benumbing spell which now hangs over it,
and regenerated to a new political existence.

DR. NEWMAN AND THE ENGLISH CHURCH.

THE great passage of arms between two of the most prominent men of our day is already becoming a thing of the past. Dares has discovered to his cost, that it was rash to provoke Entellus to resume the gauntlets. Hard hitting and ardent impetuosity have proved no match for the keen eye and masterly hand of the veteran controversialist. The bystanders have pronounced their ' Habet ' on the aggressor in the fray. But it is not as a mere trial of strength that the controversy has been watched so eagerly, not only by the partisans of either champion, but by that outer unsympathising world, which is usually too busy to attend to theology. It was easy enough for Dr. Newman to refute the random imputation of words which he had never spoken. But his ' Apologia ' * goes far beyond this. He undertakes to clear himself and his career, as well as the Communion to which he now belongs, from the general charge of duplicity; and, with this view, gives an account of his reasons for submitting to the Church of Rome. That two public men, so thoroughly uncongenial to one another, that they

* 'Apologia pro Vitâ suâ,' Longman, 1864.

K 2

might argue for ever without approaching in any degree to a mutual understanding, should come into collision, like two thunderclouds, was a thing to be expected sooner or later, and of comparatively small moment in itself. But it is a great thing that the character of a man so pre-eminent as Dr. Newman should be cleared even from suspicions, not only for the sake of himself and his friends, but because the world at large has a stake in the reputation of its leading men. It is a great thing also, to have a vindication of the Roman Church from a notorious reproach by so competent an advocate; and to have the reasons of so remarkable a change of creed from the lips of the person himself.

The personal accusation is disposed of for ever. Even those who may hitherto have doubted Dr. Newman's sincerity must acknowledge now, and gladly, that they were mistaken. The career, which the 'Apologia' retraces, strange as it is and erratic, is transparently that of a true man. If any one can be proof against such evidence, he is past being convinced at all. In particular, Dr. Newman's letters to several Roman Catholics, during the critical time just before his secession, show plainly his sincerity both in taking the final step, when he did, and in remaining where he was, till then. Together with this charge of disingenuousness, other personal questions are set at rest once for all. No one can say again, that Dr. Newman has not found rest in his new Communion; nor that he is unloving towards old friends and old associations, however unable to sympathise with them.

He has vindicated himself triumphantly. The ' Apologia,' so far, is no Apology ; no retractation, no hesitating or qualified attempt at self-excusing. It is a downright denial of what is alleged : a defence of himself as complete as that inimitable ' Apologia,' in which Plato vindicated his master's innocence, by merely being his biographer. Whether Dr. Newman is equally successful in vindicating the Roman Church is another question. In fact, it is only by holding aloof from entire adhesion to such casuistry as that of Liguori, and by drawing a distinction between Italian and English ideas of truthfulness, that he saves himself from a verdict of complicity, not indeed with practices, but with a theory, which Englishmen are apt to stigmatise as ' jesuitical.'

But the ' Apologia ' is most important as a deliberate record of religious convictions and experiences. Even if it were divested of the charms of a style that is almost faultless in its exquisite propriety, and of all its gossiping reminiscences of men and things fast fading into the twilight of oblivion, it would still be one of the most perfect autobiographies ever penned. In this ' votive tablet ' the life and the man himself are laid bare ; for, in narrating his growth and changes in religious belief, he is speaking of what has been to him, not merely, as with all good men, the first thing in life, but almost the sole object of interest, the drift of the whole current of his being. Persons who neither know nor care much about Leo and the Monophysites are yet fascinated by so unreserved a revelation of man's real inner life. This knowledge of himself, this rare power of dissecting and analysing himself, is one chief characteristic of Dr. Newman; one great source of his weakness alike and strength. He uses the same freedom, or more, about himself, as he would about others, when he calls himself 'vacillating,' 'impetuous,' 'fidgety.' Overpowering indeed must have been the force of long suppressed feelings, thus to burst open the flood-gates and to constrain him to pour forth the secrets of his heart before the crowd. It is in no carping spirit, nor with any want of reverence for the fore-most theologian in Christendom, that the attempt is made to touch on a few of the salient features thus presented, especially as they relate to those great ques-tions of the day which concern the English Church.

The controversies of 1840 seem now superseded by others. Their sound falls on our ears as from a distance, as stories of the War of Independence on the ears of the belligerents lately standing face to face in Virginia and Georgia. The question of 1840 in the English Church was 'Rome or England?' In 1865 it is 'dogmatic or undogmatic Christianity?' The 'Apologia' will do good service if it reminds those who are now contending amongst us for the truth, that there are other questions of importance besides that of inspiration; and that the basis of the Christian faith is not in the naked letter of Holy Scripture alone, but in the whole testimony and tradition of the Church. Here is the answer for those who ask, 'How are we to know what to believe without a theory of literal inspiration?' Those who hold fast the faith once delivered to the saints, and the form of sound words, preserved and transmitted by the Church from earliest times, cannot be at a loss what to believe, nor disturbed in mind even by controversies about the Bible.

In this way the 'Apologia' is very useful. But for direct assistance against the onset of infidelity we look in vain. Say what they will, there is something in their position, as soldiers of Rome, which hinders her ablest men from wielding their weapons freely. They are cramped and hampered by the exigencies of their system. They fight with their hands tied. Instead of vanquishing the enemy with his own weapons—like those great protagonists of the Church in early days, who subjugated man's rebellious reason by persuading and convincing it—they fall back in lieu of argument on the perilous and unwarrantable antithesis of faith and reason, and on the suicidal dilemma of believing everything or nothing. Their one reply to their adversaries is an appeal to the infallibility, the very existence of which is admitted only by themselves.

In this one word we have the key-note of the 'Apologia,' and the clue to the career of its author. Men who are naturally sceptical and restless, and yet willing to believe, crave for the repose which infallibility promises, as a nervous person craves for his opium or his dram. It has the same attraction for them as a gorgeous ritual for minds less predominantly logical and more æsthetical. This characteristic comes out strongly and prominently, indeed, in the 'Apologia,'

but not for the first time there.   We had a glimpse
of it in the deeply interesting story of 'Loss and
Gain.'   Charles Ridding's conversion to Rome is
there explained and justified by his need of something
which should silence his perplexities and doubts for
evermore, by giving to faith an authority altogether
independent of reason.   The real biography only
delineates more fully what had been already adumbrated by the fiction.   Dr. Newman appears throughout his life, and by his very nature, in the attitude
of a man protesting—as one moved by an irrepressible
sensitiveness to protest against the things around him
—in the beginning of his Oxford life protesting almost
as warmly against Sir Robert Peel and his Roman
Catholic Emancipation, as at the last against the
Bishopric at Jerusalem.   It was natural to him to be
isolated, intellectually, and eclectic; and to pass from
phase to phase, from Puritanism, along the 'Via
Media,' through his attempt to reconcile certain
Roman tenets with Anglican doctrine, till he reached
his goal.   Intensely self-conscious, he longed for
infallibility, like those 'who feel the weight of too
much liberty,' and doom themselves of free choice to
the restraint and coercion which they feel to be salutary.   The tendency is scarcely ever latent.   He made
the Bishop of his diocese his Pope, so long as he
could, and bowed eagerly to his decisions, not with
any affectation of humility, but as if heartily glad to
be rid of a heavy responsibility.   When the Bishops
'charged' against him it was a shock to the very
ground under his feet.   When a general outcry of

dissent and disapproval was raised against his interpretation of the Articles, it was more than he could
bear. A more obstinate temper might have been
hardened in its own convictions by all this opposition.
But he yearned for consent and unanimity. To his
mind the antiquity of a system was valueless without
catholicity. That was the crucial test: that alone
inspired confidence and rest. A sense of his own
innate proneness to doubt made him suspicious
of everything like it. What is called 'Liberalism,' a
readiness to entertain new ideas, an aptitude for
change, he regarded instinctively from the first as a
deadly foe, deserving no truce, no quarter; not as a
tendency in which good and evil are mingled, but as
thoroughly bad, dangerous, anti-Christian. Even
when he had almost made up his mind to join the
Roman Church, the alliance of that Church with
O'Connell, more than anything else, deterred him.
He desiderated in the Church of England the voice of
an 'oracle;' and he sought what was to him a necessity of his being, where alone the semblance of it could
be found. To him, as to Wesley, the 'world' was
'bad:' he wanted, if not perfection, at least the assertion and profession of it; naturally he gravitated
towards that communion which, disdaining the common processes of reason, arrogates to itself a supreme
authority, and looms on the mind with a grandeur of
proportions and discipline to which less organised
and less extensive portions of the Church Catholic
make no pretension.

True, there is a great deal of special pleading in

his way of explaining this submission of a defiant
and distrustful intellect to a supremacy which admits
of no questions.   Under his hands the infallibility
of St. Peter's chair resolves itself into something
very like the elective empire of the present day in
France, which professes itself the exponent and representative of the popular will, even while domineer-
ing over it, at once its creation and its idol; or like
the subtle influence of the *Times* newspaper in England, half leading, half following, public opinion,
always moving with it.   Still the fact remains.   The
perfect repose of intellectual irresponsibility amid the
storms of controversy seems to have been from the
first the haven to which he was floating, even una-
wares; the unacknowledged loadstone of his course.
For the sake of this he is content, if not to embrace
cordially, yet to acquiesce without a murmur, in all
those details of doctrine over which infallibility throws
its shield.

If infallibility attracted him to Rome, there was
something in the English Church which repelled him
quite as strongly.   All the associations of what is
called the ' Establishment ' were alien and repugnant
to him.   The outward conditions of the Church in
England, and its relations to the civil power and
society, are indeed only accidental, not essential to
her being, and seem in many ways providentially
adapted to her place and her work.   But to him they
were utterly distasteful.   Like Wesley, he thirsted
for something more intensely and purely spiritual,
impatient of the mundane element, which is inse-

parable from the alliance of Church and State, of soul
and body. He seems intolerant of the intrusion of
anything earthly, however innocent, in the personal
life of the soul, in the corporate life of the Church.
After shaking off very quickly the other trammels of
a narrow Puritanism, he retained this Manichæan
abhorrence of matter; for it was not so much part of
his training as of his innate self. In theory he
doubts, like Berkeley, the positive existence of matter;
in practice he seems to regard it with suspicion and
dislike. He speaks of the world, not as a field in
which wheat and tares wait together for the sickle,
but as a vast growth of noxious weeds, in the occupation of the enemy. Whatever in the English
Church especially marks it as established and pro-
tected by the State provokes his keenest sarcasms.
The Hebdomadal Board at Oxford, the Heads of
Houses, regarded him as an enthusiast and fanatic.
They were in his eyes obstructive, secular, unspiri-
tual. In 'Loss and Gain,' the sight of an English
clergyman driving his wife home in their pony-
carriage after stopping in Bath, elicits a pitying,
contemptuous smile. In the 'Apologia,' the height
of incredibility is the idea of an Anglican Bishop
working a miracle. Clearly the wonder is, that a
man so uncongenial to the English Church remained
faithful to it so long as he did. For the Church of
England, though allowing a wise latitude in every
direction to the zeal of her members—tolerating, on
one side, Scripture Readers, and, on another, Sisters
of Charity—is yet inclined by circumstances and by

the force of hereditary associations towards a type of organisation distinctively peculiar to herself : and, though never forgetting nor relinquishing for one moment her own spiritual independence of the State, has characteristics, which appear Erastian to those who take the words ' in the world but not of the world' in the sense of Loyola or Whitfield.

Those who are well acquainted with Dr. Newman and his writings, and whose judgment is not warped by their predilections, will hardly fail to concur in this estimate of him.   But we cannot wonder that strangers and opponents have been hopelessly bewildered by such a character, in which the lofty traits of the saint and the philosopher are individualised so strongly by the eccentricities to which genius is ever liable.   It is a web in which the colours are not merely varied, but violently contrasted; in which the intersecting lines cross and recross one another in endless confusion.   What could be more enigmatic to most people than such a man, whether addressing them from his pulpit or from the seclusion of his study?   We may compare him in some features to Origen or Chillingworth, but after all

> None but himself can be his parallel.

We may find other instances of a man fearlessly honest in principle being accounted disingenuous by his contemporaries; for the greatest men are misjudged in this way more often than in any other during their lives.   The foremost orators and statesmen have, in their day, too often been subjected to similar misconstructions. A subtle intellect, though guided by the purest sincerity of purpose, often leads a man into paths which look very tortuous to his neighbours. But this real honesty, with an appearance of disingenuousness, is the least of the contradictions which meet us in Dr. Newman. So impetuous, and yet so shrewd and caustic;—so fond of irony and reserve, not in conversation only, but in more deliberate and solemn utterances also, and yet so gushingly outspoken and communicative at times;—so candid in argument, and yet constitutionally so unable to enter into the feelings and views of the school of Professor Kingsley;—so pugnacious and yet so tender-hearted;—so prone to dispute about every thing, and yet acting usually on the *laisser-aller* rule of letting people be, if they do not agree with him;—truly a character like this is more than enough to perplex a British public.

The same contradictoriness comes out in his line of argument. Ordinarily, he is most fair; but, if once persuaded of a thing, his ready ingenuity supplies him with any number of pleas for its truth. His tone and manner are those of a practical man; but, as in arguing from the Monophysites, he trusts himself implicitly to an uncompromising theory. In him the practical and the speculative habits of mind seem coexistent without being harmonised. He warns us, in his ' Arians,' against logic as a dangerous instrument in controversies of religion, and yet himself follows to the death a ruthless and impracticable logic, which refuses to make any allowance for the

Church of England, and which, at the last, abdicating
its functions, consigns him to the care of a Church
claiming to be irresponsible to reason. He repudiates
sentiment as a guide, and yet seems, as in his manner
of accepting the infallibility of the Roman Church,
with all that this involves, to believe first, and to
reason afterwards.   He depreciates the Anglican
system as a mere system on paper (and such it might
well seem to a man living among books and bookish
men, and intolerant of anything less perfect than his
ideal), and yet overlooks the inconsistencies in doctrine and practice of that more imposing system
which allured him from us.   Keen-sighted and logical
beyond others, we yet find him gravely arguing that
if a conviction shall recur to his mind, it will thus
prove itself trustworthy because supernatural—as if
all such impressions came invariably from a good
source, always emanations of truth, never a delusion
and a lie.   Calmly reviewing his public life with the
light which his own disclosures throw upon it, we
may trace in all these apparent contradictions a self-
conscious spirit, ever on the watch against its own
proclivities.   But the feeling at the time of lookers-
on, and even of adherents, vainly endeavouring to
keep pace with him, was one of amazement and con-
sternation.   The 'Apologia' has explained what
seemed inexplicable.   While scattering to the winds
all insinuations of duplicity or crookedness, it shows
that an idiosyncrasy of no ordinary kind accounts for
his secession from England to Rome.

    It is important to estimate Dr. Newman's secession

rightly, and to see clearly what it is really worth in its theological bearings. It has been said by others, and by himself too, that he was never adapted, with his self-questionings and misgivings, for the leadership of a party, and, when he crossed the Rubicon, very few of his followers crossed it with him. But many of those who had hitherto felt the confidence which he seemed to feel in the English Church recoiled from the brink of the chasm with a shock, which even now thrills and reverberates through England. It is therefore of importance to realise clearly the true causes of a defection which has done more than anything else of late years to unhinge the faith of intellectual Englishmen. Those causes, we have endeavoured to show, originated in a peculiarity of temperament, and were, first, a craving for infallibility as a sedative for doubt, and next, a dislike to some traditional characteristics of the Church of England, for example, in its social life, and as being a civil as well as an essentially religious institution. It is sometimes said that Dr. Newman was persecuted out of the Church of England. No doubt there was much to harass him in the obloquy that he encountered, and his was a nature to shrink from the unsympathising coldness of the few, even more than from the coarse invectives of the many. But the root of his defection was that he never was heartily an English Churchman, never in accordance with that type of which the 'Country Parson' and the 'Christian Year' are representative. The openi g stanzas in either book, redolent as they are of social affections and of social wisdom, are thoroughly unlike that view, of life and of the world which presents itself through the gratings of a cloister.   Here we have one cause of his estrangement.   But its mainspring was the attractiveness to him of the Roman system in its colossal proportions and systematic organisation.   It promised him what he wanted—the guidance of an unerring hand—and step by step he allowed himself to be thus led onwards to the destination, which was all the time, though he was unconscious of it, his foregone conclusion.

On both these points the mind of the English Church is at issue with Dr. Newman.   It does not exalt, whilst it does not disallow the monastic type of excellence, and, instead of holding out the panacea of an infallible guidance, it treats the doubts and difficulties of faith as part of man's probation, to be handled wisely and tenderly, not to be rudely cauterised nor exscinded.   Instead of peremptorily silencing every question by the assumption, that she alone is the Universal Church, she alone inspired with oracular certainty, she appeals to antiquity, and is content to abide by that decision.   Dr. Newman himself has told us in time past, that communion with other parts of Christendom is not necessary to the life of a national Church, however conducive it may be to its health; and that the life of a Church consists in holding the tradition of Apostolic doctrine, and the grace of Apostolic organisation.   If those who are deputed by Providence to steer the Church of England through the troubled waters, which now surround her, will but firmly grasp these great and cardinal principles, the panic of the moment will soon subside. It is our privilege to enjoy the inheritance of the Creeds transmitted to us from our forefathers in the Church Catholic. We are

The heirs of all the ages, in the foremost ranks of time.

This priceless legacy we hold in trust, to be bequeathed in turn to our posterity, enshrined in the pages of that 'Book of Common Prayer,' which comes to us Englishmen, of the nineteenth century, in substance, if not in very words, from the Saints and Martyrs of ancient Christendom, from the chosen twelve, and from the truly infallible lips of Him, who is the Truth, their Divine Lord Himself.

THE SCHOOL OF PROFESSOR KINGSLEY.

THOSE who are addicted to the habit of 'tabulating' the public men of the day, must be not a little puzzled in which pigeon-hole of their classification to put Professor Kingsley. A mere glance at the list of his published writings shows at once his popularity as an author, and the versatility of his powers. Novels, sermons, poems, politics, theology, physical science succeed one another in a profuse disorder, which culminates in the utter chaos of his 'Water Babies.' But even thus we gain some insight into the writer. The first impression is one which a closer intimacy will not dispel, of a repugnance to whatever is artificial, conventional, systematic. Whether or not this antipathy exceeds its proper limits, and what other elements must be taken into account in order to form a just conception of the author, are questions not to be solved from the title of his books. If the endeavour to indicate some of his characteristics should lead, in any degree, to a freedom of speech which is more permissible about public men whose career is over, than about those who are yet among us, Professor Kingsley himself will be the first, it is hoped, to excuse it, so long as criticism confines itself to what is patent to the eyes of the world, to that conception of him which arises from his published writings.

It must have been a surprise even to Mr. Kingsley's friends, when the vacant chair of modern history was offered to one, whose literary pursuits seemed to lie in other fields. But this very variety of attainments is simply so much gain for the historian or professor of history, unless it interfere with that special knowledge of his subject which is, of course, the first requisite of all. To the historian, as to the barrister, no sort of knowledge comes amiss. He must be moralist and philosopher, or history becomes dry annals ; he must be poet and orator, or he cannot bring his narrative home to the hearts of his readers. Scott in his novels, for example, and Shakespeare in his plays, have an unconscious art of teaching history which professed historians may envy them. The new Professor may not be pre-eminently learned ; but he has the faculty, which is peculiar to genius, of seeing familiar things in a new light, and of making others do so too. In this, and in other ways also, he resembles Dr. Arnold. We may look in vain through his works for passages such as abound in Arnold's, of grave and majestic beauty ; the dignity of style is wanting, the energy all the more intense, because repressed and restrained ; there are continually spasmodic jerks and joltings as the steam-engine fights its way, with many an impatient snort, to its destination ; but there is the same ardour for the right, the same combativeness against evil, the same liking for the simplest and homeliest phrases, the same distaste for the cant of mere conventionalities.   If Kingsley is ruder, blunter in speech, and at times shrill and noisy in his passionate denunciations, he has a richness of humour and fancy, which Arnold had not, and for want of which he never could have written ' Two Years Ago,' or the ' Saint's Tragedy.' It is a curious fact that a stranger to the personal influences of Arnold and Rugby, should come nearer to the likeness of Arnold than any one even of those among his favourite pupils who cherish his memory most reverently.   The most distinguished of them all, the one usually taken as the representative of Arnold and his school, has far less in common with his master than the Cambridge Professor.   For Kingsley, though more tolerant than Arnold, more comprehensive in his philosophy, more genial and hopeful in temperament, is yet, like Arnold, a 'good hater.'   None can say that, either in praise or dispraise, of the Dean of Westminster.

An author's style, like the personal appearance, the dress, and manner of any one, is a tolerably fair criterion of the man himself.   The marked preference for words of Saxon origin in both Arnold and Kingsley is indicative of that Teutonic impetuosity, of that sturdy downright earnestness of purpose, which, whether right or wrong, goes straight to its mark, disdaining periphrases, and overlooking, too often, all that is not obvious from its own point of view.   Again, Kingsley's nervous grasp of words, that ring like the hammer on the anvil, the broken

and uneven run of his sentences, the bursts of eloquence verging on rhapsody, chequered by collo-
quialisms and slang, the quaintness and grotesqueness
which 'crop out,' as he would say, in the midst of
true sublimity and pathos, are all expressive of the
mind which inspires the diction. This reckless defiance of proprieties, this absence of elaboration and
polish, are essentially part of the writer's self. This
looseness of language is the result, as well as the
cause, of a corresponding looseness and inexactitude
of thought. A closer reasoner would not so hastily
take up analogies, attractive at first sight, but which
will not bear handling ; as when he compares the
barbarian Goths, who conquered the Roman Empire,
with the disciplined and civilised Englishmen who
conquered India. Like Arnold, he can always make
his meaning clear ; but, unlike Arnold, he is diffuse
and discursive, apt to wander from his subject, and to
waste himself in redundant reiterations.

But, with all these points of personal resemblance
to the great Head-master of Rugby, Kingsley is no
'Arnoldite.' However strongly he may assert the paramount importance of practical godliness, as the one
thing needful above all others, and though his tendency
may be to keep doctrine in the background, he cannot fairly be accused of being indifferent to dogmatic
truth, of despising creeds and catechisms. The
Arian struggle is not, in his eyes, a question of races
and localities ; it is 'an internecine struggle between
truth and falsehood.' Still less can any other ecclesiastical party claim him for its own. Like a knight-

errant of old, he holds his lance eagerly poised for
the fray, ready to take whichever side appears to him,
for the moment, in the right, especially if it be
the weaker. He is no 'free companion,' selling his
prowess for hire. The party which has least of his
sympathy is that which has exaggerated the doctrine
of the corruption of human nature. The old Puritans,
Cromwell's Ironsides, or the Covenanters of the
Pentland Hills, he can admire and revere ; but their
modern representative, with stereotyped phrases that
have outlived their meaning, and one who looks on
the whole universe as 'very good,' stand far as the
poles asunder. He is too abhorrent of discipline,
too careless of form and ceremony, and, in a sense,
too undogmatic to sympathise heartily with the great
Oxford movement of thirty years ago. Nor is the
difficulty solved by labelling him as one of the ' Broad
Church' party. He is no latitudinarian, after the
manner of Dr. Rowland Williams, Mr. Wilson, or Professor Jowett. He holds a position of his own, mid-
way between Archbishop Trench and Mr. Maurice ;
less ecclesiastical than the one, and more dogmatic
than the ingenious theologian, to whose mind every
categorical statement seems to suggest, as a matter of
course, a counter statement to cancel it. After all,
we must look to the past for Professor Kingsley's
affinities. Strange as it may sound, a fox-hunting
parson of the last century, if he was, as some were, a
good parish priest and a man of education, comes
nearer to him than any thing else. Their political
creeds may differ as widely as Magna Charta and

Mr. Bright's Charter for Working Men, but the tone and temper of the men is not unlike. Though Professor Kingsley hates the intrusion of self-interest into the conscience as the motive for doing right, yet no man insists more constantly on that inseparable connexion between 'wealth,' in the old-fashioned sense of the word, and 'godliness,' which formed the staple of sermons like those of Paley. If we go back further still, to the robust geniality of the Elizabethan era, we shall find traits of character which resemble him still more closely.

Professor Kingsley, with all his rare endowment, writes, after all, like a great boy. His sweeping statements, the extravagance, at times a puerile extravagance, of thought and language, which breaks out even in his lectures, as if the shooting-jacket were peeping out under the Professor's gown, the exuberance of animal spirits which explodes in slang, his fearless championship of what he believes to be truth, are the characteristics of one who retains the freshness and elasticity of mind which others have left behind them. Here we have the secret of his hero-worship, of the exaggerated value which he sets on the study of biography, of his rare gift of sympathy with the boyish temperament of the sailors at 'Aberalva,' and of the sunburnt, hard-handed sons of toil everywhere. Not long ago he stood forward to advocate in the *Times*, with his usual fervour, the cause of the Dorsetshire labourers; and it was he, unless we mistake, who volunteered, in a short-lived periodical, some fifteen years ago, to be the

Cicerone through our National Gallery, not of the rich and educated, but of the hardworking artisan and his fellows. He has a thoroughly boyish relish for the wonders of physical science;—like a boy, he prefers all which is external and objective in nature to what belongs to the inner life. His novels, original, vivid, life-like as they are, and instinct with the creative power of imagination, fall short of the highest standard, because they are put together like the awkward, loosely-compacted limbs of a great hobble-dehoy. His failings are those of boyhood. He carries the principle of 'calling a spade a spade' to its utmost limits. In 'Hypatia,' in the 'Roman and Teuton,' in his novels generally, while reprobating vice indignantly, he thrusts it forward into the foreground of his picture, bestows on it a lavish amount of colouring, and, in short, expresses it with a coarseness unnecessary and unbecoming. There is also sometimes a tone of levity and apparent irreverence, such as boys are apt to assume in disgust at cant and unreality. It is no wonder that he can describe so well the long-haired young Kempers, with their rude chivalry and their scorn of what is dishonourable and base. Like them he is a thorough boy, impatient of check or control, a loud advocate for fair-play, impulsive, and fearless of ulterior consequences.

We have said that Professor Kingsley is, what Johnson admired, 'a good hater.' The especial object of his hatred is evidently whatever makes men prim and starched, artificial and unreal. We need not dwell now on those earlier and more fragmentary writings, one of which is only too fitly entitled by its author, ' Loose Thoughts for Loose Thinkers.' The crude speculations of ' Yeast,' ' Phaeton,' and ' Alton Locke ' may be taken for what they are worth, as the effervescence of genius. He is too sensible a man, as indeed may be gathered from his inaugural lecture, not to have modified, by the experience of an active and useful life, theories of an unsettling and destructive kind. But the antipathy to discipline pervades all his writings; and when the aspiration after discipline takes refuge within the walls of the cloister, he has no patience with it.* ' Naturam sequere ' is his motto; pushed at times beyond all reason. The ' Saint's Tragedy ' turns on this. In ' Westward Ho ' even his vocabulary of invective seems inadequate for the contrast which he would draw between Sir Amyas and his Jesuit brother, between, to use his own contemptuous expression, ' the man and the monk.' In the glowing pages of ' Hypatia ' he seems simply to despise the Egyptian monks, with their blind fanaticism; but he manifests something more than mere contempt for Cyril's sanctimonious chaplain, ' Peter the Reader.' In ' Two Years Ago ' we have another variety of the same thing—the poet, absorbed in dreams of developing himself and his own capacities, and whose morbid self-consciousness so blunts his perception of things as they are, that he can neither enter into the thoughts and feelings of those around him,

---

* In his last work, the ' Lectures on Modern History', Mr. Kingsley shows more tolerance of monks, at least of those like St. Benedict.

nor enjoy fairly and honestly the beauties of nature; while, by way of contrast, we have for a hero 'Tom Thurnall,' a sort of 'bull-terrier,' tough and hard as any destroyer of rats that ever was. In his 'Lectures' all the writer's sympathy, in the death-struggle between Rome and the Barbarians, is with the undisciplined children of the northern forests; he has none to spare for those who, with all their grievous sins, were yet the representatives then of civil order in the world.

In one shape or another he wages a fierce crusade against self-discipline, and, as usual, with more zeal than discrimination. He gives no quarter to the habit 'of constantly fingering the spiritual muscles' to see how they are getting on. He has no words bad enough for the belief that celibacy is a higher state than marriage. He abhors the cowardly selfishness, as he regards it, of those, and they are not confined to any one section of Christendom, whose idea of religion consists in 'saving themselves.' He distrusts asceticism altogether. His ideal of a Christian Saint is something very unlike the stiff and emaciated figures which are too conventional with stainers of glass: something more robust and athletic. Now, to say the least, it is illiberal and unphilosophical not to see that asceticism, even in its extreme developments, in the recluse or the visionary, tends, if recognised as exceptional and abnormal, to preserve the equilibrium of society, by its energetic protest against those evils in social life which repel good men from the world; just as a comparatively secular tone among some of the clergy in any country tends to preserve the clergy, as a body, from being unduly isolated from their fellow-countrymen. Besides, he fails to make allowance for the varying dispositions of men, for the innate fitness of some for a contemplative rather than an active life. Above all, in his dread of the unreality which sometimes results from living too strictly by rule, he forgets that a certain amount of this discipline is the only possible foundation of that manliness and unselfishness which he prizes so highly. While the world lasts, no wise man will forego the use of external aids and supports because foolish people get a fall through leaning on them too heavily.

Another instance of this one-sidedness, this want of due regard to both aspects of a question, may be seen in Professor Kingsley's tone about the cholera. Because it can be traced back to causes under man's control, and for which man is responsible, therefore, he seems to argue, special prayer is out of place; and instead of fast-days and litanies, we ought to mend our drains, and purify our cottages and lodging-houses. The fallacy is too egregious to escape detection, except in a mind pre-occupied by the one idea of ' Sanitas sanitatum omnia sanitas.' It is as if he were to tell a sick person that, because he ought to send for the doctor, therefore he had no need to pray; or, as if a waggoner with his cart-wheel in the mire, ought only to put his own shoulder to the wheel, without seeking or accepting other assistance. That it is a mockery to call to Heaven for help, without also doing all that

prudence enjoins, none but a fanatic or a hypocrite
will deny; but to speak as if the one duty clashed
with the other is an inconsistency in one, who has
so well asserted the great truth, that the spirit which
dwells in man is not, as materialists pretend, the
slave of the inexorable laws which sway the material
universe. In his 'Inaugural Lecture' Professor
Kingsley has done good service to the cause of truth
and morality, by his eloquent and forcible refutation
of those who, like the late Mr. Buckle, would degrade
man into a self-calculating machine, and history into
a pedantic enumeration of averages and statistics.
When any, the most expert of chess-players, shall be
able to calculate with unerring certainty his antagonist's next move, it will be time enough to take
seriously into consideration the doctrine, that man's
free-will is a dream, and that he is the unconscious
creature of the circumstances which surround him.

If any one shall object that Professor Kingsley's
share in the great controversy which he recently provoked with Dr. Newman is inconsistent with this
estimate of him, as eminently generous and truth-
loving, we can but admit, while we regret, the inconsistency. It is one more to be added to the list,
already too long, of similar inconsistencies even in
great and good men; it is an instance how a positive
and overbearing habit of mind blinds even a truthful
man to the truth, as it concerns himself, and hinders
him from frankly acknowledging the error which he
cannot see. But, on the whole, there is not much
danger of overstating what we owe to Professor

Kingsley. The danger is rather lest those whom his peculiarities offend should fail to do him justice. His influence is unquestionably a weight in the right scale. He is not, strictly speaking, the founder of a school. He is naturally too unsystematic to act otherwise than as a pioneer, as one breaking up the ground for others. Among those who admire and imitate him there may be, as often happens, a tendency to reproduce those traits in him which, though most conspicuous to a superficial observer, are not the most worthy of imitation; and his 'healthy animalism' may too often degenerate into a mere cant, or even into 'muscular *unchristianity.*' But if we look deeper we see in him a man fearless in asserting the truth, as he conceives it, for its own sake, and at all hazards, without being the slave of party; who, in an age of fastidious luxury, not merely writes and talks about the poor, but shows that he indeed feels with them and for them; who keeps a practical aim in view, while many lose themselves in unpractical doubts and purposeless questionings; and who, while the world at large is more prone than ever to bow the knee to mere intellectual ability, is not ashamed to pay the honour which they deserve to obscure labourers in the cause of duty, rather than to those who stand above their fellows in pride of knowledge and refinement. He leads men back from unprofitable attempts to grasp what is beyond their reach, to see that religion is really, as our Catechism teaches, the mainspring of morality, and that the creeds of the Church Catholic find their fittest counterpart in all that is noblest in man. He reminds us that men are most truly 'manly' when they are 'godly,' that true manliness and true holiness are one. An influence like this is especially efficacious among young men, whose moral sense revolts from pharisaical denunciations of the world as unmixedly evil, and from the narrow timidity which, as in the Donatists of old, so now in certain quarters merges Christianity in the cry, 'Shall I be saved?' They welcome in him a thorough Englishman, not exempt indeed from the weaknesses of his nation; an Englishman in politics, averse alike to a centralising Imperialism, and to a Republicanism equally subversive of domestic life; an Englishman in his religious belief, with nothing of Italian sentiment, of German scepticism, or of Calvinistic austerity about him, and whose watchword is that of our English Prayer-Book, 'Fear God and love your neighbour.'

WESLEYAN TENDENCIES WITHIN THE CHURCH.

THERE are few things with a more pressing claim on the attention of the English Church than the subject of Wesleyanism. In numbers, in popularity, in all that is denoted by the word 'respectable,' if not in intellectual ability, they stand in the front rank of Dissent: or rather, they hold a position aloof from their allies on the great battle-field, and look with divided sympathies on the contest between the Church and the sects. Hence, of all the varieties of Dissent, Wesleyanism alone has left its mark within the Church, even in quarters where it was least to be suspected. The teaching of John Wesley has tinged with its own sombre hue, more widely and deeply than is generally acknowledged, the inner life of the Church, against which the attitude of his followers is a continual protest. The ordinary habits of religious people, even within our own pale, and their sentiments on points both of doctrine and practice, are often flavoured with the leaven of Wesley far more than they themselves are aware. In this point of view, especially, it is important to analyse the essential elements of Wesleyanism, and to discriminate as fairly as we can between the good and the evil which are there blended so perplexingly.

The man and his system are here more than ever inseparable. All good men have a certain influence, tacit or avowed, on others; from all great men this influence radiates widely. John Wesley was not merely, with all his aberrations, a great and good man, but one framed and fitted by nature to be a leader of his fellows, strong in the faculty of organising. The very nick-name which fastened itself from the first on the society which he founded, and which has clung to it with such tenacity, is curiously appropriate. Wesley was a worshipper of 'method;' and could not rest without forcing his idol on others. This passion for drilling the rest of the world he inherited from his mother, who seems to have been what is called 'strong-minded,' in a day when woman's mission as a teacher and expounder was not yet so loudly trumpeted as it is nowadays by Miss Cobbe and her philosophic sisterhood. Wesley had also that propulsive power within him which always sweeps others along with it irresistibly. With his keen, fearless logic, there was combined a zeal for making proselytes which is seldom found in keen logicians; and with all the restless, fervid energy of Edward Irving there was in him an imperious and autocratic will peculiarly his own. Wesley would never have abdicated his leadership as Irving did.

In the minuteness * of his directions to his disciples

* There is a characteristic story of Wesley betaking himself to an accountant, after trying in vain himself to discover an error in his accounts amounting only to *sixpence*.

the founder of many a monastic order may vie with
Wesley. But in one respect he stands alone. He
carried out to the utmost the saying, that he who
wants a thing done must do it himself. By an
activity of mind and body almost beyond belief, he
retained the reins over every department in his own
hands to the last. In cases where he was compelled
to delegate his authority, he would still have every
thing done precisely in his own way. In fact, he
dogmatised without hesitation about everything.
His audacity in laying down the law about medicine
is an amusing instance of his rare self-confidence.
He knew by experience what sort of diet and what
sort of remedies suited himself. By conforming carefully to these rules he enjoyed, like the great lawgiver
of Israel, health and strength unabated to the end of
an unusually long life. But he could not be satisfied
without obtruding his theories on everybody else.
He would have all men dieted and doctored on his
method, or not at all. He was indeed a Pope to his
followers; dictating to them how to pronounce their
syllables in singing, and prescribing the most trivial
domestic regulations for their school at Kingswood.
Wesley was always positive in the opinion of the
moment. In his early days he was all for rebaptising
Dissenters, and quite indifferent, in the plenitude of
his infallibility, to the fact that the usage of the
Church Catholic was against him. The same narrow
exacting intolerance animated him always. Here lay
the strength and weakness of his character. Here is
one main source of the mingled strength and weak-

ness of the society which he moulded so strictly, so elaborately, after his own pattern.

The influence of Wesley's chief coadjutor has been comparatively evanescent. Whitfield beside Wesley is a mere orator for the mob — half Cleon, half Diogenes. His preaching produced, it seems, a greater sensation at the moment; that is, with the uneducated, or with persons of higher rank weary of themselves, and languidly longing for a new excitement. But his sermons, unlike Wesley's, in reading are simply nothing. The greatest orators, from Cicero downwards, have seldom been men with great strength of character. John Wesley is an exception. His style betrays indeed the faults incidental to one who is incessantly speaking in public—the dangerous fluency, the facility which degenerates into commonplace, the waste of words, the tiresome reiteration of favourite phrases. But on the whole his style is singularly chaste and forcible. The cause is obvious. Though he rarely passed a day without delivering several sermons, he was as regularly alone for seven or eight hours of each day, with no companion save his book and his own meditations. For he was perpetually on his circuits: and a journey on horseback or in a chaise was a very different thing from our railway travelling, and tended rather to concentrate thought than to distract and dissipate it. Besides, John Wesley had a good deal of his eldest brother's shrewd and practical sense. Samuel Wesley's dissuasive protests against the course which he saw with regret his younger brothers pursuing are clear and cogent.

John Wesley showed this sagacity even amid the extravagances which resulted more or less directly from his teaching. He could see the evils of religious excitement in others, for instance, in the French and German fanatics with whom he was at one time in close contact. Even among his own disciples he made an effort from time to time to put some sort of restraint on their hysterical paroxysms. He discouraged the screaming and raving and convulsive gesticulations, which are as contagious as a panic in an excited crowd. That the Frankenstein which he had called into being did not always obey its master is no disparagement to Wesley's power of governing; it was simply an inevitable consequence of the principles which he was sowing broadcast. Still he persisted in asserting his supremacy in the teeth of all opposition. He was a thorough martinet in discipline. Inconsistent as it appears in one who was himself defying the constituted authorities, he repressed with a grasp of iron every attempt at insubordination in his own camp. He would have no rebels, no murmurs there. The independence of our American colonies he mistrusted as subversive of law and order. Antinomianism he fought against manfully; and when it claimed, as it did reasonably enough, to be the legitimate offspring of his doctrine, he repudiated it with abhorrence. He was too sensible not to foresee the dangers that would arise out of the schismatical spirit which he had evoked. He refused to vest the appointment of his preachers in local trustees, in order to avoid the enormous evil of making the ministers dependent on their flock: he preferred to keep them responsible to himself and to the Conference only. In short, in the ecclesiastical policy which he devised with so clear a head and worked with so steady a hand, he evinced the genius of a statesman. Granting his premises, his first principles of action, it must be allowed that he displayed tact and adroitness of no ordinary kind in carrying them into practice. It is no wonder that, to this day, we see the venerable features of John Wesley, with glance, notwithstanding the hoary locks, bright and keen as ever, adorning the mantelpiece of even his humblest followers.

Wesley, moreover, was a man morally and physically brave. Once, in his sleep, he fell overboard from the deck of his vessel into the Atlantic, but even in that strange awakening he did not lose his head for a moment. Often and often he had 'to fight,' almost in the literal sense of the words, 'with wild beasts,' hemmed in on every side by an infuriated mob; but his presence of mind never failed him. He was self-possessed and imperturbable always. He was a scholar too, having made good use of a liberal education ; fond of questions in philosophy, and ready at any moment with an apt quotation from his Virgil. A poet he cannot be fairly called by any stretch of courtesy. His younger brother Charles had more of the poet in him, as the hymn shows, 'Come, O Thou Traveller unknown :' but John Wesley's imagination was rather that of the orator. Very seldom indeed is a great orator a great poet. To be a convincing and persuasive speaker, a man must be too intent on the end in view, and too careful about the steps which lead to it to allow his fancy to linger by the way, or to follow at will its own capricious devices. Like the great controversialist of our day, whom in many respects he so much resembles, Wesley was too strictly logical for a poet. It is simply absurd to say as has been said, that John Henry Newman, any more than John Wesley, could under any circumstances have developed himself into a poet in the true sense of the word. Both are logicians and orators essentially. As an orator, and especially in the inexhaustible fertility of his applications of Scripture, Wesley in his best passages is not very far behind Jeremy Taylor, or even St. Augustine himself. In fine, in John Wesley we have a man courageous, eloquent, sagacious, and with all his rare natural endowments subjected as completely, as human infirmities permit, to the law of conscience. Whence and how are we to account for the eccentricity of his orbit, and for the fanatical excesses which alienated the man and his influence from the Church in which he was born and bred, and within whose walls at first the flame of his devotion shone so brightly?

We have already indicated the answer. Wesley was emphatically what is termed 'doctrinaire:' a man possessed with an idea, bent on realising it without rounding off one obtrusive angle, or softening one repulsive feature; and quite resolved, if need be, to ride roughshod over what seemed to him the foolish prejudices of the rest of the world. This predominant idea was the attainment by a method of his own of a perfection beyond the reach of man in this life. Everything was to be squared to the pattern in his mind; everybody, willing or unwilling, was to be elongated or curtailed, as might be necessary, on this Procrustean model. Instead of taking human nature as it is, and moulding its plastic elements slowly and tenderly into what it ought to be, with wise and loving heed to the circumstances wherein it is placed by Providence, he would refashion it harshly and abruptly according to his own standard of propriety. Dissatisfied with the broad fundamental rules laid down by the Church, he would impose on others a code of his own, more minute, more rigorous, more 'methodical.' Instead of a thankful acquiescence in the ordinances which the Church has provided, he would invent something more directly efficacious, more instantaneous in its results. With his head full of this idea, and with much around him to stock his sense of right, Wesley had nothing of Hamlet's feeling—

> The times are out of joint! O! cursed spite,
> That I was born to set the world aright!

He felt himself equal to the occasion. His was not a mind to waver or hesitate in following his principles to their logical conclusion, from regard to the manifold intricacy of the conditions under which GOD's Providence has placed us, and in accordance with which, if at all on earth, the longing for perfection can only be realised. Clear-sighted, narrow-minded, ardent, and indefatigable, conscious of the loftiness of his aim, Wesley was the man to set the world to rights, supposing only that the world were something entirely different from what it is. It is no wonder that Wesley's career, in spite of his many excellences, ended as it did. Self-will is a grave fault even in its aspirations after holiness ; it is the vital principle of Dissent. The censorious, inquisitorial spirit which characterised Wesley is characteristic of Wesleyanism.

One of his favourite tenets was, that unless a man has perfect faith he has none at all. Between the elect and the reprobate he presumed to draw his line of demarcation with an unfaltering hand. He would not see how in the realm of spirit as in that of material nature light fades into darkness, and tint melts into tint by an insensible gradation which mortal eye cannot penetrate. According to him, the soul is either in utter darkness or illuminated by the instantaneous flash of Divine assurance. Till a man can

> Read his title clear
> To mansions in the skies

he is an alien and outcast in God's sight. It is a bold thing thus to separate the wheat from the tares in this life. With the same Draconic severity he condemned as sinful whatever was not directly and manifestly conducive to the glory of God. He would speak in the same breath of adultery and the wearing of jewels, as heinous offences. The mere act of touching a card, or of going to a theatre, was denounced as an enormity. 'No amusement is innocent' was one of his sayings. Recreation in his eyes was unnecessary and wrong even for little children. Others have taught men to be 'merry' at once 'and wise:' or, like good Bishop Hacket, to 'serve GOD and be cheerful.' Wesley's motto, even for little children, was, 'Be serious.' Need it be added, that so flagrant a violation of the laws of Providence failed signally? His school at Kingswood proved a great disappointment. It would have been almost a La Trappe for the innocent victims of his theory, if that theory could have been carried into practice. Wesley might have learned from the great moralist of pagan Greece, as well as from higher sources, that virtue resides in the adaptation of a general law to particular circumstances, and that it is invariably equidistant from the extremes which lie on either side of it. But he was too intent on a visionary perfection to attend to the warnings of experience. Certainly it is not by a scornful defiance of the limitations which the All-wise Ruler of the universe imposes on our human nature in its ever-varying conditions, that we can hope to fulfil in our daily lives His precepts of perfection. These are to be fulfilled in the spirit, and in the intention, not in a servile idolatry of the letter. It is not for us

> To strive to wind ourselves too high
> For mortal man beneath the sky.

The pursuit even of holiness in such a method is after all a refined form of self-will and self-love. When the mind is for ever asking of itself, 'Have I faith?' 'Am I saved?' it becomes irresistibly absorbed in its own self-consciousness. The transient phases of feeling are scrutinised and analysed till they die under the process, instead of leading on to something to be done. Everything is regarded as it affects self. Worship, instead of being the offering of prayer and praise to One above, becomes 'a religious exercise.' People speak of preferring one place of worship to another, ' because they feel that it does them more good.' Questions such as, ' Will this or that course be best for me ?' recur continually in the diaries of Wesley and his admirers. Here is downright veritable selfishness, hardly disguised at all. Perhaps it comes out most glaringly in the Wesleyan hymns. Like those of the Moravians, with whose spirit Wesleyanism has been inoculated largely, the love which they breathe for the SAVIOUR resembles rather an hysterical passion, than the manly, chivalrous devotion which longs to pay its reverent homage without seeking any thing for itself in return. Any one who will take the trouble to contrast one of the favourite hymns of the Wesleyans with one of George Herbert's devotional poems will see at once the difference. The sentimental cravings engendered and fostered by erotics like the former are well described by Southey * as ' a spiritual ague.' Under such a system the man who sets himself to serve GOD degenerates from the free and willing service which He approves into a self-tormenter like the ' Heautontimorumenos' of the old drama. Even childhood, robbed of that sweet unconsciousness which is its

* 'Life of Wesley.' By Southey. New Edition. (Bell & Daldy). 1865.

especial charm, is taught to be always sifting and scrutinising its motives with a precocious distrustfulness. Wesley forgot that the seed grows silently and in secret. With his weekly classes for mutual examination and confession, he was for ever pulling up his plants to see how they were getting on. The healthiest state of mind is, when a man does his duty without thinking too much about it.

This exaggeration of one's own importance, this disregard of every thing except the end in view, is of the very essence of fanaticism. Never was a better definition given of fanaticism than by Wesley himself. It is the pursuit of the end without the means. His own system is essentially fanatical. It begins at the end instead of the beginning. Instead of commencing with a sound morality and raising the spiritual edifice, step by step, on this sure foundation, every thought is merged in the one paramount idea of 'saving the soul.' Instead of acting on the Divine precept, that they who do the will of Heaven shall have more and more of light shed on their way, the soul is incited to expect to reach the goal at once, and all the suggestions of prudence and expediency are put aside as impertinent and evasive. A fanatic will not see, for example, that in renouncing at one stroke all his worldly advantages he may be curtailing all his future power of being useful, nor that by intruding into another man's sphere of work his well-meant exertions may be doing more harm than good in the long run, and sacrificing permanent progress to results immediate but transitory. Wesley would not see that the feverish craving which he was exciting for personal assurance of salvation was a very different thing from patient obedience to the will of God because it is His will: nor, that by disorganising the Church he was in the end retarding, not advancing, the cause of true religion. The fanatic shuts his eyes to all this. He is always presuming on some Divine interposition, some miraculous aid in the work which he has in hand, as if the world could not go on without him. Wesley, for instance, was in the habit of taking a verse haphazard out of the Scriptures, and applying it blindfold to his own circumstances at the moment, as if he had any right to reckon on such extraordinary illumination. In fact, this bibliomancy or sortilege goes on the principle that we may at any moment expect omens and portents from on high, to show what we ought to know by the voice of conscience. The tendency is to make a Pharisee or a Fetish-worshipper, or both at once. It is worth noticing, that Wesley's tenets found a readier acceptance in the naturally superstitious temperament of the Welsh, the Irish, and the Negroes, than among the 'canny' denizens of North Britain.

Faith and fanaticism are distinct as the ruddy glow of health and the hectic flush of fever; as the deliberate energy of a sound mind in a sound body, and the spasmodic violence of delirium. True faith is distinguished from its parhelion by the due regard which it has for the consequences of its actions: not solely nor chiefly for the consequences which may result to self immediately or in the future, for that is cowardice or merely selfish prudence, but for the consequences, as they concern the glory of God and the good of man, which a calm and unbiassed judgment discerns rising in the distance. The fanatic in his infatuation despises this circumspection, this attention to circumstances, and sees only what he wishes. What is really meant by forsaking all things for Christ's sake is a question which has perplexed earnest hearts in every age. That we must renounce actually all things forbidden, and that we must be ready at any time to renounce even things permitted, if they interfere with any duty, does not satisfy the scruples of the fanatic. Teachers like Wesley take for their text the sons of Zebedee forsaking all things to follow the call of Christ, and insist that everything is wrong which is not directly and consciously aimed at edification. Our Prayer-Book on the other hand teaches us, in the Collect for St. James's Day, ' forsaking all worldly and carnal affections to be evermore ready to follow God's holy commandments.' The fanatic overlooks the obvious fact, that the fishermen of Galilee could not pursue their ordinary occupations and at the same time be companions of Him whose Apostles they were to be, simply because they could not be in two places at once, and proceeds to enforce on all who would follow Christ in any capacity the renunciations which belong to the case of those who like the Apostles have actually to forsake home and kindred for their Master's sake. In short, he denies practically the distinction between the use and abuse of a thing, and substitutes his own law of total abstinence for the Divine law, with its higher and more arduous discipline, of temperance in all things. Thus he denounces every amusement as sinful on the ground that every particle of time must be devoted to things directly spiritual. But in the end these good intentions defeat themselves, by defying consequences. The experience of history shows, that such a theory, so far as it can be carried into practice, must end in eliminating from the world at large the elements which preserve its pleasures from degenerating into vice, and in exposing those who try the experiment on themselves to the danger of falling hopelessly from their giddy height, and to that worst kind of temptation which comes in the shape of spiritual pride.

Conspicuous examples of an utter withdrawal from the world and its pursuits may be useful exceptionally, as a counterpoise to that dead weight of apathy to unseen things which is ever dragging downwards the nobler impulses of our nature. But as a rule and in all ordinary cases there are limits not to be transgressed even in what appears to be the purest self-denial. The counsels of prudence are never to be slighted with impunity; for in the end true expediency and true rectitude are one. To live strictly by rule; to order the disposal of time, money, every thing with a view ultimately to the service of our Master; to give up for His sake not the least that may suffice but the very most that we can, is very different from trampling under foot the prudential considerations which point out the way to the end.

It cannot be denied that this tendency of Wesleyanism, which may be characterised as a craving for results immediate and palpable, is at work at the present time beyond the pale of that sect, and fraught with dangers, which are all the greater for being latent and below the surface. Just as in the question of education there is a cry for something which may make boys into men at once, giving them a smattering of everything, instead of the old-fashioned aptitude for future development; so in other matters, there is danger of an unwise precipitancy, and of that recoil and exhaustion which invariably follow it. Who can watch the vagaries of those among ourselves who imitate the vagaries of the revivalists, or of the mediæval friars, without being reminded of John Wesley with his little band of enthusiasts in their back room in the Horsefair at Bristol? There is the same fussy disquietude, the same eagerness for 'high pressure.' There is a cry for more of excitement, more of sensation in our services, and a chimerical idea of making the Prayer-Book more popular by tampering with it. Those who make unauthorised innovations, whatever may be their intention, are, like John Wesley, undermining the stability of their Church. There is a cry for an afternoon celebration of the Holy Eucharist, as if the reasons which have ruled the practice of the Church Catholic otherwise were not as weighty now as ever. There is a cry in Ecclesiastical music for something more attractive than the severe beauty of our old English music, and for a style of hymnody which is really inane and frivolous. It is to Wesleyanism mainly that we owe this debased style of hymnody. The same subtle influence has much to do with that idolatry of the mere letter of Holy Scripture which prevails in England, and with those austere notions about the Day of the Resurrection which degrade it from a great Christian Festival, 'an Easter Day in every week,' into a Jewish Sabbath; so that 'the day of days,' is now too often an object of aversion to the young, from the injudicious restraints which have made it of late years not so much a day of rest from labour, as of abstaining from everything like pleasure. Wesleyanism, again, lies at the root of the exaggerated scruples which are felt in some quarters against what is termed the indiscriminate use of the Burial Service; for it is characteristic of Wesleyanism to arrogate to itself the awful prerogatives of the great Omniscient Judge, daring to pronounce on its fellow-men the doom which should be left to His unerring lips to utter. It is mainly owing to the influence of Wesleyanism, that family prayer, even among Church-people, has tacitly supplanted the public services of the Church, to which it ought to be subordinate and subsidiary; and that an exaggerated reverence for the day which closes one year and opens another, has thrown into the shade the other landmarks of time which the Church has set up along the course of the Christian year.

Even when primitive usage is alleged for the revival of some obsolete practice, we must discriminate between the principle and its details, between that which endures for ever and that which belongs to a particular phase of things. Wesley was fond of appealing to the Church of the Fathers, but he disregarded this distinction. The rigorous discipline of the Church in its infancy, numerically small and external to the world, affords no true analogy to the Church in England, established by law and national. The marked severance in what were still heathen countries between the ' catechumens ' and the ' faithful,' is no warrant for such arbitrary demarcations, as Wesleyanism favours, among those who are all alike Christians. The doctrines of the ancient Church are a κτῆμα εἰς ἀεί. Like the principles of morality, they are immutable in their nature. But details of practice vary from time to time, like the social usages of mankind.

SWEDENBORGIAN TENDENCIES WITHIN THE CHURCH.

THERE are few more signal instances of a prophet confuted by the stern reality of facts than that of Swedenborg. He claimed to be inspired in the plenary sense of that term. He enounced his doctrines as a direct revelation from Heaven. He was, according to himself, clothed with the attributes of a Messiah, commissioned to found a new Church and to inaugurate a new dispensation. More than a century has elapsed since the commencement of this new era, and his predictions are as far as ever from fulfilment. Even in America, the hotbed of all that is eccentric and anomalous in creed, 'the New Church,' as its adherents call it, numbers only some forty preachers; in England and in other European countries, fewer still. The very excuse alleged by Swedenborgians for this want of vitality is curiously inconsistent with the claim of their founder to be the regenerator of the world. When they say that they do not care to make converts, on the ground that theirs is 'an internal, not an external Church,'* whatever that

* Life of Emanuel Swedenborg, &c.' By Nath. Hobart. Boston.

N

may mean, they allow, in fact, that their pretensions are a failure.

Yet for all this the phenomena of the 'New Jerusalem' are worthy of consideration. Insignificant and absurd as they may appear to a casual observer, they throw a strong light on principles which are at work in other parts of Christendom. They exhibit these principles no longer in the germ, but in all the maturity of flower and fruit. To a Roman Catholic like Mœhler, Swedenborgianism seems the legitimitate development of the principles which he loosely classes together as Protestant. In one sense of that very equivocal term so it is. Whether or not this can be said of a Church which is essentially built on primitive catholicity is quite another question. But even the English Church may learn something from Swedenborgianism. It may learn to be on the watch against insidious errors, which are apt to insinuate themselves into the popular theology of the present day. The floating spars and fragments of the wreck ought to warn other vessels off the rocks and quicksands, which might otherwise lurk unseen.

Perhaps there are few, even among the well educated in England, who know much more of Emanuel Swedenborg than that he was a Swede, as the name imports, by birth, and the founder of a sect holding some very extraordinary notions. He was the son of a Lutheran 'Bishop,' who carried his reverence for the letter of Holy Scripture so far as to object to all such Christian names as are not to be found there; like the man who objected to the title

'Archdeacon,' that it does not occur in the Bible; or like those who make a point of quoting the Psalms from the Bible version, as if there were some virtue inherent in that translation and not in that older and more beautiful translation with which we are all familiar in our Prayer-Books. The Swedenborgians pride themselves to this day on using no prayers in their public worship which are not taken word for word from the Bible. Swedenborg himself, in the latter part of his life, kept no other books on his shelves than the Bible 'in Greek and Hebrew.' His 'illumination' dates from 1745, the year marked in our annals by the last effort of the Stuarts to regain the throne. He was then almost sixty years old. From that time he turned his back completely on his former pursuits, which had been chiefly of a scientific kind, and lived thenceforward in a world of his own, holding daily conversations, as he imagined, with angels and disembodied spirits. He lived unmarried, and died at a good old age, esteemed and loved by all who knew him.

It would be a great mistake to call Swedenborg an impostor. A more unworldly person can hardly be conceived; simple and retiring in his habits, gentle and loving as a child. He seems to have been thoroughly sincere, even in his wildest assertions—the unconscious dupe of his own hallucinations. The portrait prefixed to his biography tells its own story. It is the face not of an ambitious, designing man, but of one kindly, unpractical, visionary. His was indeed such a character as is often nurtured in the seclusion

of the cloister or of the library, especially among
those who give themselves to the study of natural
science; fond of retirement and meditation; idolising
knowledge in the abstract more than for its influence
on his fellow-men; unfitted by long and sedentary
communings with books to try things which concern
man as man on the touchstone of reality. His im-
passive, unexcitable nature, like that of our Sir
Isaac Newton, was singularly undisturbed by ordinary
emotions. He seems not so much to have overcome
the temptations of ambition or sensuality, as really
not to have known what they were. But, in his own
amiable way, he was a great egotist; blindly confident
in his own opinions, and serenely indifferent to what
others had to say against them; and, unless we may
impute the extravagancies of his old age to an intellect disordered by overwork, he cannot be acquitted
of spiritual pride and of a blasphemous presumption.
Happily it is the most reasonable, as well as the most
charitable supposition, that he was beginning to dote
when he began to think himself a prophet.

Up to this time Swedenborg had been a devoted
student of physical science: and in this direction his
learning was vast and multifarious. Twenty-seven
volumes published anonymously attest at once his
erudition and his love of learning for its own sake;
and he is said to have anticipated several discoveries
generally ascribed to subsequent investigators. Un-
fortunately he had a great distaste for those sciences
which are concerned with man and his organisation.
He knew nothing of metaphysic, and strictly speaking

not much of ethic. If he had taken more pains to examine the microcosm of human nature, he would not have dogmatised so rashly on points which, more than any others in science, require a delicate and cautious handling. Instances abound in his works of a gross confusion between the material and immaterial parts of our nature. Sometimes, for instance, he speaks of intellect as distinct from spirit, sometimes as identical with it. There is no science where it is more dangerous to reason *à priori*, or, in other words, to argue that a thing is because it must be, than the science of metaphysics. The facts which form the starting-point of the inquiry are so few; and these few are so impalpable, so slippery when grasped, so impatient of being arranged into order, that there is all the more necessity to make the most of them. Without a careful and accurate induction of such facts as are within its reach, the study of metaphysics becomes pure guesswork. But Swedenborg was addicted to this seductive mode of reasoning.

Even on subjects which he understood, there was something radically wrong in Swedenborg's method. To use his own metaphor, he was like a person endeavouring to make out the plan of a labyrinth by climbing up to some position whence he may command a bird's-eye view of the whole. But his illustration breaks down hopelessly in fact. There is no such point of vantage to which man may ascend, and whence he may enjoy this omniscience. The very attempt is an infatuation. Rather it is by holding fast the clue bequeathed by previous explorers, and by the slow, laborious process of experiment, that the maze is to be unravelled, and thus only. Doubtless the guessings of intuition, as we call them, checked and corrected by patient induction, lead to great discoveries; but unless so verified they are worth nothing, except by the merest accident. *Scientia longa, vita brevis.* Science is too long, and life too short, for each successive generation of students to start afresh on its journey from the beginning.

But Swedenborg was one of those who take every thing as an open question. He acted on the principle which some would apply even to the hereditary traditions of revealed truth, that no pioneers had cleared his way before him, that no fellow-labourers were working in his field. The *ignis fatuus* of self misled him. Relying on this, he saw only the side of a question which happened to be nearest. While teaching, for instance, wisely and well, that the 'mind forms the body,' he lost sight of the converse truth that our lower nature acts and reacts largely on the mind. He seems to have had only the dreamiest perception of the relation which subsists between matter and spirit, and to have been ignorant of the great truth, which the advance of physical science tends more and more to establish, and which is in perfect harmony with the dictates of morality and religion, that in the exquisite mechanism of our being the will alone is purely immaterial. In short, he aimed at too much, and thus accomplished little. With all his acuteness and comprehensiveness of intellect he resembled a man seeking the philosopher's stone. He was the slave of an unbridled imagination, of an imagination—not like that of Shakespeare, robust and vigorous from continual contact with life in its myriad forms—but sickly, unreal, and idiosyncratic as that of Shelley, seeing everything in the deceptive light of its own hallucinations.

When a man like Swedenborg comes to apply a method like this to theology, the consequences are obvious. Even in physics he was an audacious theorist, laying down the law, for example, on the manner and process of the Creation as if he had been an eye-witness of it. In his religious theories he was the same, and with results more disastrous, as the subject is of an incalculably graver importance, and as it transcends more completely our human faculties. He objected altogether to dogmatic theology, forgetting that, after all, he was but substituting a system of his own invention for one resting on general acceptance and on its derivation from the fountain-head of truth. He discarded even the help of commentaries. He was to be the architect of a New Church, the founder of a New Jerusalem. 'The Bible, and the Bible alone,' was his motto; but, as with others who repeat the same cry, it was the Bible as he was pleased to understand it. Who can wonder, that on the vast ocean which it had to traverse, the gallant vessel, rudderless, and without a pilot's guiding hand, foundered on its voyage of discovery?

There is no need to dwell long on Swedenborg's visions. They belong to his declining years, and are the not unnatural growth of an imagination so undis-

ciplined and so egotistic, where the vapours of its own
conceits were seething so busily. His latent tendencies to mysticism betray themselves, even before 1745,
in some of his physical treatises. When we read of
' the hieroglyphic key to representatives,' of ' corre-
spondences and influxes,' with grave disquisitions
worthy of old Ephraim Jenkinson in the ' Vicar of
Wakefield,' on ' cosmogony,' with its ' forms, and
orders, and degrees, and series,' we are prepared for
that which too often follows overmuch learning. But
the actual ' illumination ' began in 1745. From that
time Swedenborg believed himself privileged to hold
frequent and familiar intercourse with angels and
departed spirits. These dialogues with the dead were
no fraudulent device. The whole character of the
man renders this more than unlikely. Nor are they
to be put aside at once and without a moment's investigation, as impossible, *à priori.* Those who deny the
possibility of any communication between ourselves
in our present state of existence and the world of
spirits, are asserting a negative which, to say the least,
they cannot prove. But, to come from the abstract to
the particular case in question, Swedenborg's ' memorable relations,' as he called them, rest, it is obvious,
on the flimsiest evidence, and present themselves with
scarcely a pretext of probability. They stand self-
convicted. The most cursory glance detects the sig-
nificant circumstance that his apparitions were persons
with whom he was acquainted personally, like the
lately deceased Queen of Sweden, or, like the poet
Virgil, in history. Those few of his ' memorable

relations' which look at first sight less puerile than the rest, will not bear a cross-examination, but vanish into the merest hearsay. Like the 'spirit-rappers' of our day, Swedenborg only saw what he knew already, with this difference, that his apparitions were the honest production of his own reflex and introverted imagination. His absurdities reached their climax when he fancied, with a characteristic confusion of matter and spirit, that he 'had not room to step among the spirits' who were in his chamber, and that he was commissioned not merely to bring back to earth the revelations with which he was favoured, but to give in exchange the results of his own inspiration to the spirits with whom he was conversing. It is worth noting, that Swedenborg was a vegetarian in diet. He used to connect his peculiar gifts as a 'seer' with a habit which he had of holding his breath for a very long time!

Were it not that unreasoning credulity like unreasoning scepticism is simply limitless, it would be inexplicable that pretensions such as these could find credence anywhere. The flames, and voices, and other portents which formed part of Swedenborg's visions may gratify an appetite for the marvellous, but cannot add much to the credibility of these stories. But even if his 'visions' were as unquestionable as, to an unprejudiced mind, they are devoid of probability, still, if unsupported by evidence of a different kind, they would not add a feather's weight to his claim to be inspired. Granting for a moment the fact of his intercourse with the world of spirits, it remains to be proved how this circumstance is to be accounted for, before it can be admitted as a credential of his mission. For the mere power of seeing farther than others into that unseen world from which we are separated by a veil so thin and yet so impervious, by itself proves nothing. It may be the result of physical causes and of a peculiar organisation; nor, even if proved to be supernatural in its nature, is it of necessity to be referred to a heavenly origin. Signs and wonders, as Christians have been warned by the teaching of Him who is the Truth, as well as by the dictates of reason, are by themselves no voucher for infallibility, no guarantee for the doctrine which they introduce.

What the doctrine was which Swedenborg had to enunciate it is not easy to say. In the tangled medley of his obscure and incoherent speculations there is much that is perfectly unobjectionable. But the old saying applies here as elsewhere, that the true is not new, and the new is not true. Swedenborg raised his voice seasonably against some dominant errors of his day. Faith had been rudely divorced in popular theology from morality and reason; and the unmeaning shibboleth of 'faith without works' was everything in popular estimation. Against this delusion Swedenborg protested. Faith, he insisted, is no mere imputation of holiness, but inseparable from charity, in the largest and truest sense of the term; in other words, the love of God and the love of man are its moving principles. Swedenborg perceived, what is often overlooked, that the law which the great Apostle of the Gentiles decries and depreciates, is the old Levi-

tical Law, not the law revealed in Christ of Christian
holiness. Again, some of his speculations on the
nature of angels, and on the severance which death
effects between soul and body, though fantastic as
usual, are singularly beautiful. There is, besides,
throughout his writings a bright and genial hopeful-
ness, a trustful anticipation of that good time which
shall come at last to remedy the ills, and to redress
the manifold inequalities of earth, which bears witness
to the simple piety which lay at the bottom of his
eccentricities.

So far well. But his system abounds with inconsistencies. How can it be otherwise when the mind
presumes to be its own guide in the pursuit of truth?
No one can travel far with a man like Swedenborg
without becoming painfully aware that he must choose
between his self-constituted teacher and the guidance
of the Church as it has been in all ages. The same
confusion of matter and spirit which clouds his philosophy reappears in his theology. The attempt to live
a life superior to the animal nature recoils upon itself.
In Swedenborg's imagination the spiritual world
assumes a grotesquely material character. He imagined that he could see his evil passions exuding as
vapours from his body, and taking the form of worms.
He began by arguing that the invisible world may be
deciphered from the analogy of things visible. He
ended by saying, so far as a precise meaning can be
attached to such vagueness of thought alike and
expression, that the sun which we see in the sky is
not merely a symbol of love and wisdom, but essential

love and wisdom itself. Coleridge has said that nature, meaning material nature, is the antitheton of God. Swedenborg's teaching, if carried out consistently, ends in Pantheism.

Can we wonder if a system evolved, in great measure, out of the consciousness of the individual, diverges more and more from the beaten track? Swedenborg's repugnance to dogmatic theology, and his disregard of tradition, issue naturally, if not in an explicit denial of the great truths of Christianity, at least in the evasion or suppression of them. In his periphrastic language they are disguised and diluted, till they disappear altogether. It is easy to quote passages in which Swedenborg professes his faith in the SAVIOUR, but in denying his eternal Sonship he practically denies that He was GOD. Whatever may have been Swedenborg's position at first, he ends in promulgating a new Christianity which is to supersede the old. His bland and philanthropic sentiments, his fervid expressions of piety, must not hinder us from allowing this. The tenets of the Book of Mormon may be more directly inimical to the truth, but the standing-point of the prophet of the Mormonites and of Swedenborg is in fact the same. It would be strange if the ultimate results were very different. A lax theology inevitably tends towards a licentious morality. Truth doctrinal and truth practical are sometimes spoken of by superficial cavillers as separate and even antagonistic, but they are one. Swedenborg, like Joseph Smith, claimed to have a revelation from Heaven, and an illumination far surpassing all previous revelations that ever were. The prophets of old, he says, were inspired, but not as he was; theirs was only an unconscious reception of the truth, while his is rational and intelligent. Forgetting that the internal senses of Scripture are manifold as the diverse aspects of truth, he insists that he alone has caught the internal sense, that his interpretation, and no other, is the right one. Forgetting that the future punishment of the wicked, like the future bliss of the faithful, is shrouded in mystery from mortal eye and ear and brain, he defines the state of departed spirits with a more than scholastic precision. He fixes a year for the end of the world, with all the audacity of Dr. Cumming, and with equal success. Those who oppose his notions are 'persecuting the truth.' Nay, he claims to be himself the representative of the SAVIOUR coming to judge the world! Certainly the career of Swedenborg is a warning to those who, with intentions as good as his, set themselves to erect a Church of the future, as if the hoary edifice which CHRIST built on the rock were tottering to its fall.

But there are other lessons to be learnt from Swedenborgianism. Its history shows what is and must be the result of taking the Bible alone as the rule of faith. It is a practical refutation of the theory, which has lately been propounded with more than usual emphasis, that we have only to take the Bible in hand and interpret it like any other book. Those who begin with the Bible alone are very apt to end with a Bible expurgated and mutilated to suit their own requirements. It will be a fatal day for education in England if ever the chaotic vagueness of what is called Bible Christianity be substituted for creed and catechism. Above all, Swedenborg's preposterous assumptions ought to deter others from that self-confident habit of dogmatising, which intrudes into regions 'where angels fear to tread.' In his wildest extravagancies Swedenborg always fell back, in default of other reasons, on the infallibility of the inspired text in its every word and letter, and of his own interpretation of it. Christians of a more sober and reverent frame of mind may be content to know, that in Holy Scripture there is indeed the voice from Heaven speaking to them, without presuming to define in what degree and manner the heavenly voice deigns to use the instrumentality of mortal speech, utterly inadequate though it be. The clear and definite teaching transmitted in the Church from CHRIST and His Twelve affords a more than sufficient guidance in the midst of this inevitable uncertainty.

GEORGE HERBERT, REPRESENTATIVE OF THE ENGLISH CHURCH.

IT cannot be denied that England of the present day is in danger of neglecting the literature of England of the past. Of course, in history and travels, except for readers who have occasion to refer to original authorities, and, most of all, amid the vast and daily increasing acquirements of physical science, this superannuation of old writers is inevitable. Not so in works of fiction; not so in poetry, endued, as all true poetry is, with perpetual youth. Yet even Shakespeare with us, though duly honoured, is, after all, seldom read, slightly known. We live too much in the present. Our ears are too preoccupied by the loud and impatient voices of the restless scene around us to listen to the calm, clear accents which speak from the far distance. We are in danger, it must be owned, of neglecting the treasures of the past, while, with contracted range of vision and hasty grasp, we care only to seize what lies close within reach as we drift along.

The particular, author whose undeserved neglect suggests these remarks, is one whose name at least is well known, if his writings are not. Some years ago, in the annual exhibition of modern paintings, not a few among the crowd which filled the Royal Academy's rooms were attracted round a small but highly finished picture, which, to say nothing of its other claims to be noticed (and these are considerable with all who can appreciate the delicacy, repose, and careful execution of Mr. Dyce's manner), certainly stood out in unique contrast to its companions, both in subject and colouring. It transported the spectator from the many-coloured silks and whispered criticisms of the gay concourse of sight-seers to a trim lawn, under the pale foliage of spreading limes, beside a smoothly flowing river. Here we see a solitary figure lost in thought, with half-opened book in hand, pacing slowly with steps timed to the peaceful flow of the stream. His refined, thoughtful cast of features, and grave clerical costume of James the First's time, together with the fishing tackle on the bank, guitar resting against the trunk of a tree, and the shapely spire of his loved Salisbury Cathedral rising in the distance, plainly identify him as George Herbert. Although far too sensible a man to attempt to give such a distracted attention to different things at once, as this collocation of rod, book, and music seem to imply, still these accessories are not out of place, as giving some idea of the extent and variety of Herbert's tastes and pursuits. But the general impression produced by the picture is inadequate. It is rather that of a recluse, a visionary sentimental bookworm, than of a man who combined with the devotion and self-discipline of a Thomas à Kempis the accomplishments of a perfect gentleman, the genial humour and shrewd practical sense of a thorough man of the world. Mr. Dyce's picture, while representing well the serenity which Herbert's impetuous nature gained by rigid exercise of self-control and resignation, illustrates only too well the popular misconception, universal among those who know George Herbert only by report. Most persons, we may venture to say, only think of him as, to borrow Mr. Spurgeon's elegant designation of him, 'a devout old Puseyite' of the time of the first Stuart, completely estranged from their sympathy, not by the antiquated manners of the period only, but by his own singular austerity of life, and extraordinary self-abnegation. Most persons merely know his poetry by a few lines culled here and there to provoke a smile at their quaintness and want of rhythm. Even among those who cherish with loving reverence the memory of his holy and beautiful life, few are aware—for it needs patient research, undiscouraged by the archaisms of a style strangely dissonant to our modern ears—how high a place he is entitled to, purely on the ground of intellectual ability. Among the rich legacies of literature bequeathed to us from the past, and fast being lost under the accumulating dust of ages, Herbert's 'Remains' especially deserve to be rescued from neglect, and restored to a place on our book-shelves and in our hearts. They are valuable, not merely or chiefly to the archæologist, but intrinsically; and, in particular, at the present time, as containing the antidote to many of the evils incidental to the tendencies of our modern literature. But we must proceed to adduce our reasons for claiming so high a niche in their gallery of worthies for one, of whom probably our readers have hitherto formed a far lower estimate.

In his own century Herbert's writings were popular enough. It is characteristic of his modesty, or, more strictly speaking, of the victory which he won over his naturally eager and ambitious temperament, that they were all posthumous in publication. The Poems seem to have been written before the 'Country Parson.' His preface to the latter is dated 1632, the year of his death; and its other name, by which it was more usually known at first, 'A Priest to the Temple,' seems to indicate that it was conceived in its author's mind as a companion volume to the already existing, though unpublished, collection of poems, entitled 'The Temple.' These poems were evidently not the work of any particular period in his life, but the growth of years; kept under lock and key, according to the wise advice of Horace, until past their nonage. 'The Temple' was first given to the world in 1633, by Nicholas Ferrar, Herbert's literary executor; under his editorship it was printed by his daughters and other members of his household, or 'Protestant Nunnery' as it has been called, at Little Gidden, in Northamptonshire, and then published at Cambridge, after being, of course, formally licensed by the Vice-Chancellor's 'imprimatur.' * In about

* Many private papers of George Herbert were lost in the fire at

forty years, so good Izaak Walton says in 1674, it passed through ten editions, more than 20,000 copies being sold: a success quite out of proportion to that of the far greater poet, of whose ' Paradise Lost,' shortly afterwards, only 1,300 copies were sold in the first two years, and only three thousand in the first eleven years after its appearance. But the unpopularity of Milton's politics and theology easily explains this disparity, to say nothing of the inevitable repugnance, which even in those laborious days a profoundly learned and recondite epic, in twelve books, would have to encounter in the majority of readers. The ' Country Parson '—it is not plain for what cause— was not published till 1652. It would naturally attract scarcely any but professional readers, yet it went through three editions in twenty years. We cannot trace the progress of either volume through succeeding editions. The men of the eighteenth century were not likely to admire George Herbert. His style was too abrupt and unadorned for their elaborately rounded periods, his religious aspirations too glowing for their decorous conventionalities, his theology too patristic for their latitudinarianism, and, we may add, his thoughts at once too profound and too rudely chiselled for their polished but superficial philosophy. Till Pickering's costly and beautiful edition in 1840—one among many other instances of the good taste and too enterprising spirit of that publisher—there was no complete edition of George

Highnam House, Gloucestershire, the seat of Sir Robert Cook, the second husband of George Herbert's widow.

Herbert's works.   But, as we begun by saying, they were honoured among their contemporaries. *Valeat quantum.*   Let us try to estimate the worth of that popularity.

The Elizabethan era, towards the close of which George Herbert was born, has been called by some, who prefer its sturdy masculine vigour to the superior refinement of Pope and Addison, the Augustan age in English literature.   It resembles rather the last days of the Republic, when the massive intellect of Rome was beginning to appropriate to itself the treasures of Grecian civilisation.   With equal avidity and with equal inexperience and awkwardness at first the great minds of Elizabeth's age, and of that which immediately succeeded it, seized the new stores of intellectual wealth laid open to them by the revival of classical learning, and by frequent intercourse with Italy, then, even more emphatically than ever, the land of art and song.   That era may be compared to that delicious season of the year, the 'jocund month of May,' of which the poets of the time were never weary of singing the praises, combining at once the freshness and transparency of spring with something of the riper loveliness, without the languor, of summer.   The ruggedness, too, of the literature of those times finds its parallel in the sharp winds of May, of which we, the less hardy descendants of the men who repelled the Armada, are, with the exception of Mr. Kingsley, as his Ode to the East Wind shows, apt peevishly to complain.   It was an age of mother wit, as yet comparatively rude and unpolished, and of learning pursued as yet with too undiscriminating a voracity. The healthy appetite of the giants of those days, uncloyed by modern profusion, delighted in whatever it found, and was discouraged by no difficulties. We see in George Herbert at times, and more often in Milton and other contemporaries, something which looks at first sight like a pedantic ostentation of learning, but is really the mere exuberance of delight at discovering a vein of hidden ore. The great minds of that day were, after all, the masters, not the slaves, of their learning. Their originality was not stifled nor dwarfed beneath its weight. The very difficulties of the work gave an additional zest to it, and stimulated their faculties to the utmost. The severity of this discipline, for there was no 'royal road' to learning then, and few of those appliances which facilitate our journey, rendered whatever knowledge was acquired more real and solid, more thoroughly assimilated to the mind of the learner. To be a 'painful scholar' was great praise, and synonymous with being a good one. Books were then scarce and dear, and prized accordingly. When George Herbert wished to buy a new book at College, he was obliged, in spite of his liberal allowance, to 'fast for it,' as he writes to his father-in-law, Sir John Danvers, in order to indulge himself in so great a luxury. In these days of cheap paper and steam presses, we can hardly conceive the reverence then felt for anything in the shape of a printed book, almost as if a sacred thing. Nor is it easy for us, living in the whirl of incessant communication by the rail, the post-office and the telegraph, to throw ourselves back even for a moment into the deliberate movements, not in travelling only, but in speaking, writing, thinking, of the men of those days. As we trace their faded manuscripts, we see in their strong, square penmanship, with every single letter firmly and perfectly defined, the nervous and muscular grasp of the writers. It is the transcript of their character, of their energy, exactitude, perseverance. The succinct and condensed sentences, formal and stiff certainly, yet terser and racier than our comparatively loose and inarticulate style, express the perspicuity and reality, as well as the narrowness and slowness, of their conceptions. Hallam calls that age, ' the most learned, in the sense in which the word was then taken, that Europe has ever seen.' The limitation is important, as reminding us that what we call 'physical' philosophy was yet in its infancy. The learned were more conversant with the unchanging laws of mind, inherited through the schoolmen from the Porch and the Academy, than with the fluctuating sciences of gases and ' strata.' In its own way the learning of the Elizabethan and post-Elizabethan ages was prodigious.

But the peculiar characteristics of that age, which essentially distinguish it from our own, were, as we have already hinted, deliberation, earnestness, concentration of purpose. Men had a more leisurely, and yet a more painstaking, way of thinking and acting, and a sense of enjoyment and repose in their work, not easily attainable in these days of high pressure.

They could realise better than we the beautiful thought with which Milton consoled himself in the forced inactivity of his blindness—

They also serve, who only stand and wait,

They could find hours, while we can scarcely spare moments, for undisturbed meditation: a habit of mind as much at variance with our mobile temperament as the stillness of the old Inns of Court is unlike the din and turmoil of Fleet Street, which roars outside the gates. The feverish spirit of speculation, which in commerce makes or destroys a fortune in a day and exercises the same perturbing influence even over our philosophy and literature, was altogether alien to the orderly and scrupulous habits of that age. The advantages of our own day are great, in the triumphal march of physical science, in the vastness of our intellectual horizon, in the richer complexity of our acquirements. But in this very diffusiveness of aims there is a great danger. We seem to want that closeness of concentration which stamps the Elizabethan age.

One among the best of our living poets, Mr. Matthew Arnold, in the preface to his volume of poems, complains of the want of ' sanity ' in modern literature. There is an unnatural straining after originality, and an impatience of authority or control, which too often disfigure even our greatest works. The clever and popular ' George Eliot, ' for example, may be taken as in many ways a typical instance of modern tendencies. The wonderfully graphic delineations of life and

character are spoilt by bad taste, an unevenly balanced
judgment, and a strange confusion in the ideas of
right and wrong.   It is a great relief to turn from
such unwholesome exhalations of a false and unreal
philosophy, to the bright, clear, buoyant atmosphere
which Shakespeare breathed.   No wonder that the
Elizabethan age attracts so powerfully the sympathies
of writers like Mr. Kingsley.   They find there a
hearty and robust geniality, a manly common-sense,
an emancipation from modern subjectivity of thought
such as they delight in, while they are lenient towards
the coarseness of speech into which that boyish
exuberance of animal spirits was apt to degenerate.
It would be great injustice to set down the age of
Elizabeth and James as licentious and immoral, on the
score of the occasion al '*grossièreté*' of its drama.
True, the continental fashions then being imported
from France and Italy, and by the Englishmen who
served in great numbers in the debauched camps of
the Low Countries, tended to corrupt the court.   If we
may judge from Howel's gossiping letters, Lord
Dalgarno, in Scot's 'Nigel,' is no unfair sample of its
profligacy.   But this laxity of morals did not taint
the great bulk of the nation—the country gentry
living at home on their own estates, the stalwart
yeomen of the country, the staid citizens of the towns.
At no other period, perhaps, was the 'middle-class'
(using that vague term to embrace both professions
and trades), so generally sound at the core.   Never
was our commerce at once so daringly enterprising
and so strictly honourable: never was the sanctity

and happiness of domestic life so fully realised. Accustomed, as we are, to the pert slang of ' governor ' for father, accustomed, it must be owned, to relegate our religion too exclusively to one day in seven we of this century may smile as we read of grown-up sons, high in office, making lowly obeisance at meeting father or mother, and may wonder that the constant presence of a chaplain was almost a matter of course in every large household. We who see the common recreations of our working-man too often of a low and debasing kind, can hardly realise the fact, that almost every family circle in those days in all classes, from the highest to the lowest, could while away the long bright summer evenings in the open air, or the dull afternoons in winter round the hearth, with glee and round, and madrigal; each age and sex bearing its own part in the manifold harmony of the strain. There is something lost in all this. The Spartan-like deference for old age, the sense of religion as interwoven with the daily affairs of life, the love of music, with leisure to enjoy its cheering and elevating influences,* these are habits which no nation can well afford to lose.

But we must return to George Herbert. We have dwelt at length on the characteristics of his age, not merely to show cause why the verdict of his contemporaries should not be set aside as valueless, but also because the man and the age cannot be separated.

* It was well said in an admirable article on ' Music,' since reprinted from the Quarterly Review, that the Elizabethan music is full of ' sound piety, broad fun, perfect freedom of speech, and capital eating and drinking.'

He is, at once, a result of his age in some degree, and one of the efficient causes of it; being himself modified by its circumstances, while contributing to make it what it is. For this reason we must pause for a few moments longer, to count the long list of illustrious names which that age unrolls.

It was an age fertile in great men. Spenser was writing his 'Faery Queene' just about the time of George Herbert's birth. Raleigh's brilliant but erratic career reached its unhappy close while Herbert was public orator at Cambridge. While holding that office, and dividing his time between the Court and the University, Herbert must have had frequent opportunities of seeing and hearing on the stage the marvellous creations of Shakespeare's genius, then in all the freshness of their first appearance. More exactly coëval with Herbert was Milton, with a galaxy of stars in the poetic firmament of far lesser magnitude and feebler lustre, of whom only a few scattered rays penetrate to us through the intervening mist of years, Daniel, Quarles, Wither, Drummond, Sandys, Suckling, and others. In theology there were Usher, Chillingworth, Hammond, Andrewes, Sanderson, and Hall, a strong array; in philosophy Hobbes and Selden; in jurisprudence Coke and Hale; in political life the Cecils, and many other truly sagacious statesmen; and, last in our enumeration, but foremost in philosophy, in law, and in affairs of state, Lord Chancellor Bacon. We may add to the list Burton, whose 'Anatomy of Melancholy' is no bad sample of the quaint and miscellaneous erudition then in repute.

But the drama was the distinguishing glory of those days. Then flourished, in the words of Southey, 'a race of dramatic writers, which no age and no country has ever equalled.' Ben Jonson the founder of the English 'comedy of manners,' and, inferior only to him, in Hallam's judgment, Massinger; with Beaumont and Fletcher, Ford, Shirley. Such were Herbert's contemporaries; some of them as Bacon,* Andrewes, Sanderson, his intimate personal friends; as were also Lord Pembroke, his kinsman, one of the chief actors in the important work of colonising Virginia, and governing the rising colony; Donne, Cotton, Ferrar, and Sir Henry Wotton, all men of no common ability, highly cultivated, and of a still more uncommon moral excellence. Certainly it was a rich soil, prolific of a healthy and luxuriant vegetation, the age in which George Herbert found himself.

It is impossible to approach Herbert's writing in an unprejudiced state of mind unless we first form a just conception of the writer. When the reader feels that he is addressed by one who has a claim on his attention, he is alive to beauties that might otherwise be unnoticed, less on the look-out for faults, can afford to overlook a few blemishes of style here and there—in a word, brings himself into that conformity of feeling with his author, which all artists exact by right as indispensable. Without this *provisional* sympathy, and even deference, no one can be a fair critic. We must divest ourselves at once of the vulgar notion of

* Bacon dedicated some metrical psalms to George Herbert; and 'usually,' says Walton, 'desired his approbation, before he would expose any book of his to be printed.

George Herbert. Far from being a mere devotee, planted like Simeon Stylites on his solitary column in unnatural isolation, inaccessible to his fellow-men, he was emphatically a man of social sympathies, sustained and directed upwards by the entire devotion of his heart to heaven, as the tendrils of the vine are taught to ascend by the elm round which it clings. He loved to watch the 'quidquid agunt' of men, their business and pleasures, not with the contemptuous indifference of a Stoic or Epicurean, but as being all, if duly regulated, component parts in the order and beauty of the universe. Gifted himself with rare natural advantages, he neither neglected nor misused them. Excepting good health (for he was constitutionally delicate, and, in particular, subject to painful and weakening attacks of the ague, then far more prevalent and serious than in our days of good draining), hardly one of fortune's gifts was wanting. He was born of a family noble in the truest sense of the word; for the name of Herbert was eminent then, as now, for the high character of those who bore it, with the difference that modern civilisation has directed to more peaceful pursuits the same high spirit which distinguished the 'fighting-men and men of renown,' of whom Lord Herbert of Cherbury, with his usual complacency, reckons not a few among his ancestors. Well born and well bred, with a very prepossessing exterior,* with accomplish-

* One of his biographers, Archdeacon Oley, 1652, describes his person, in rather ludicrous terms, as 'a contesseration of elegancies, and set of rarities to the beholder,' and speaks of 'his exquisite carriage.'

ments of many kinds, and a sweetness of disposition which could not fail to win and retain friends, with abilities which raised him to one of the highest posts in the University at the early age of twenty-five, he started in the race of life with a bright prospect of success before him. His only fault, according to his brother, Lord Herbert, was that he was naturally quick-tempered, 'not exempt from passion and choler;' and Walton tells us, that 'if in his undergraduate life he expressed any error, it was that he kept himself too much retired, and at too great a distance from his inferiors; and his clothing seemed to prove that he set too great a value on his parts and parentage.' His allowance at college, we gather from his letters, though liberal, was not always sufficient for his rather expensive habits. Certainly, in his after-life, as the 'country parson,' denying himself in every way for his parishioners, identifying himself with their homely lives, and lending a patient ear to every poor old woman who came with a story of distress, we see no traces of this reserve or exclusiveness, natural as it was to his fastidious delicacy of taste. He was the youngest but one of seven brothers, all men of note, and all apparently marked by a strong family likeness in high spirit and ability. The eldest, who raised himself to the rank of Lord Herbert of Cherbury, is well known to this day for his versatile talents as diplomatist and philosopher. The two next, Richard and William, after receiving a liberal education, served with distinction in the Low Countries, and were renowned according to the punctilious code of honour then in force, as duellists, Richard carrying twenty-four wounds with him to his grave at Bergen-op-zoom. Charles died young, a Fellow of New College. These four were George Herbert's seniors. But he seems to have been more closely drawn to the brother next after himself in age, who afterwards became Sir Henry, a favourite at Court, at one time 'Master of the Revels,' and of course, like all the fine gentlemen of the day, famous in 'affairs of honour.' The youngest, Thomas, was a brave sailor. The brother of such men was not likely to be a bookworm.

George Herbert's naturally high spirits are evident in the few letters which remain, mostly belonging to the early part of his life. They are chiefly addressed from Cambridge to his brother Henry, and are very racy, considering the stiffness of letter-writing then in vogue. It is an instance of the chivalrous respect then paid to ladies, that while signing himself to Henry 'your loving brother,' he is 'your loving brother *and servant*' to his poor sick sister Elizabeth, wife of Sir Henry Jones. Writing to his brother at Paris, he tells him, 'be covetous of all good, which you see in Frenchmen, in knowledge, in fashion, in words;' and particularly in that 'wittiness of speech' which has always been a specialty of that nation. 'Let there be no kind of excellency which it is possible for you to attain to, which you seek not.'

About the same date he writes from Cambridge of having 'some forty businesses on hand,' and with equal relish of 'the gaynesses' incident to his office of public orator. In those days the Universities were in close communication with the Court, and to be distinguished at Oxford or Cambridge was a sure passport in political life. The office of 'public orator' was especially valued as an introduction to the Court; and a bright vista in that direction was opening itself to the young scholar courtier.* At first he hailed it gladly. Looking back afterwards on those sunny days from his quiet parsonage at Bemerton, he says:—

> —my birth and spirit rather took
> The way that takes the town.

But it is not in the tone of vain regret. He thanks the guiding Providence which diverted him by his bad health from the glittering prizes of that highway to greatness to the 'fallentis semita vitæ,' in which he was to serve God and his country. His intention of taking Holy Orders was clearly an afterthought; but that of leading a strictly religious life, even in the midst of secular avocations, clearly was not. He was not one of those who, as Carlyle expresses it, 'go through a mud-bath in youth in order to come out clean.' The dedication of all his powers to their highest use, whatever his way of life might be, at Court or in the University, was his fixed purpose from first to last, formed in very early life, and never laid aside for a moment, even in his 'fierce' youth, 'eager, hot, and undertaking,' as he himself describes it. In his first year at Cambridge he complains, 'many love-poems are daily writ and consecrated to Venus, few

---

* Oley says, ' he might have had a secretary of state's place, *like other Public Orators.*'

that look towards God and heaven.' His delicate health was, no doubt, one cause that determined him to retire from the stirring scene of the Court. But he was also moved by a strong longing to raise the country clergy from the low estimation in which they were generally held, as the coffee-house squibs of that day show too plainly. Oley attributes this contempt of the clergy partly to the too indiscriminate admission of candidates first into the Universities, and thence into Holy Orders—for, as sometimes happens now, testimonials were given too much as a mere form —and partly to the general poverty of the country clergy, and the dearth of men of high family among them. It was a common thing then for their children to be apprenticed to trades. Herbert's ' Country Parson ' is described as ' taking care not to put his children into vain trades, nor unbefitting the reverence of their father's calling, such as taverns for men and lace-making for women.' Elsewhere chaplains are warned against being ' over submissive and cringing,' and the rural clergy against haunting ale-houses and taverns.* Herbert resolved to set himself to rescue the high vocation of the clergy from this loss of caste and consequent loss of influence.

But it was not without a severe inward struggle

---

* Clearly it was not their poverty so much as their low tastes and pursuits that degraded them. The circumstances of the present day seem imperatively to require that neither low birth, nor scanty means, nor even a less perfect education than usual for gentlemen, should stand in the way of the admission of fit persons into holy orders, at least into the diaconate, for missionary work at home and abroad. An easy examination for deacon's orders with a stricter examination for priest's orders would make this practicable without danger.

that he decided on that renunciation of pursuits, otherwise innocent, which the consecration of a man's life to the work of the ministry demands. If he came late to the work, he did not come empty-handed. Crowned with academical honours, and graced with the prestige of high social position, he brought his abilities, his reputation, his prospect of worldly success, and freely devoted them all to the work. He could truly say in a short poem, called ' The Pearl,' that he knew the ways of learning, the ways of honour, the ways of pleasure, of love, of wit, of music, and, as Walton adds, ' he knew on what terms he renounced all these for the service of his Master.' In another poem, ' The Quip,' he personifies, ' Beauty, Money, Glorie, and Wit,' as severally assailing him with raillery for his neglect of their fascinations; to each and all he replies by turning to his heavenly Master :—

But Thou shalt answer, Lord, for me.

Not as one seeking in the cool shadow of the Church a refuge from the glare of worldly disappointments, but with humble thankfulness, as feeling unworthy of the office, he undertook the responsibilities of the ministry. After retiring for a year to his brother Henry's house in Kent, there to pause before taking the irrevocable step, he was ordained deacon in 1625; and after four years passed in deacon's orders (for he imposed on himself this unusually long period of probation, and his diffidence was hardly overcome at last by the persuasions of Lord Pembroke and Laud, then bishop of London), he was ordained priest, and

P

appointed to the small rectory of Bemerton, in 1630, being then in his thirty-seventh year. His resolutions formed on the eve of induction, and the rules which he then laid down for himself are recorded by Walton. We must extract part of them. 'I beseech that God, who hath honoured me so much as to call me to serve at His altar, that as by His special grace He hath put into my mind these good desires and resolutions, so He will by His assisting grace give me ghostly strength to bring the same to good effect. And I beseech Him that my humble and charitable life may so win upon others as to bring glory to my Jesus, whom I have this day taken to be my Master and Governor. And I am so proud of His service that I will always observe and do His will; and will always call Him *Jesus my Master.* And I will always contemn my birth or any title or dignity that can be conferred on me, when I shall compare them with my title of being a priest, and serving at the altar of *Jesus my Master.*' In one of his poems he turns again and again with fresh delight to these words :—

How sweetly doth '*my Master*' sound '*my Master.*'

With all his self-discipline and devotion George Herbert was not a man to be happy alone. Some little time before this crisis in his life he married a daughter of Mr. Danvers (a name well known in the county), of Bainton, in Wilts, a member of the same family as Lord Danby. It was a very short courtship. Walton naïvely says, 'she changed her name into Herbert on the third day after their first interview.

But, to say nothing of love at first sight, their families were already connected, and they had heard so much of each other through friends that they met for the first time not as strangers, but as if long acquainted. ' They wooed so like princes,' Walton explains, ' as to have select proxies, such as were true friends to both parties. One is reminded for a moment of Richard Hooker and his extraordinary marriage. But the cases are quite different. That learned, but for once *in*judicious divine, simply acquiesced in the choice of the landlady of his lodgings, who took the opportunity of nominating her own daughter. The proof of marriage is of course in its consequences. Every one knows how poor Hooker was found by a former pupil vainly endeavouring to give his mind to the great treatise which he had on hand, while rocking the cradle amid the objurgations of his Xantippe. But Herbert's married life was singularly happy. His wife proved herself worthy of such a husband.

The rest of his life is soon told. For little more than two years he lived and worked among his parishioners, and then his short, but useful and happy, life was closed by a death-bed in perfect unison with all that had preceded it, serene and hopeful as a cloudless sunset. Two years and three months may seem a disproportionate space of time for his work in the ministry, after so long and so careful preparation for it. But it is not for us to call his death premature. To himself the old adage may safely be applied —' his wings were grown;' and, as for his work, it was ended. ' Non diu sed multum vixit.' His contemporaries complained that 'he lost himself in that humble way, while devoting his energies to that obscure little parish. But his influence, like that of the saintly poet of Hursley, whom he resembles in so many ways, in forming the highest type of Christian character for laity as well as clergy, has been extended by his example and writings, far beyond the narrow limits of that little parish on Salisbury Plain, with its ' twenty cottages ' and ' less than a hundred and twenty souls '—far beyond the age in which he lived.

It is not difficult, from hints contained in Walton's life and in his own sketches of the ideal ' country parson,' to form a tolerably complete idea of Herbert's daily life at Bemerton. The picture is a delightful one. His little church has lately been restored at a great cost by the munificence of a lady worthy to bear the name, which he and others like him have ennobled in the highest sense of the word. As it stood in his day, with its low dovecote-like bell turret and narrow irregular windows, it must have been very like the homely but picturesque little churches which may still be seen often enough in Herefordshire, lingering amid other vestiges of the past in that old-fashioned district, and bearing witness, by their contrast to the statelier structures of the eastern counties, to the inferiority of western England in wealth and population. The romantic hills and dingles of Herefordshire are certainly as unlike as can be to the gently undulating plain about Bemerton. But there is, perhaps, no county which, at the present time, so nearly realises the truly pastoral relation which subsisted two

centuries ago between a country parson and his
people. In spite of the close vicinity of rampant
Dissent in Wales, the old traditional respect for the
Church and the clergy is still half-unconsciously
cherished there among the peasantry and farmers
while each little parish seems to constitute only one
large family, as described in Herbert's ' Country
Parson,' with the parson himself acting *in propriâ
personâ*—not as in towns, through the mediation of
curates and committees—the head and centre of everything that is going on, not excepting even the lesser
and more trivial affairs of common life. In a little
world of this sort we may imagine the poet-rector,
loving and beloved by his flock, and reverenced by
them not only for his office, but for his rank, learning
and sanctity—holding much the same position among
them as the late Augustus Hare in his little parish on
another of the Wiltshire plains. Herbert brought
all the weight of his personal advantages to bear on
his work, incommensurate to his powers as it may
seem in worldly appreciation. He made his knowledge
of the Platonic dialogues useful in the public catechising of the young people in church—a practice on
which he set great store—borrowing the method of
the sage, ' who taught the world as one would teach
a child.' He used to entertain all his parishioners in
turn at his Sunday dinner-table, welcoming the poorest
with an especial share of that high-bred courtesy for
which he was eminent even in a day when the etiquette
of chivalry was still observed, and ' the grand manner '
was more common among gentlemen than it is now.

We may fancy him seated in his study, digesting his omnigenous stores of learning into a large common-place book—so he advises in the 'Country Parson'—but turning at any moment from the congenial occupation to encourage any poor applicant for relief, who came to unfold a simple story of petty anxieties. His influence with the higher classes, always less amenable to such an influence, was as great as with the poor. ' There was not a man in his way,' writes Oley, ' *be he of what rank he would,* that spoke awry in order to God, but Herbert would wipe his mouth (!) with a modest, grave, and Christian reproof.' He had a singular graciousness in reproving —always a disagreeable task—' a dexterity in sweetening this art ;' a gentle yet uncompromising manner; a delicate tact in guiding conversation, which is wanting in persons of equal zeal, but less discretion. The eighteenth chapter of the ' Country Parson' gives some idea of this suavity and tenderness with unflinching firmness of manner: and, if such an art can be imparted by any rules, it may be by those laid down in the ' Church Porch.' Walton tells a story, illustrative of Herbert's winning manner, of his gaining a lasting influence for good over a gentleman living in Salisbury, by a short, casual conversation as they walked together, being previously unacquainted, on the road to that city. There must have been an irresistible charm about him, not the result of merely outward polish, but of innate sweetness of disposition and unselfishness, disciplined by the 'self-reverence, self-knowledge, self-distrust,' which were the results of his religion. It is no wonder that his flock followed him willingly, instead of being driven. 'When Mr. Herbert's Saints' bell [Sanctus-bell?] rang to prayers,' his neighbours, rich and poor, loved to resort to the little chapel adjoining his house where the Church-service was daily performed 'at the canonical (?) hours of ten and four.' Men 'would leave their plough to rest awhile, that they might offer their devotions to God with him, and then return to their work.' In our days of busy competition, even George Herbert would find it difficult to collect a large congregation in a small rural parish on a week-day. Herbert describes the country parson as ob-serving the stated times of fasting and abstinence. The passage is characteristic of the man and his age. 'As Sunday is his day of joy, so is Friday his day of mortification, which he observes not only with abstinence of diet, but also of company, recreation, and all other outward contentments; and, besides, with confession of sins and all acts of humiliation.' It was the general practice then. Of late years many religious persons have neglected fast-days from fear of an observance which, more easily, perhaps, than any other, degenerates into formalism; while persons less serious have been only too glad to be freed from its restraint. Plainly, with George Herbert, it was no mere 'opus operatum.' There was no idea of any-thing meritorious in it. It was an ethical discipline for relieving the 'divinæ particula auræ' from the depressing burden of the 'corpus onustum.' His remarks in the tenth chapter show that he felt the obligation in the spirit rather than in the letter. 'If a piece of dry flesh at my table be more unpleasant to me than some fish, then, certainly, to eat the flesh and not the fish, is to keep the fast-day naturally. He goes on to say that fasting must never interfere with health, the preservation of sound mind in sound body being a paramount duty. We have dwelt at some length on this point, because the idea of Herbert and his contemporaries would be incomplete without it.

George Herbert was not one of those who sacrifice common everyday duties to those of a more directly religious kind, and who are so intent on the far distance, as in their abstraction, to be unconscious of the ground under their feet. The good parson is portrayed as exercising a general supervision, even over those departments of the household which do not usually belong to the 'pater-familias' to regulate. The following passage is very quaint: 'As he is just in all things, so he is to his wife also, counting nothing so much his own as that he may be unjust to it. Therefore he gives her respect both afore her servants and others, and half, at least, of the government of the house, reserving so much of the affairs as [may] serve for a diversion for him; yet never so giving over the reins but that he sometimes looks how things go, demanding an account, *but not by the way of an account.*'

His religion was not something distinct from the daily routine of life; it penetrated and ruled every action. If beggars, for example, come for alms, the parson takes the opportunity, 'before giving, of making

them say their prayers, or the Creed, or the ten Commandments; and as he finds them perfect, so rewards them the more.' His own household was managed in the same spirit. The tie between master and servant was closer and more affectionate then:—
' Besides the common prayers of the family, the parson straitly requires of all to pray by themselves, before they sleep at night and stir out in the morning, and knows what prayers they say, and *till they have learned them makes them kneel by him.*' Herbert knew well the truth of Michael Angelo's great saying, ' These trifles make up perfection; and perfection itself is no trifle.' His devotion, being sober and unfanatical, never obscured the homelier duties of life. When some friend objected that he was spending too much in alms-giving he could answer that 'a competent maintenance was secured to his wife after his death.' His parish never made him forgetful of friends or relatives.

> Meliorne amicus, sponsus, an pastor gregis
> Incertum est,

is the verdict of Dean Duport.

To complete our sketch, inadequate at the best, of George Herbert, at Bemerton, we must think of him as gracefully unbending at times from the tension of work, and joining in such social recreations as accorded with his profession. Twice a week, after walking in to Salisbury for the cathedral service, which it was ' his heaven upon earth ' to attend, he would spend part of the evening ' at some private musical meeting, where he would usually sing and play his part.'

We may imagine him, as really happened once, stopping on his walk, 'like the good Samaritan, and putting off his canonical coat to help a poor man with a poorer horse that was fallen under his load.' He arrived in Salisbury in such a state that his musical friends there 'began to wonder that Mr. George Herbert, who used to be so trim and neat, came into that company so soiled and discomposed.' We may fancy him, rod in hand, strolling along the river side, one of the ' gentle anglers ' whom his friend Walton commemorates, shaping into verse his sacred meditations. Certainly a life like this, in which work and rest, self-discipline and natural impulse, secular duties, and heavenly aspirations, are blended into harmonious unity, as in one of those rich strains of music, now grave, now joyous, but always duly measured, which he loved to follow: a life in which the coarser threads of existence are inextricably intertwined with, and transfigured by the radiance of, the more ethereal filaments; in which the calmness and equanimity which the Roman poet vainly longed for seems attained ; is among the highest and most complete developments of human nature possible on earth. Monastic seclusion may secure peace by eliminating the elements of discord. ' They make desolation and call it peace.' A life like Herbert's calls into action all the component parts of our organisation, and consecrates them severally to their appointed use.

It is his largeness of mind, quickness of sympathy, and practical sense, that we have been especially endeavouring to illustrate in George Herbert, for of his learning and piety there can be no question. We commend his life and works to the admirers of ' muscular Christianity.' True, Herbert had no share in Mr. Kingsley's horror of anything like asceticism, nor so unreserved a confidence in the undisciplined impulses of nature; still they agree well in the warm appreciation of whatever is noble and beautiful, whether in the moral or material universe, and particularly in the great truth that the work and excellence of man lies *in* the world and not *out* of it, and has a fruition in this life, though not in this life only. We might often fancy that we are reading the more didactic parts of ' Westward Ho! ' or ' Two Years Ago,' in the genial, plain-spoken, thoroughly fresh and real moralisings of Herbert. Some few extracts we must give (for his condensed wisdom loses much by dilution), chiefly those bearing on the secular aspects of life. In the ' Parson's Survey,' not of his own parish only, but of what is now called ' the spirit of the times,' for the good parson is described as being also a good citizen, Herbert speaks of idleness among the young nobility as the ' great national sin of the times.' It seems to have been one of the newest fashions imported from France and Italy; as Shakespeare writes of a lackadaisical youth—

> For I remember, when I was in France,
> Young gentlemen would be sad as night;
> And all for wantonness.

To remedy this evil (one not peculiar to that century), Herbert prescribes manly occupations. He recom-

mends the young nobility to learn farming; to act as
magistrates; to study civil law, the basis of interna-
tional relations; and therefore especially useful to
statesmen and diplomatists; to improve themselves by
travelling abroad; ' to ride the great horse '—that is,
to acquire the accomplishments of the tiltyard.   No
doubt, if alive now, he would add the rifle corps to
his list.   His wisdom is not of a cloistered tone.   On
the other hand, it is far removed from the sharp practice of mere worldlings.   It is, like the prudential
maxims of the Book of Proverbs or Ecclesiasticus, the
identification of duty with expediency.   The ' Church
Porch,' an introduction in verse to the other poems,
reminds the reader of the best parts of Horace's
Satires, not less by its ' pedestrian muse ' than by its
shrewd wit and graceful pleasantry.   It abounds in
pithy sayings, such as may give a man not the manners only, but the principles and feelings of a true
gentleman.   Mr. Willmott well says, ' The " Church
Porch " is a little handbook of rules for the management of temper, conversation and business.   Every
child [?] ought to get it by heart.'   Here is good advice tersely given :—

> Pitch thy behaviour low, thy projects high ;
> So shalt thou humble and magnanimous be.

Here is a word for the over-sensitive :—

> Think not thy fame at every twitch will break.
> By great deeds show that thou canst little do :
> Then do them not.

Beneath all the lighter raillery lies a profound vein

of sentiment, the utterances of which sound like the voice of that great and wise king, who tried all things under the sun, and found them vanity. It is this keen sense of the ridiculous, as well as of the awful side of human life, which is one chief characteristic of Shakespeare, and which he portrays so well in the melancholy Hamlet, and in the cheerier Pantagruelism of the young prince, the future hero of Agincourt. Herbert, in the same way, was one of the few who can realise at once the utter nothingness of even the greatest affairs of this life in one point of view, and the immeasurable importance of even the most trivial as forming the moral destiny. It is characteristic of him, that he translated the sensible little treatise on 'Temperance and Sobriety' of Ludovicus Cornarus, known to Italian scholars as Luigi Cornaro, of Padua: a delightful sketch of a hale and hearty old age, with rules for attaining it. Herbert seems to have had a peculiar aptness, both by nature and education, for casuistry; not for hair-splitting and sophistries, but for the 'noble art,' as he rightly calls it, of solving the perplexing cases of conscience which occur every day. His way of cutting these knots, or rather of disentangling them, is thoroughly English. It is the evidence of a healthy moral sense practised in logic, but with its own unerring instincts unblunted. A few examples must suffice. He shows when it is wrong, and when not, to take usury—to inform against a neighbour—to omit customary acts of devotion; how far tears and other physical accom· paniments of contrition are really essential or only accidental to it—how persons may test their motives in seeking preferment.   On the question which often perplexes the benevolent, of giving relief to unworthy applicants, he advises to give *most* to those of best character, but *something* to any in distress; for evident miseries 'have a natural privilege and exemption from all laws.'   His 'proverbs,' some apparently his own, others merely collected by him, which the reader will find among his greater works under the title of 'Jacula Prudentum,' leave hardly anything in life untouched.   We quote at hazard two of the pithiest :—

> Marry your *son* when you *will*, your *daughter* when you *can*.
> Buy at a fair, sell at home.

We refer our readers to the rest, if they value the guidance of Herbert's aphorisms in the mazes of life.

The 'Country Parson' is, of course, the book by which Herbert is best known.   Though intended primarily for the clergy, it is a book to delight readers of any profession by the charming series of portraits which it unfolds of the good pastor in almost every conceivable attitude and grouping.*   Oley, in his day, feared only that an ideal so faultless 'would make the laity discontented.'   The literary merits, too, of the book are great.   There is no fine writing in it; there are no grand passages.   But

---

* There is *one* curious omission. Not a word is said on the delicate relation between incumbent and curate. A chapter on the 'Parson and his Curate' would have been useful to both parties. Herbert's silence on this point is the more surprising from his having had a curate himself.

the language throughout is choice, scholarlike, and equable; singularly simple, exact, and terse; above all, it is in perfect keeping with the ideas to be conveyed. If, indeed, the great thing in style is, as Aristotle teaches, to be 'clear and pleasing,' if the language ought to fit as closely yet easily to its ideas as a well-made dress to the limbs, then Herbert's prose must be ranked high. It is like a well-dressed person. The reader is unconscious where its charm lies; but if he change a word, or the place of a word, or add or take away anything, he discovers how exquisite, yet, to all appearance, unstudied, is the composition. In this 'curiosa felicitas,' Herbert's style resembles that of his friend, Lord Bacon. It is entirely free from the euphuism then in fashion at court, and its graceful ease is the more remarkable, considering the ponderous manner of the learned men of the day. Hallam, in his 'History of Literature,' passes by the 'Country Parson' too summarily. While allowing to it the faint praise of being 'a pleasing little book,' he objects that 'its precepts are sometimes so overstrained according to our notions as to give an appearance of affectation.' So much the worse, then, for us and 'our notions.' But a book on the life and habits of a country parson was not much in Hallam's way; nor was he likely, from the associations which environed him, to free himself from an unintentional prejudice against the theological school, in which, according to his 'notions,' Herbert would be classed. To the charge of being 'overstrained,' it is enough to answer that the precepts in question were laid down by the author as 'rules and resolutions' for his own guidance. 'He set the form and character of a 'true pastor,' he says, 'as high as he could, for himself to aim at;' and he practised what he taught. Many useful manuals for the clergy have been written lately, testifying to their revived earnestness in their professional duties: Evans' 'Bishopric of Souls,' Oxenden's 'Pastoral Office,' Monro's 'Parochial Work,' Heygate's 'Ember Thoughts,' Bishop Wilberforce's 'Ordination Addresses,' and Blunt's admirable 'Lectures on the Parish Priest.' But the 'Country Parson' can never be superseded. Short as it is and unassuming, it is inexhaustible in its suggestiveness. Walton says, 'He that can spare twelve pence and yet wants a book so full of plain, prudent, and useful rules, is scarcely excusable.' It will never be obsolete. Here and there may occur something inapplicable to modern usages. Now that the ties of neighbourhood are less binding, it is not likely that, 'in case of any calamity by fire or famine to a parish,' all the inhabitants of an adjoining parish would go in procession, with the parson at their head, 'to carry their collection of alms themselves, to cheer the afflicted.' Nor would it be generally practicable now, though something similar is customary in some hotels, for the 'parson on journey' to assemble his fellow-travellers 'in the hall of the inn' for family prayers, 'with a due blessing of God for their safe arrival.' Still, in both cases, the principle holds good. Generally, his advice may be taken literally. His advice, for example, on the way of reproving, is as true now as then, and much needed by many zealous young clergymen. 'Those whom he finds idle or ill employed, he chides *not at first*, for that were neither civil nor profitable, but always *in the close*, before he departs from them: yet in this he distinguisheth; for if it be a plain countryman, he reproveth him plainly, for they are not sensible of fineness; if they be of higher quality they commonly are quick and sensible, and very tender of reproof, and therefore he lays his discourse so that he comes to the point very leisurely, and oftentimes as Nathan did, in the person of another, making them to reprove themselves.' Again, his remarks on reading the prayers in church are very seasonable, while complaints are heard continually of the bad elocution of the clergy; of their 'gabbling' in one church, of their 'drawling' and 'mouthing' in another. The parson's manner is thus described:—'His voice is humble, the words treatable [*sic*] and slow; yet not so slow as to let the fervency of the supplicant hang and die between speaking; but with a grave earnestness between fear and zeal, *pausing, yet pressing*, he performs his duty.' It is not, however, to be desired, that modern preachers should follow him implicitly, when he assigns no less than 'one full hour' as the time not to be exceeded in preaching; for the diffusion of books has changed the functions of the pulpit. There are preachers who may profit by his advice against over-analysing a text. The old story of 'let us *tap* this ' " *but* " ' finds its counterpart in some pulpits in our day. On the difficulties of parochial work, there is much to be learnt from the 'Country

Parson;' for example, on avoiding the danger of bribing the poor into an unreal profession of religion, while rewarding the most deserving.

One of the most beautiful and characteristic chapters in the book is 'the parson on Sunday.' In the description of Sunday as a joyous, as well as holy day, equally free from the interruption of worldly cares, and from the dull vacuity and gloom of ultra-sabbatarians, we see the cheerfulness of his religion. 'On the Sunday before his death,' writes Walton, 'he rose suddenly from his couch, called for one of his instruments, and having tuned it, he played and sang——

> The Sundays of man's life,
>   Threaded together on Time's string,
> Make bracelets to adorn the wife
>   Of the eternal glorious King.

Very beautiful, again, is the chapter on 'the parson in contempt.' Few, if any, clergymen can expect to go through their pastoral duties without incurring some degree of obloquy; too often in proportion to their fidelity to their charge. Those who, as the author of the 'Christian Year' says,

> feel bowed to earth
> By thankless toil, and vile esteemed,

may gather strength from Herbert's picture of a man, naturally sensitive like himself, raised above the susceptibility of injuries or affronts, 'showing that reproaches touch him no more than a stone thrown against heaven, *where he is and lives.*' But it is endless to make extracts. We must refer our readers to the book itself. Only one word more for the younger clergy, and we have done. They are in danger of becoming too much absorbed in their secular duties, of growing shallow and fussy, amid the countless distractions incidental to these days of penny magazines and penny savings' banks. They may learn from the 'Country Parson,' with his huge 'body of divinity, a book digested by himself out of writers old and new, the store-house of his sermons,' that they must rescue some portion of every day from such secular avocations, however laudable, as may be discharged as well or better by lay agency, in order, by patient study, to lay a solid foundation of learning especially in that great province of knowledge which is peculiarly their own.

Herbert's contributions to our controversial theology are less than might be expected from so learned and profound a theologian. He was naturally averse to publishing; and many of his manuscript papers were lost in the fire at Highnam House: besides, his early death may have prevented more. All that remains is gold, fine and unalloyed. In his short preface to his friend Ferrar's edition of the 'Divine Considerations of John Valdesso'—the companion of Charles V., first in his campaigns, afterwards in his retirement from the world—he touches cursorily, but with a master-hand, on several of the very questions now agitating men's minds in England, his candour and comprehensiveness of intellect, and what may be called philosophical intuition, qualifying him pecu-

liarly to answer such doubts and difficulties as are
propounded in the 'Essays and Reviews,' so far as
they came before him.   He is so free from the conventionalities of religious phraseology, so philosophical, so calmly judicial, and, at the same time, so
thoroughly real and earnest in his convictions, that
whatever falls from him in defence of received truths
carries no slight weight.   Thus, while expressing the
deepest reverence for the written Word of God as
unfathomable in its meaning, or, to use his own words,
' ever teaching more and more,' he does not shrink
from using the plainest language about such actions
there recorded even of eminent saints, as would be
censured in ordinary men.   But he adds, 'it is one
thing not to judge, another to defend them.'   It is
not, however, by passages directly bearing on the
questions mooted in ' Essays and Reviews,' so much
as by his general characteristics as a theologian, that
Herbert's writings afford a solution of them.   What
especially marks his theology is, that reverence and free
thought go hand in hand.   He applies his consummate
powers of reasoning to the question discussed, not as
if himself standing aloof from it, or merely theorising
on paper, but with intense personal conviction, and
as qualifying the laws of thought by the plain dictates
of common sense and common morality.   He seems
capable of realising a mystery, without its mysterious
nature evanescing in his grasp.   Whatever truth,
however abstruse, he handles, ceases to be a mere
bodiless abstraction, and becomes a living reality.
Thus, with him every article of the Creeds is a sub-

stantial verity, incorporated into his very existence. Though well versed in all the philosophy of the schools, there are no cobwebs of idle speculation in his reasoning to be brushed aside before arriving at the truth. All is real, definite, actual, so far as regards the knowledge within the reach of man; beyond that he does not presume to pronounce. His superiority to that habit of mind which wastes its energies in objectless unsatisfying speculation, and his repugnance to the intrusion of unauthorised definitions and dogmatisings into the illimitable field of heavenly mysteries, are evidenced in these quaint lines. He is speaking of—

> Divinities' transcendent sky,
> Which with the edge of wit they cut and carve;
> Reason triumphs, and faith lies by.
> Could not that wisdome, which first broacht the wine,
> Have thickened it with definitions?
> And jagged his seamlesse coat, had that been fine,
> With curious questions and divisions?
> *Love God, and love your neighbour. Watch and pray.*
> *Do as you would be done unto.*
> O dark instructions, ev'n as dark as day!
> Who can these Gordian knots undo?

It is the combination in Herbert's character of the practical and imaginative elements which renders him so eminently and thoroughly English.

He was by no means a partisan in theology. His orthodoxy was not of a partial and exclusive cast. He was one who would have symbolised heartily with the 'Evangelical' party in the fulness of their assertion of justification by faith: only, without losing sight of the other great truths handed down from apostolic times.

He assents freely to Valdesso insisting on the supreme importance of faith; only adding, that from real faith all other graces are sure to spring. The words, 'I am less than the least of Thy mercies,' were ever in his thoughts and prayers. When his friends round his death-bed were reminding him of some good deeds which he had done, he replied, 'Not good unless sprinkled by the blood of Jesus.' He seems to have been as far removed from Arminian self-righteousness as from the licence of the Antinomians. Perhaps nothing better, in small compass, has ever been written on the great problem, how to reconcile free will and grace, than his lines, which begin—

Lord, Thou art mine, and I am Thine.

Again, on the vexed question of election, these few words speak volumes :—' The thrusting away of God's arm doth alone (and nothing else) make us not loved by Him.' It is a great loss that no copy remains of his ' Letter on Predestination,' which Bishop Andrewes valued so highly, that he always carried it ' in his bosom.' Herbert was one of the few who can appreciate the manifold aspects of every question as it may be regarded on this side or on that. He resembles Pascal in many ways; in fine wit, in profound, yet clear insight, in freedom from the narrowness of party spirit. His short poem against the invocation of saints is a remarkable instance of feeling duly balanced by judgment. He protests, elsewhere also, against Romanist errors, but always with temperance and consideration. No one need be surprised to find

George Herbert identifying Papal Rome with Baby-
lon, as if the matter did not admit of question. It
was the way of his generation: a fact, which exposes
the fallacy of an assertion, too often allowed to pass
unchallenged, that our old divines clung to the errors
of Rome, and would have made a more sweeping reformation if living in these days. But this is not the
place to pursue these theological questions. It is
enough to repeat what no student of George Herbert's
remains will deny, that it would not be easy to find a
more perfect representative than in him of the spirit
of our English theology as embodied in our English
Prayer-Book.

It remains to speak of Herbert's poetry. As might
be expected, we find it almost ignored by critics like
Ellis and Warton. ' Apage sus; non tibi spiro.' The
former, in his ' Specimens of the Early English Poetry,'
superciliously dismisses Herbert with a laboured antithesis, which betrays equal ignorance of the facts of
Herbert's life and of the most salient features in his
character. ' Nature intended him for a knight-errant
but disappointed ambition made him a saint!' Any
one less Quixotic than George Herbert, or less like a
man soured by worldly disappointment, can hardly be
conceived. Warton, in a strange confusion of metaphors, speaks of Pope 'judiciously collecting *gold*
from the *dregs* of Herbert, Crashaw,' &c. It would be
nearer the mark to say, that Pope had penetration to
detect the rich unpolished ore, strewn at random in
Herbert's elaborate workmanship. Hallam passes by
Herbert's poetry without a word. Campbell, in his

' British Poets,' while devoting two or three pages
a-piece to the merest poetasters, can only spare the
corner of a page, and half a dozen lines of preface, for
George Herbert. But we must bear in mind the prejudices which rendered Herbert's writings ' caviare to
the general' of late years. More surprising is it that
Southey, in his continuation of Ellis, should mention
Donne, Wither, and Quarles, without any notice of
one certainly their superior as a poet. On the other
hand, as we have seen, Herbert's poems made a great
impression on the minds of the seventeenth century.
Henry Vaughan bears witness to Herbert's influence
as the originator of a new school in poetry. Baxter,
the nonconformist, a man of no common ability, was
a warm admirer of Herbert's poems. Even in our
own day, the great poet-philosopher, Coleridge, again
and again extols George Herbert, not as a man only, but
as a poet. ' Let me add,' he writes in ' The Friend '
[vol. i. p. 53], ' that the quaintness of some of his
thoughts, not of his diction, than which nothing can
be more pure, manly, and unaffected, has blinded
modern readers to the general merits of his poems,
which are for the most part *exquisite in their kind.*' In
the ' Biographer Literaria ' he speaks of the ' weight,
number, and compression of Herbert's thoughts, and
the simple dignity of the language.' He writes to his
friend Mr. Collins, the Academician, ' Read " The
Temple," if you have not read it.' Certainly, this is
high praise from a great critic. Still, it must be owned
that there is much in Herbert's poems to account for
distaste on a first perusal. At first sight they seem,
not here and there only, but throughout, stiff, obscure,

fantastic. Perhaps the reader casts aside the 'Sunday Puzzle,' as the late Bishop Blomfield nicknamed 'the Christian Year,' in utter perplexity, or with the exclamation which Plato provoked from a despairing student, 'Si nonvis intelligi, non debes legi.' But on a closer approach, and with patience, the mist clears off; and what seemed to be unsubstantial and impalpable conceits, 'airy nothings,' prove to have a form and substance well worth some trouble in deciphering. Coleridge says, truly, that the difficulty arises not from any fault in the expression, but from the very nature of the thoughts to be expressed. 'The characteristic of our elder poets,' and he cites Herbert as an instance, 'is the reverse of that which distinguishes more recent versifiers; the one (Herbert and his school) conveying the most fantastic thoughts in the most correct and natural language; the other, in the most fantastic language conveying the most trivial thoughts. The latter is a riddle of words, the former an enigma of thoughts.' Great allowance must be made for the influence of the Italian poets, with that fondness for quaint fancies, which may be seen in the frigid conceits and extravagant metaphors of Tasso and Ariosto—an influence from which Shakespeare himself was not exempt, as his atrocious puns show, and to which we may attribute the wretched acrostics of that period, in which it was the fashion for a lover to express his ardour, or a mourner his sorrows on the memorial stone. Something, too, is owing to his patristic studies. As Oley says, You find in him the choicest passages of the fathers bound ' in metre.' Keble, again, characteristically traces much of this redundance of imagery, ' and constant flutter of his fancy, for ever hovering round his theme, to an instinctive delicacy which shrank from exposing his religious feelings too openly before the eyes of the world.* It is evident also that Herbert's neglect of poetical propriety was in part a reaction from the smoothness and unreality of the popular love-songs of the day. In the last lines of a short poem, entitled ' Grief,' he gives way to the feelings of devotion struggling for a free utterance :—

> Verses, ye are too fine a thing, too wise
> For my rough sorrows ; cease, be dumb and mute ;
> Give up your feet and sorrows for mine eyes,
> And keep your measures for some lover's lute,
> Whose grief allows him musick and a rhyme,
> For mine excludes both measure, tune, and time—
> Alas ! my God !

In the same spirit he describes himself as at first seeking out ' quaint words and trim invention,' as fitting ornaments ' to deck the sense,' in speaking of ' heavenly joyes,' but at last abandoning the vain attempt, and resolving that he will, since

> There is in love a sweetness ready penned,
> Copy out only that.

Elsewhere he seems to long to rescue all the flowers of poetry, 'sweet phrases,' 'lovely metaphors,' 'lovely, enchanting language,' from all lower purposes, for a worthier use. We must remember also, in criticising ' The Temple,' that it was not originally intended for

---

* Prælect, xxiv. quoted by Mr. Willmott.

publication. It was the literal transcript where he found relief in recording his own religious experiences. On his death-bed he left 'this little book' for the hands of his friend Ferrar, adding, 'He shall find in it a picture of the many spiritual conflicts that have passed between God and my soul, before I could subject mine to the will of Jesus, my Master. If he can think it may turn to the advantage of any poor dejected soul, let it be made public; if not, let him burn it.' The too frequent recurrence of anti-climax, and even downright bathos, at the end of many of the poems, indicates that they were never properly revised by the 'last hand' of the author. All these considerations tend to avert the hasty condemnation which might otherwise fall on Herbert's poems as abrupt, rugged, and enigmatical; at any rate, they excuse the poet, even where they cannot alter our opinion of his poetry.

After all, it cannot be denied that Herbert, as a poet, never will and never can be a general favourite. The want of poetic diction—and it must be remembered that in his day the language of poetry was not yet recognised by tacit consent as distinct in many points from that of prose—the quaintness of his thoughts, and the homeliness of his phrases, are grave faults in the eyes of most people. Even the multiplicity and compression of his ideas make him unpopular, though it may satisfy a more critical taste, just as a thorough musician enjoys a closely compacted fugue more than flowing airs and melodies. His subject, too, is against him. The very names of his poems—' Faith,' ' Prayer,' ' Virtue,' 'Obedience,' ' Conscience,' to say nothing of other titles positively ludicrous to our modern ears—are a stumbling-block on the threshold, except to those who approach in a devout, or, as Coleridge preferred to say, 'devotional' spirit. To all others, the pervading sense of the unseen world in every line is as an unknown tongue, an unintelligible rhapsody. His words are, as the old Greek dramatist says, ' eloquent to those who go along with them,' but to none else. They are not likely to attract the uninitiated; their influence is rather in deepening and quickening religious feelings already existing. Like music in a minor key, his poetry does not command attention by a full burst of sound, but quietly instils congenial musings into the attentive ear. All these causes are more than enough to relegate Herbert into the class of poets whose lot it must be ' to find fit audience though few.' He would himself gladly acquiesce in such retirement, in the same spirit as that in which Wordsworth sings,—

Shine, poet, in thy place, and be content.

Herbert's poetry can never be popular. But all true lovers of poetry will find hidden treasure there, if they have patience to search below the surface. There is the difficulty. It must be read *leisurely* to be appreciated. The eager, bustling spirit of our times is incapable, without some self-restraint, of comprehending those compressed utterances, the result of undisturbed meditation. Just as in a dimly lighted

room he who gives only a hurried glance, may turn
away disappointed from a really fine painting, so it is
only after a mental effort of fixed attention that the
latent beauties of poetry like Herbert's can be descried.
Then, and not till then, what seemed confused and
meaningless comes out in light and shadow, disclosing
the significance of even the minutest details. A short
poem called 'Aaron' is an instance. Herbert is pour-
traying the Christian minister as unworthy in himself,
but as rendered worthy by the indwelling gifts of the
great High Priest :—

> Holinesse on the head ;
> Light and perfection on the breast ;
>   Harmonious bells below, raising the dead,
> To lead them unto life and rest :
>   Thus are true Aarons drest.
>
> Profanesse in my head ;
> Defects and darknesse in my breast ;
>   A noise of passions ringing me for dead
> Unto a place where is no rest :
>   Poore priest thus am I drest.
>
> Onely another head
> I have, another heart and breast,
>   Another musick making live not dead,
> Without whom I could have no rest :
>   In Him I am well drest.
>
> Christ is my onely head,
> My alone onely heart and breast,
>   My onely musick, striking me ev'n dead ;
> That to the old man I may rest,
>   And be in Him new drest.
>
> So holy in my head,
> Perfect and light in my deare breast,
>   My doctrine turned by Christ (who is not dead
> But lives in me, while I do rest),
>   Come people ; Aaron's drest.

On a hasty reading, these lines sound as the merest extravagance. They are full of meaning to those who care to find it. The metre, too, is characteristic. At first, it seems cramped and inelastic; when grown more familiar to the ear, it has a plaintive sweetness of its own. Take, again, 'The Call':—

> Come my Way, my Truth, my life ;
> Such a Way, as gives us breath ;
> Such a Truth, as ends all strife ;
> Such a Life, as killeth death.
>
> Come my Light, my Feast, my Strength :
> Such a Light, as shews a Feast ;
> Such a Feast, as mends in length ;
> Such a Strength, as makes his guest.
>
> Come my Joy, my Love, my Heart :
> Such a Joy, as none can move :
> Such a Love, as none can part :
> Such a Heart as joyes in love.'

It only requires thought to see the deep connection which underlies this string of apparently disconnected images.

Religious poetry is seldom of the highest order. The subject transcends human capacity: and the religious poet is in danger of having his sensuous perceptions dimmed by the superior brightness of the immaterial world. Exceptions, indeed, there are few, but glorious. Among our countrymen, Milton stands alone in this category; Cowper, Keble, Trench, and some few others, occupying the next places. Many persons, who would otherwise never have dreamt of versifying, have published what is meant for poetry solely under the promptings of strong religious feeling, as the prolific doggrel of our innumerable hymn-books testifies. To compare Herbert with the colossal genius of Milton would be preposterous. He is more nearly on a par with the others whom we have mentioned. If he wants their polished and musical diction, and is comparatively deficient in the variety of natural imagery, and the tenderness of domestic pathos which belong to the poets of Olney and Hursley, he may be ranked above Keble in terseness and animation, while his manly cheerfulness is a delightful contrast to the morbid gloom which throws its chilling shade over many of Cowper's most beautiful passages. In the general characteristics of profound and reflective philosophy, Herbert and Trench may be classed together. Between Herbert and Keble the resemblance is still more striking. The influence of the older poet is very perceptible throughout the 'Christian Year'—here and there in the very words of it.

It is interesting to trace the coincidences of these kindred minds. In the 'Flower,' which Coleridge calls 'a delicious poem,' Herbert rejoices in the return of spring to the earth, and of spring-like feelings to his own heart, and proceeds:—

> These are Thy wonders, Lord of power,
> Killing and quickening, bringing down to hell,
> And up to heaven in an houre.
>> We say amisse
>> This or that is;
> The Word is all, if we could spell.—P. 174.

In almost the same words, Keble exclaims:—

These are Thy wonders hourly wrought,
Thou Lord of time and thought ;
Lifting and lowering souls at will,
Crowding a world of good or ill
Into a moment's vision.
Sixth S. after Trinity.

In another place, Keble expresses the longing, such as
even heathen philosophers felt, for the glorious emancipation of the immortal nature of man from its earthly
elements :—

Till every limb obey the mounting soul,
The mounting soul the call by Jesus given :
He, who the stormy heart can so control,
The laggard body soon will waft to Heaven.
Twenty-third S. after Trinity.

The same thought occurs in Herbert :—

Give me my captive soul, or take
My body also thither !
Another lift like this will make
Them both to be together.

In both poets alike we see a natural inclination towards the attractions of the world checked by self-discipline :—

I thought it scorn with Thee to dwell,
A hermit in a silent cell,
While, gaily sweeping by,
Wild fancy blew his bugle strain,
And marshalled all his gallant train
In the world's wondering eye.

I would have joined him, but as oft
Thy whispered warnings kind and soft
My better soul confest.
' My servant, leave the world alone :
Safe on the steps of Jesus' throne
Be tranquil and be blest.'
First S. after Trinity.

So in 'The Quip,' which we have already referred to :—

> The merrie world did on a day
>   With his train-bands and mates agree
> To meet together, where I lay,
>   And all in sport to jeer at me.

And the 'merrie world' in the person of his representatives, 'Beautie,' 'Money,' ' Wit,' tries all his allurements, but in vain. Herbert writes, in his poem on ' Giddinesse :—

> Surely, if each one saw another's heart,
>   There would be no commerce,
> No sale and bargain passe : all would disperse
>   And live apart.

Keble has expressed the same idea more fully in his beautiful lines for the Twenty-fourth Sunday after Trinity :—

> Or, what if Heaven for once its searching light
>   Sent to some partial eye, disclosing all
> The rude bad thoughts that in our bosom's night
>   Wander at large, nor heed love's gentle thrall,
>
> Who would not shun the dreary uncouth place?
>   As if, fond leaning where her infant slept,
> A mother's arm a serpent should embrace ;
>   So might we friendless live and die unwept.

In both poets the consecutiveness of the ideas is often far from obvious, and must be sought beneath the surface. In Herbert there is less periphrasis in the expression of devotional feelings. Such outbursts as—

> Oh ! my dear God, though I am clean forgot,
> Let me not love thee, if I love thee not !

R

cannot be paralleled in Keble; they are characteristic of Herbert and of his age.

These parallel passages are interesting as marking the similarity of character which subsists in great and good men, even of very distinct individualities. The admirers of the 'Christian Year' will find much in ' The Temple ' to remind them of their favourite passages. If ' The Temple' is never likely to exercise the extraordinary influence of the ' Christian Year,' —an influence on the religious mind of England greater than has ever been exercised by any book of the kind, an influence extending itself imperceptibly even to quarters seemingly most alien—still it is a book to make a deep impression, where it impresses it at all; and its influence is of a kind to percolate through the few to the many.

The resemblance between Herbert and Cowper is fainter; or rather a strong resemblance is qualified by equally strong traits of difference. Both poets have much in common with Horace, strange as any comparison may appear at first sight between them and the pagan poet of the licentious court of Augustus. They have no small share of his lyrical fervour, his adroitness in the choice of words, and in the adaptation of metres; and, in satire, the same light touch, the same suppressed humour, the same half-sportive, half-pensive strictures on the anomalies of life. Both Herbert and Cowper love to dwell on the transitoriness of earthly pleasures; but there is this difference: Herbert oftener adds that man may enjoy them in moderation while they last:—

Not that he may not here
Taste of the cheer :
But as birds drink, and straight lift up their head,
So must he sip, and think
Of better drink
He may attain to, after he is dead.—P. 134.

Both poets complain alike of times of religious depression; but Herbert's lyre is more often tuned to joy and thankfulness for refreshment and relief. He was naturally of a more hopeful temperament. But there are other causes to account for the difference. That distrustful dread of alienation from the favour of Heaven, which, in religious minds of Cowper's school, seems even to overcloud the sense of reconciliation through the cross, was no part of Herbert's creed. On the contrary, it was the very essence of his faith, a source of unfailing strength, to regard himself and his fellow Christians as having all the privileges of adoption within reach freely to enjoy. Again, while poor Cowper's mental vision was for ever introverted on himself, and busied with that dissection of transient phases of feeling which paralyses the healthy action of the soul, Herbert's glance was oftener turned to the great objective truths of Christianity, deriving from them support in the consciousness of infirmity. Here is the secret of the *cheerfulness* of his poetry. This vivid realisation of the great external facts of Christianity is what distinguishes him from the 'erotic school' of Germany. But for this, he might be classed with many of the poets of the 'Lyra Germanica.' But his poetry, though instinct with the same glow of seraphic love, is more definite, more

practical, less sentimental.   There is in it more substance for the mind to take hold of, more suggestiveness of something beyond, less evaporation into mere
transports of emotion.   His expressions of devout
love, however eager and impulsive, are always (as
in a short poem called 'Artillerie') profoundly
reverential.   Love and obedience, faith and duty, are
with him inseparable.   This habitual attitude of mind
toward the Deity, this filial feeling of love tempered
by awe, is beautifully apparent in the closing lines of
another poem :—

> But as I grew more fierce and wild,
>   At every word
> Methought I heard one calling '*Childe!*'
> And I replied 'My Lord!'—P. 160.

We have endeavoured to illustrate particular traits
in Herbert's character, rather than to select his finest
passages.   Some few of these we feel that we ought
to cite before concluding, especially as our author
is one not so well-known as he deserves to be.   The
beautiful lines on 'Virtue,' beginning

> Sweet day, so cool, so calm, so bright,
> The bridal of the earth and sky.
> The dew shall weep thy fall to-night,
>   For thou must die.'—P. 85.

are perhaps the best known, being quoted in Campbell's 'British Poets' and elsewhere.   They are
singularly applicable to Herbert's own life and
character, and are redolent of the sweetness and
brightness of his disposition.   The 'Sonnet,' if we

may use the word out of its strict signification, on ' Time,' and the lines on ' Love Unknown,' were both favourites with Coleridge. The former has been well compared to a collect in the Prayer-Book in its perfect rhythm, and in the fulness and compactness of its meaning. The latter is a short allegory, highly imaginative, and rich in devotional feeling. We subjoin a specimen of Herbert's more philosophic poetry, not unworthy of Wordsworth :—

> Man is the world's high priest ; he doth present
> The sacrifice for all, while they below
> Unto the service mutter an assent,
> Such as springs use that fall, or winds that blow.
>   *   *   *   *
>
> We all acknowledge both Thy power and love
> To be exact, transcendent, and divine ;
> Who dost so strongly and so sweetly move,
> *While all things have their will yet none but Thine.*
>
> For either Thy permission or command
> Lays hands on all.—P. 118.

Again in ' The Search : '—

> Where is my God ? what hidden place
>   Conceals Thee still ?
> What covert dare eclipse Thy face ?
>   Is it Thy will ?
> O let not that of anything !
>   Let rather brass
> Or steel or mountains be Thy ring —
>   And I will passe.
> Thy will such an entrenching is
>   As passeth thought :
> To it all strength, all subtleties
>   Are things of nought.
> Thy will such a strange distance is,
>   As that to it,
> East and west touch, the poles do kiss
>   And parallels meet.

Many similar passages might be cited, not of a kind, perhaps, to make an immediate impression, but such as will approve themselves gradually more and more to a thoughtful and sympathising mind, and from which it may derive solace and strength.

Herbert's Greek and Latin poems need not detain us long. They evince his mastery over the idioms and metres of those languages; but like most classical compositions of his day, they seem harsh and strained from the effort required to force the old languages to adapt themselves to modern ideas, for which they have no equivalent. His Latin letters are open to the same criticism. The redundance of flowery compliments in them is also a fault of the period.

In our quotations we have referred to Pickering's * edition of 1850, as being, in our opinion, the best extant. It is, as may be expected from the publisher's name, carefully and beautifully executed; in type and general effect, perfectly in keeping with the author's age. The old spelling is retained, as in Keble's Hooker, and for the same reason, as assisting the reader to carry back his thoughts to the associations amid which the author lived and wrote. Willmott's edition † betrays haste by its unpardonable inaccuracies both of spelling and punctuation, especially in the Latin letters, without even any list of the errata. In not a few poems the sense is quite obscured by their not being printed in form of

* 'The Works of George Herbert.' In two volumes. (Pickering) 1850.
† 'The Works of George Herbert.' In one volume. Edited by Rev. R. A. Willmott. (Routledge) 1859.

dialogue. The notes, scanty and misplaced, are of little service, being attached generally to words that need no explanation, as, for instance, ' shrewd,' ' callow,' ' diurnall,' ' oblation,' ' glozing,' while passing by the few phrases that really present any difficulty. Mr. Willmott deserves thanks for adding a few short Greek poems: not that they are of any great value in themselves, but because they show the versatility of Herbert's genius, and his proficiency, not in Latin only (a common accomplishment in his day), but in the less trodden field of Greek literature. Mr. Willmott has done well in omitting ' The Synagogue,' a poor imitation, almost a caricature, of ' The Temple.' The omission of Walton's inimitable life is unaccountable; nor is it compensated for by the editor's own ' Introduction.' It might have been hoped, that some light would be thrown on the connexion between the poet's life and particular passages in his writings. These omissions are the more to be regretted, as this edition is entitled to the credit of introducing an undeservedly neglected author in an attractive and popular form for general reading.

Men like George Herbert are rare. It is not his wide learning, nor his refined taste; not his high spirit, nor his amiability, nor even his strictness of life; it is not any of these qualities singly that distinguishes him; but the rare combination in one person of qualities so diversely beautiful. He was ' master of all learning, human and divine.' So writes his brother, Lord Herbert of Cherbury; and his remains, few as they are, confirm this eulogy; yet his learning is not what strikes the reader most, it is so thoroughly controlled and subordinated by his lively wit and practical wisdom. He was exemplary in the domestic relations of life, 'tender and true' as son, husband, friend: yet he seems to have lived as a 'home-missionary' among his parishioners. He was a man of letters, yet ever condescending to the petty concerns of his poor ignorant clients; an ambitious man; yet he relinquished all worldly objects for the humble work of the ministry. He was, in a word, a man of extraordinary endowments, both personal and such as belonged to his rank—not lost in indolence nor wasted on trivialities, but all disciplined and cultivated to the utmost, and then devoted to the highest purposes. Men of a less evenly balanced genius may create a greater sensation in the world, as the eccentric course of a comet may attract more notice than steadier and less startling luminaries. But it may be questioned whether the influence of men like George Herbert and John Keble is not wider and deeper, though less perceptible, in the end. From them issue the hidden wartercourses of thought and action that irrigate the world with ever fresh supplies of life and vigour by innumerable, unnoticeable rills, preserving its morality from corruption and stagnation. The influence of those who possess Herbert's natural ability, combined with his *solidity* of character, cannot be measured by what we see. It is to men of this metal that England owes her greatness—men, like him, of high spirit, strict principle, genial, practical energy—men who, over and above other fine qualities, are strong in that reality and earnestness on which we are apt to pride ourselves as peculiarly English. Such a hero, in the truest sense, England lately lost in Lord Herbert of Lea; such, in a different sphere of life, was his kinsman, the country parson of Bemerton. May the race of men like these never be extinct among our statesmen and our clergy!

The most promising young men in the universities, it is asserted, draw back from ordination, and prefer other professions. They may learn, from the example of George Herbert, how to devote their talents to a worthy end.

POSITIVISM.

THE word 'Positivism' is one which requires explanation for most people. They may be more familiar
than they are aware, in one way or another, with the
thing implied by the word. But the word itself is a
sound without meaning to many even of the educated,
or with a meaning too vague and indistinct to be of
any service. The ordinary associations of the word
are not at first sight, very pertinent. Further consideration will show how far the name corresponds to
the thing which it stands for, and whether Positivism
deserves acceptance or rejection at the hands of those
whose aim is the truth. The question is of the
deepest and widest importance. Positivism claims to
supersede the traditional belief of Christendom; it
speaks of this as having lasted its time, as being now
effete and obsolete, as merely stopping the way; and
though avowed Positivism may be confined to very few
in England as yet, the indirect influence of its principles tends to undermine received habits of thought
in every direction. Before, however, proceeding to
discuss its practical consequences, it is necessary to
look the theory itself fairly and steadily in the face.
The metaphysics of one generation, as Coleridge has

said, become the ethics of the next, and the popular morality of that which comes after.

The inquiry, which we are instituting, must, if it is to be of any use, be pursued dispassionately; for truth needs no favour; and whatever is not truth sooner or later confutes itself. It must be pursued from the philosopher's point of view, waiving for the moment the prescriptions of authority however sacred, if it is to carry conviction into quarters where those prescriptions are not recognised. It must be pursued as far as possible without the technical phrases which belong rather to the laboratory than the lecture-room; for it is quite possible to be exact without being pedantic. As for the details of Positivism, they may be left out of sight and out of mind, until it has been first ascertained how far the principles are true in which they originate. Unless the foundations are sound, the superstructure, tall and stately though it may be, rising tier above tier with a superficial symmetry, must fall to the ground. If the very rudiments of the system involve a fallacy, we need not trouble ourselves much about its subsequent performances. It will save time and trouble in the end to begin at the beginning.

On the great fundamental principles which underlie, not merely this or that philosophy, but the very existence of man, and which the conditions of his existence compel him consciously or unconsciously to put to the proof daily, appeal may reasonably be made to the practical sense of mankind at large. All great truths, like the air which we breathe, or the light which warms and guides us, are essentially common.

It is true indeed that communities as well as individuals err continually; but this comes, speaking generally, from the judgment being warped either by the predilection of the feelings, or by defective knowledge of the particular object under its consideration. Galileo is persecuted, and Stephenson derided, not because the process of reasoning differs at different epochs, but because their cotemporaries have not yet learned the laws of the material universe, have not yet advanced so far as they in the sciences of astronomy and mechanics. Socrates must drink the hemlock, and Athanasius has the world against him, because their lofty teaching clashes with the lower propensities of human nature. But the blindness is transient; the error corrects itself; truth asserts its sovereignty. When the case has been fairly stated, its principles expressed clearly, and their application traced legitimately, the consentient voice of collective humanity is, to say the least, entitled to a hearing.

The philosopher in his closet is apt to forget this. His dreams must be confronted with the rude light of day, before they can take their place among realities, as the mental image of a substantial truth. If they fade away at the touch of daylight, they must be relegated, the sooner the better, to the world of phantoms, as the spectral exhalations of an illusive consciousness. After all, the proof of every thing lies in the actual. Even the most abstract propositions must be verified by fact. From the contact of the mind with the external world, by the medium of sensation, they spring originally; and thither they return at last. It is the actual application, and nothing else, of the rule or the principle which gives it currency, and which establishes, so far as anything in this life can be established, its validity and its practical certainty. Here only is the test in which the mind instinctively acquiesces; and, provided that the experiment be made on a commensurate scale, the test is a safe one. Expedience, for instance, if only we look far enough and widely enough into the network of consequences, invariably coincides with the true and the right. *Judicet orbis terrarum.* Let the world give its verdict. The appeal is made, not indeed to mere numbers, but to the corporate intelligence of the great family of man.

Positivism, in one sense, is no new thing. Its axiom, that we must start from what we know, and thence move onwards to that which we either know not at all or know less well, is as old as the time of Socrates, and older still. In fact, although philosophical systems have often developed themselves very inconsistently with it, this is the basis of all philosophy and of all knowledge whatever. Socrates taught it more explicitly than his precursors, and practised it more consistently. The keynote of his teaching is, that we must make each single step of our journey sure, if we hope to arrive at truth. Aristotle inculcated it as emphatically: indeed, in his strong grasp this, the only clue through the labyrinth of speculation, was held even more firmly, because he was more content than his master to abstain from those ethereal mazes where it could not avail him. He erred ludicrously in details of material science, though sometimes even there anticipating modern discoveries by the marvellous power, which is the birthright of genius, of imagining the whole from a part; but his method was the right method, and he was true to it. The fault was in the insufficiency of the data which lay within his reach, in the scantiness of the material phenomena from which he had to generalise. Bacon and Locke trod in the footprints of Aristotle, with a larger area of the material world open to their observation. All alike taught, that induction must precede deduction, if the latter is to be of any value. We must take particular instances one by one, and mark the several points in which they differ or agree,* in order to extract the laws of their being. Analysis must clear the way for synthesis, disintegration for construction. We must take our stand on what we know best, and make our footing sure there, before we can make one step with safety towards those dim regions which are more remote from our cognition. So far as this, the ' New Philosophy,' if not as old as the hills, is at least as old as the human faculties of thinking and judging; and what it has to tell us is barely more than a truism

---

* This sense of the likeness or unlikeness, identity, or non-identity of things by which we affirm ' This is that,' or ' This is not that,' seems to be the ultimate point, beyond which the analysis of the mind cannot go; and to be, strictly speaking, the only real intuition that we have. It is the basis of the syllogising, which, though unconsciously for the most part, always takes place in the act of reasoning: and it seems to be analogous to that sense of liking or disliking which is the primary form into which all the emotions may be resolved.

though, like many other truisms, too often disregarded.

The difference so far between Comte and Aristotle, or Comte and Plato, is chiefly this. The old philosophy closes its researches with the confession, that the mind of man, unassisted by some direct revelation from a source external to itself, cannot fathom the mystery of the universe, cannot unriddle our strange and complex existence, cannot reconcile the jarring elements of our nature, cannot pretend to have caught more than the faintest glimmering of the answer which the inexorable Sphinx demands from each and all of mortal race as they pass beneath her stony gaze, cannot say why man finds himself where he is and what he is, cannot account for him or his surroundings. The new philosophy, on the other hand, has a system of its own, independent altogether of a revelation from without, which it propounds as amply sufficient for all our requirements.

Here we come to what is essentially distinctive of Positivism. In order to attain, if possible, this certainty, and to subjugate all things to his own unaided intellect, the positivist begins by excluding from his notice whatever does not, in his opinion, admit of demonstration. He professes to take things simply as they are. Practically, he refuses to recognise the existence of whatever has no visible and tangible phenomena to produce as its passport for admittance into his universe; as if a certainty could be attained thus, which cannot be attained in any other way. Positivism is in fact materialism in dis-

guise. Mathematics of course are its starting-point.
For the first principles of mathematics can be demonstrated by an induction which we may call universal;
and in the application of its first principles there is
no possible risk of mistake, because the numerals
which are its symbols are precise and invariable. In
the language of logic, the major premiss—for example,
that one and one are not one, but two—is verified by
the universal sense of mankind, and from this are
evolved all the ramifications of the science with
certainty, just as Bach's most complicated fugues are
evolved out of seven simple notes, because there is no
possible ambiguity in the middle terms employed, no
risk of their being inexact or equivocal. In mathematics the proposition is perceived in the concrete at
first, and its terms remain immutable through all
subsequent reasonings. But the positivist has nothing
to say to sciences which are less definite, because
more abstract in their nature. He closes the door
peremptorily against logic, because it is concerned,
not with things which can be seen and handled, but
with the processes of thought. Metaphysic is even
more abstract, and therefore even more to be regarded
with suspicion. Withdrawing itself even further than
logic from things tangible, it investigates, not the
manner in which the mind works, but the very nature
of the mind, and of all those impalpable attributes in
which man differs from the brute. Sciences such as
these can have no place in Positivism.

Comte was as jealous as Swedenborg himself of the
intrusion of metaphysic within the pale of his theories.

Both aimed at a certainty and an infallibility beyond what is accorded to man. The Swede argued from his own inner consciousness; the Frenchman from his own observation of things without. Each starts with the assumption, that he can achieve certainty for himself. Each in his own way rejects the mental sciences. Because the phenomena which belong to these sciences are immaterial; because they are less sharply defined, less easily grouped into system; because they cannot be adjusted into his scheme for re-arranging the universe, the positivist, like the mystic, puts them aside, and makes his calculation with more than half of the figures omitted. Yet there is a voice within man which tells him, that the things which are seen are for a time, the things which are not seen are for ever.

There can be no room at all for a science of ethic or of theology in a system like this. The Greek philosophy bowed instinctively, though with an unconscious reverence, to the sense of duty,* and through the dimness of its vision stretched forth its hands towards a deity more worthy of its homage than the fantastic denizens of Olympus. But such abstractions as those of GOD and of duty are not precise enough for the cosmology of Positivism. Comte can rebuke as they deserve, the chemist and the botanist, who boast that they have found the cause because they have found the law of operation. But he will not allow that, by a just analogy, the law implies a law-

---

* The frequent recurrence of δεῖ in Greek philosophy without explanation is remarkable.

giver.   The idea of Deity transcends those limits
within which the positivist flatters himself that he can
know with certainty, and therefore it cannot be
admitted.   He will not take the trouble to deny, nor
will he attempt to disprove, the existence of a GOD.
He argues only that such a thing is not proved, and
therefore to us and for all practical purposes non-
existent.   Instead of the old *De non apparentibus,*
et de non existentibus eadem est ratio, his motto is
De non procul dubio demonstratis et de non existentibus
eadem est ratio.   He insists that a thing must be
demonstrated for certain before he can receive it.

But human nature, even in the positivist, requires
something to which it may pay allegiance, and to
which the sense of obligation may be attached.   Man
needs a 'religion', in the oldest and truest sense of the
word : he needs something, the restraint of which may
control his conscious instability of purpose.   The religion of the positivist is not a religion without a GOD;
for that is impossible.   But it is a religion with a
nonentity which it calls the Human Race, enthroned
where the Christian sees Him, who is perfect wisdom
and perfect love.   So the philosophy, which repudiates
abstractions, bows its knee to a shapeless, lifeless abstraction, which, if it represents anything at all, is
but a ghastly impersonation of our own imperfections.
With this idea of a GOD, the idea of duty is exploded;
for duty involves responsibility to a superior being;
and the word ' ought,' with all its associations, must
be expunged from our vocabulary.   The substitute
is ' Altruism.'   In place of that old-fashioned sense

of responsibility which, even among heathens, made
Aristides and Phocion what they were, and to which we
owe not one Wellington only, but thousands like him,
though less known to fame, we are exhorted to act
as members of a great co-operative society, and to
remember that we must seek the good of all, if we
seek the good of each in particular. The very life
is gone from devotion and self-sacrifice, when their
object is that which is but another name for ourselves.

In truth Positivism, with all its vaunted philanthropy, is a colossal selfishness. Professing to
regard only what really is, it says practically—'I am
and there is none beside me.' Men of generous hearts
there may be among its ranks. What system or creed
however erroneous, is there, without such? But of
the philosophy which we are considering the mainspring is self. That which animates and directs its
speculations is confidence in self, distrust of all but self,
impatience of authority external to itself, or superior to
its own consciousness. In systems of philosophy, as in
ordinary matters, we must look into the emotive part
of our nature for the causes of error. The reasoning
of the intellect goes straight to its mark with the
rapidity and accuracy of a ball from a catapult, if the
object is fairly in view, provided that no gusts of
passion cause it to swerve from its course. The
intellect guides our reasonings, as the helm guides
the ship through the water: but it is the hand of the
helmsman which gives a tendency to this or that
direction. The idolatry of self gives a wrong bias
to 'Positivism;' and the consequent fault in its

reasonings is twofold; first, in excluding from its idea of the universe whatever is irreconcilable with itself; next, in supposing that, even with the help of this elimination, it can attain a greater degree of certainty than is possible to others.

There is a great fallacy in the word *nature* as used by the positivist: and the fallacy is countenanced by those who, in defending the truths of revelation, use the word *supernatural* when they should rather say *supermaterial.* The twin hemispheres of spirit and matter are alike integral parts of nature; but the positivist shuts his eyes to the world of spirit, because it cannot be coerced into his complete system of the universe. Yet that world is as real as the other, although its phenomena are indemonstrable, because they are intangible. ' There are more things in heaven and earth than are dreamt of' in the philosophy of Positivism. The will of man, manifesting itself in his free agency, and the Divine Will, of which the will of man is an indication, are as truly facts, though facts of a different kind, as the star which Leverrier watches through his telescope, or the insect which Darwin places under his magnifying glass. The consciousness of freedom, which even a child experiences in every movement, and the consciousness of responsibility to a superior being, which even a savage is not altogether without, are facts which the philosopher must take into account, although they are too indistinct to be stereotyped in an arithmetical formula.

But we need not pause to consider how far the existence of the spiritual world can be proved by reason

without revelation. If the revelation, which affirms
it, is itself authenticated, it is enough. The positivist
forgets that knowledge may be received through the
ear as well as through the eye. Provided that its source
be trustworthy the faith which 'cometh by hearing'
is quite as reasonable as the faith which comes from
our own observation. Every day of our lives we
put faith in others as to matters beyond our own
observation. This faith is reasonable or unreasonable as the person in whom we place it is
worthy or not. The faith of a Christian in his LORD
differs from this ordinary faith, not in kind, but in
degree only. The stake is greater, for it is happiness
now and for ever; but the act of believing is the
same. The Christian reasons that he has in CHRIST
One worthy of all credence, and therefore believes.
The positivist reasons that he may trust his own
impressions or those of others like himself, and
believes accordingly. It is the same method really
in both cases. Analysis discloses attributes of holiness
and power in the person of CHRIST, which induction
shows are never found in one who is merely man;
and the superstructure of the Catholic Faith rests
on this foundation. But the positivist rejects the
supermaterial without further inquiry, because it
transcends his comprehension.

The positivist aims at certainty. Does he attain
it? One science only can claim to have attained it;
and that is the science which more than any other
holds itself aloof from those affections and interests
which make the life of man what it is, and without
which it would be indeed colourless and blank.

Mathematics are certain, not because the mathematician reasons by a different method, but because the symbols which he uses are the only symbols which cannot vary in value and in meaning; and because a mathematical proposition is so entirely disconnected with our likings and dislikings, our motives of attraction or repulsion, that it is as undisturbed by them as the quicksilver in the barometer by a rise or fall of the funds on the Stock Exchange. Other sciences have words for their counters; language is the currency of thought: and our words, like our coins, in passing from hand to hand, are continually defaced by use, and imperceptibly passing from one gradation of meaning to another. Other sciences may be swayed by the prejudices of passion. Mathematics are certain because they are free from these two causes of error; but mathematics cover only a very small portion of man's doing, and suffering, and being. Man is something more than a mere calculating machine. No class of men, as a rule, is less practical than the mere mathematician. Beyond the pale of mathematics there is demonstrable certainty nowhere. Astronomy approaches most nearly to it; and astronomy is most remote in its practical bearings on man. The further science recedes from pure mathematics, and the closer it draws to the real springs of man's destinies, his hopes and fears, his loves and hatred,

Quidquid agunt homines votum, timor, ira, voluptas,

the more is the positivist under a necessity of abandoning certainty. Even in what are called 'physical sciences,' loudly as they proclaim their superiority in accuracy to theology or metaphysics, we meet with variations as perplexing as the caprices of our English climate. Even there, in the language of one[*] well qualified to speak, we find only 'empirical generalisations,' only 'materials for science.' We find Comte himself, the great teacher of Positivism, arbitrarily assuming a chemical hypothesis, which subsequent experiments are said to have disproved, 'in order to satisfy an instinctive predilection for order and harmony.' We see theories and systems, in geology for instance, displacing and demolishing one another like dolls in a puppet-show. The 'certainty' which Positivism has to offer to the Christian is but a poor exchange for the moral certainties of his religion. The positivist is himself drifting on a shoreless ocean without chart or compass, excepting such as he can make for himself. He is trembling on the brink of the abyss, and clutches the tuft of grass which yields in his grasp, instead of accepting the hand which is stretched forth from Heaven to uphold him.

It is not to be denied, that the world of spirit, as the world of matter, may have laws of its own to which it is conformed, and to which it pays obedience. If the analogy from the sense implanted in man of order and harmony is worth anything, so it is. But to say that these laws can be apprehended, is a very different thing. A hybrid term, half Greek, half

[*] J. S. Mill. 'Auguste Comte and Positivism,' pp. 36 and 61.

Latin, has been invented. 'Sociology,' we are told,
is a science by which the ever-changing habits and
opinions of men may be referred to laws as immutable
as those, according to which light follows darkness,
or summer winter. Such a sequence of opinion there
may be, clear as the day to Omniscience. But the
causes at work, even without taking the eccentricities
of the will into account, are too manifold for man to
make them out. Those who argue that the formation
of character depends on circumstances either within
or without man, forget that in every moment of his
career, he is shaping and determining them for himself.
One of the strongest instances of his dependence on
the external world, is the influence of soil and climate
on the character of a people. But these very circumstances are themselves a result, as well as a cause.
They are susceptible continually of modification, for
better or worse, from industry and ingenuity, or from
the sloth and incapacity of man.

We hear much nowadays of averages. It is
argued, that if we can only get together statistics
enough, we have got the key to the laws which regulate the course of human actions. But, by all the
principles of true induction, these averages are worth-
less, unless derived from observation which is at once
exhaustive and discriminating. They must not be
taken from an incomplete induction, nor from one
which fails to distinguish among the various causes
which are at work.* Even if it can be proved that,

---

* The evil consequences which attend vice in this life, for instance, the
physical degeneracy which luxury or sensuality causes, are more manifest

under certain predisposing conditions, certain forms of vice recur with periodical intensity in the history of the world, the responsibility of man remains where it was, unless his free will can be got rid of. For the duty of each to do his utmost against the evil remains the same, whether the effort is successful or not. It is enough for practical purposes, that, without the attempt to repress it the evil would be still more rampant than it is; and, even if this were not so, heathen philosophy as well as Christianity teaches, that the ἐνέργεια not the ἔργον, the doing, not the thing done, the honest endeavour, not the success consummated, is what really concerns us. The practical inference from such statistics is, that there is an evil agency at work in the world, which cannot be counteracted without incessant vigilance.

The same principle applies to the estimation of character, whether in the individual or in communities. Praise or blame is due, not to the character as we find it absolutely and in itself, but relatively and in proportion to the advantages which are enjoyed, or the hindrances which are to be contended with. Allowance must be made for the force of hereditary temperament within, as well as of education and other associations without. The practical inference from averages and statistics on this point is, that it is not for man to judge his fellows, but for Omniscience alone.

in a community than in the individual; because in the individual the collision of conflicting causes may produce an exceptional result, while a broader view throws out into strong relief the rule and its ordinary working. Thus the old pagan idea of a Providence was of a national deity, visiting men as a nation with retributive failure or success.

In truth, the problems of 'Sociology' are too complex and too intricate to be solved by 'Positivism.' The restless play of human passions makes them difficult enough, even without the insuperable difficulty of the human will. But the will multiplies the difficulty in a tenfold degree, because it defies analysis and baffles investigation. It is vain to prognosticate what course it will take. It can and does violate antecedent probabilities. The most skilful chess-player cannot be sure beforehand what his antagonist will do even after arranging his own movements so as to leave him scarcely an alternative. Placed between two rival attractions, it does not of necessity gravitate towards that which is to all appearance the stronger; nor does it, like the ass in the fable between the two bundles of hay, stand unable to move because of the attraction being equal. It is mere tautology to say, 'that the will always obeys the strongest motive.' Of course the will always chooses what it chooses. It is true that a man's propensities have a reacting power, and that, as this or that propensity is encouraged, it gains strength for the future. But, after all, the will is rather their creator than their creature. In forming our habits we are insensibly forging fetters for the will; but the fetters, however strong, are not too strong to be broken. Everything else in the organism of man may be surrendered to materialism.* The faculties of his mind may be mechanical in their operation, and thought may succeed thought by a law of

---

* The will of man differs from the will of brutes in this spontaneity and consciousness.

association; but, as the wheel revolves, the will exercises its right of selection, adopting or rejecting as it pleases. The emotions of his heart may result from his bodily structure, from a subtle combination of the nervous fluid with other kindred elements; but, as each emotion in turn demands to be gratified, the will assents or refuses as it pleases. Experience may show how largely both the intellect and the affections depend on the health of the body; but it cannot and does not show, that either affections or intellect are the will itself. Though intimately connected with it, they are extraneous to it; they are, to borrow Plato's imagery, the horses that draw the chariot, not the charioteer who guides them. Materialism may claim all else. But that something which is the man himself, his personality, his incorporeal life, his volition, his soul, which uses at pleasure the ministry of all his faculties, which cannot altogether, if it would, shake off the sense of responsibility in using them, which in every thrill of its consciousness bears witness to itself that it is an emanation from eternity, has never yet been proved to be of the earth in its origin and nature. Laws of its own even this may have, but they are not to be deciphered by man.*

It is sometimes objected that the virtuous man is merely pleasing himself, ' because he finds pleasure in his virtuous actions.' But here is a twofold fallacy. To find pleasure is not the same thing as to seek it.

---

* The universal sense of free agency which is expressed in ' Sic volo, sic jubeo ; stet pro ratione voluntas,' is a stronger proof of personal existence than the well-known ' Cogito, ergo sum,' of Descartes.

A really good action is not done for the sake of giving
pleasure or anything else, but from a sense, not
indeed always conscious or explicit, for the law which
is habitually obeyed need not be quoted on every occasion of obedience to right. Again, there is a
fallacy in the word ' self.' The will of course pleases
itself in choosing either what is virtuous or what is
vicious. It would not be the will otherwise. But
it pleases itself by gratifying in the one case an evil
desire, and in the other case a good one. In this preference and in this renunciation, which even in the
most happily constituted temperaments are never too
easy, resides the essence of virtue.

The same argument applies with even more force to
that manifestation of the Divine Will which we call
Providence. Here, again, unless our sense of order
and harmony misleads us, there is law in all its perfection. But who shall dare to say that he has
spanned the laws of Providence in all their breadth
and length and height, has fathomed their depth, has
comprehended the infinity of their bearings? A
miracle is a miracle, a thing which man can simply
' wonder' at, a thing beyond his power to contrive,
even though proved to result from the ordinary laws
of material nature, provided that these laws have been
so controlled and harmonised as to concur in pro-
ducing a particular event at a particular moment, as
no devices of man could have brought it to pass.
Again, a miracle is a miracle, if it results from a spiritual law counteracting and cancelling for the time a
material law. In either case the thing is miraculous,

although in perfect accordance with the laws by which the Omnipotent exercises His sway; and, although foreknown and foredoomed, not an abrupt and abnormal interference. The tender watchfulness of GOD over the special needs of His creatures severally, is perfectly compatible with law; and any theory which involves negation of law is incompatible with His prescience. These laws are not GOD, as the materialist persuades himself; nor are they above GOD, as Time and Space in the older Greek Mythology were above the Gods of Olympus; but they are, if our conceptions may be trusted, a part of the Divine economy by which the world is administered. In proportion as the will of man is in conformity with the Divine Will, it has power thus to control inanimate nature. In the perfect conformity of the Will of the SON of MAN to that of His Heavenly Father, we see this power displayed in all its fulness.

The objection of the Positivist, that a miracle is contradictory to reason, is based, as usual, on his assumption that there are no laws in the universe but such as he can comprehend. *Non est*, he argues, *quia non explicitum.* So with regard to prayer. The objection is twofold; and much confusion arises, unless we are careful to distinguish the one from the other. There is the objection, that man's prayer is incompatible with GOD's foreknowledge; that it is unreasonable to pray concerning things which have been already determined in one way or the other. To this it is enough to reply, that the objection applies as much and as little to every one of our actions; and that the prayer is as truly a link of the predetermined course of events as anything else. The difficulty is also very much diminished, if we bear in mind that our conception of time may be only the consequence of our inability to think of events, which are really co-existent, otherwise than as successive.

But the objection of the positivist is rather, that events follow one another by an inherent order of their own, and that this order cannot be affected by anything so irrelevant in his eyes as prayer. Here again is the assumption, as usual, that there is no Divine Being ready to hear prayer, that there is not

——a divinity which shapes our ends,
Rough hew them as we will.

It is false to say, that the Christian expects a miracle in reply to his prayer. A stone thrown from the hand obeys, primarily, the impulse given by the will, and obeys at the same time, secondarily, the material laws which regulate the muscular agency employed, and the motion or rest of a ponderable substance. Similarly, the overruling Will of Providence guides and governs the course of the storm or of the pesti-lence, not by violating the laws of matter, but by using their submissive instrumentality. We need not en-deavour to explain how, and by what *modus operandi* prayer can affect the course of other things. It may be that as earthly parents wait to be asked before giving, so the Heavenly Father would quicken in his children their love for Him. Anyhow, the duty of prayer follows inevitably from that sense of relation to a Superior Power of which the positivist takes no account. For a Christian there is, besides, the special command and the special promise of his incarnate LORD.

The main argument of Positivism, as of all other neologies, is drawn from the progress of the human race. It is the same fallacy again. Concentrating his attention on the huge strides of that knowledge, which relates to the material world, the positivist will not see, that in other respects man remains essentially the same, although

—the great world spin for ever down the ringing grooves of
change.

True, man is no plant vegetating for ages on the same spot and in the same way. There is a progress. Every year sees more and more of the material world reclaimed from darkness and chaos and subjected to the intellect of man, just as fen and common are every year enclosed, drained, and broken up by the plough. But the progress is only here; although it may seem to a superficial observer to extend to other things. The change of opinion, for example, on the subject of witchcraft is simply because men have discovered, that results, which in their ignorance of 'physical' science they attributed to other causes, are really due to causes of a material kind. The change of feeling, again, on the subject of persecution, is simply because experience has taught men, that they cannot attain their end by those means. The change which history discloses, is in the adjuncts and circumstances with which man is environed, not in himself; it is in the scenery of the play, not in its *personæ.* As the great drama of life unrolls itself slowly to its consummation, man, the chief actor in it, preserves his individuality to the end—

Qualis ab incepto processerit et sibi constat.

The intellect, indeed, may grow keener and more polished, but it remains the same in shape and temper as before; and in all its marvellous discoveries it plays the part of a servant, not of a master; it is an implement, not the hand of the pioneer which wields it. Civilisation may seem to effect a great change in man; but the unlikeness between the civilised and the uncivilised man is on the surface; the likeness is deep and at the core—'Grattez le Russe le vous trouverez le Tartare.' Those who say * that Watt and Stephenson have effected a revolution in man, confound his external aids and appliances with his real inner life.

One touch of nature makes the world akin.

The philosopher of the nineteenth century is after all, as the life of such men as Comte shows, not very different from his fellow-men of very different condition. Cæsar Borgia and the costermonger who murders his wretched paramour, though separated by a gulf of years, are at heart the same. The African squaws who ministered so lovingly to the sickness of Mungo Park, felt the same pity for the helpless as the gentle ladies who sailed to the Crimean hospitals with Florence Nightingale.

* Lecky's 'History of Rationalism.'

There are few plainer lessons in history than this; that the good and wise of every nation resemble one another, and, in their way, the wicked and foolish. When Comte speaks of mankind as having passed through, first, a 'theological' and then a 'metaphysical' stage, before crowning their 'progress' with his 'Positivism,' he regards mankind from a material point of view. So far as that goes, he is right. While ignorant of material laws, men are apt to refer everything, first, to the arbitrary interposition of some deity, and, afterwards, to the force of some idea. In any other sense, his words have no meaning; for they speak of things as successive which are really going on at once; they imply an imaginary demarcation between conditions of society and habits of thought which are really blended together. But there are few things easier, especially to a French philosopher, than to construct any number of theories of history. If facts stand in the way, so much the worse for them. Comte speaks of an upward progress from the worship of Fetish to that of deified men. Where are the instances? History speaks rather of a gradual declension, as in Greece and Rome, from a higher and purer worship. History shows men before Christianity looking back ever regretfully to the past. Horace, surrounded by the refinement and voluptuousness of his Augustan era, sighs for the old 'age of gold.' In the pages of Juvenal and Tacitus, and in the profligacies which are there unveiled, we see that mere civilisation by itself is no better security against utter degradation, than is the rude life of the savage in his

T

primeval forests. Left to itself, and without the re-
novating influences of Revelation, the progress of
mankind, as history shows, is not onwards to perfection, but tends to revert to the very evils which it
seems to have left far behind in the past. In one
word, it is cyclical. History is apt to repeat itself.
But his idea of progress is indispensable to Comte's
theory.

It would be tedious to follow Positivism into its
full development. Inconsistent as this may seem
with its first principles, it is in one sense their legitimate issue. For it is the fate of error to complete
its circle, and to end by contradicting the very
principles from which it started. So, not unfre-
quently, the man who will not believe the Evangelists,
can believe anything however preposterous, that
comes to him in the shape of 'spirit-rapping,' or
' table-turning : ' so, very often, the man who begins
with the severest spiritualism ends by embracing
materialism in its grossest form. Positivism begins
by discarding psychology; it ends by embracing the
guesswork of phrenology instead. It begins by
mapping out the universe of thought into departments each duly squared and labelled; it ends by
merging them all in the chaos of mysticism. It
begins by refusing to notice whatever is not visible
and tangible ; it ends by raving of an Anima Mundi
and the Loves of the Planets. It begins by rejecting
whatever cannot be demonstrated ; it ends by affirming a proposition to be true because it is symmetrical
and edifying. It begins by preaching unchecked

license of speculation; it ends by handing over the rest of mankind to the irresponsible despotism of a philosophical clique. It begins by renouncing GOD; it ends by preferring a Fetish to Him. Is this progress? Is it not rather a retrogression and relapse into that darkness and shadow of death, from which One came down from heaven to set men free?

Positivism promises to reconstitute society, and remodel the politics of the world. Its founder predicted that all this should be done within some twenty or thirty years from its inauguration. The world is to be governed henceforth by philosophers; * a new calendar is to supersede that which Europe has used for ages; and a septimal coinage is to be adopted universally because of some mystic excellence in the number seven. Some, if not Comte himself, will add, that woman is to be transplanted from the domestic retirement whence her gentle influence insensibly radiates over the world, to the glare and turmoil of public life. In short, the 'Cloudcuckooland' of Athenian burlesque is realised at last. Positivism undertakes to regenerate the world,

——sese attollit in auras,
Ingrediturque solo et caput inter nubila condit.

Babel menaces heaven; but it is in vain that the builders pile stone on stone in the frantic expectation of scaling it. The image, as in the great king's

---

* In Comte's Utopia, the philosophers are to direct the nominal rulers; the latter are to hold the reins; the former are to drive.

dream, towers from the plain; but its feet are only of perishable clay, and fall it must.

As we have seen, Positivism has a religion ready as well as a system of philosophy and of politics. For the void which it creates must be filled up somehow. It provides new priests, new sacraments, a new worship. For prayer it substitutes ' effusion,' or reverie; for that ' resurrection to life eternal,' which is the ' sure and certain hope ' of Christians, it holds out the chance of 'living in the remembrance' of survivors; in place of that Triune Deity, whom Christendom adores, it worships Humanity, Earth, and Space. The parody is complete. The parhelion is a mockery of the true sun. Man asks for bread, and the positivist gives him ashes.

It is in France that the evil expands itself most exuberantly. The passion for precision and minuteness of regulation is gratified by a system which professes to explain everything. Each turn and twist in the mental kaleidoscope presents to the eye new combinations, each more ingenious than the last; and though it may prove in the end to be merely an optical illusion, for the time there is the charm of novelty, and the still greater fascination of symmetry and completeness. There is less danger of Positivism thriving in English soil, as a whole. There is not the same sublime disregard of facts, when they stand in the way of a theory; not the same idolatry of method here. But tendencies akin to Positivism are at work among us. For ' the world is waxing old:' and there is that in ' Positivism ' which approves itself at first sight to the temperament of old age. The cardinal principle of Positivism, as we have seen, is to take things as they are. This is the flag under which it fights, at least in theory. While the optimist affirms that things are best as they are; the fatalist, that they must be as they are; and the mere dogmatist, that they are because they are; the positivist confines himself to saying that they are as they are. He avoids the question of causation, and the question of a morally better or worse. Now the habit of mind which Positivism thus expresses, is exactly what suits the old age of the world. As with the race, so it is with the individual. As time goes on, and the hair is streaked with grey, experience brings disappointment, disappointment brings patience, and the fervid enthusiasm of youth is apt to subside into an apathy, if not of contentment, yet of acquiescence. The lawyer will not waste his energies on points not directly bearing on his brief. The statesman accepts the inevitable compromises which practice exacts from theory. The controversialist is satisfied if he can throw the burden of proving on his opponent. The pride of indifferentism retires into itself from the clamour of tongues. ' Things are as they are.' The jaded spirit takes refuge from the violence and acerbity of the strife in words like these, as France, exhausted by the schemes of wrangling visionaries, prostrates herself at the feet of a dictator.

Who can deny that something, which in this way answers practically to scientific Positivism, shows itself in the literature of the day? The influence of

men like Arnold and Coleridge, who, whatever else
they were, were certainly anti-positivist, is giving
place to influences of a less earnest, less uncompromising kind.   Goethe may fairly be taken as representative of this school, with which the external
restrictions of right and wrong are nothing, if they
seem to interfere with the free development of human
nature as it is.   Goethe's Autobiography is a very
masterpiece of practical Positivism.   Self is the key-
note of the book; the gratification, the expansion, the
elaborate cultivation of self.   All other claims must
give way to this.   Goethe in love is thinking much more
of himself and of the effect which his passion may have
on the formation of his own character, than of his
poor 'fräulein.'*   He dissects himself lovingly.   The
habit of taking things as they are, without reference
to an unswerving law imposed from above, intrudes
from the material sciences into questions of ethic and
of religion.   History is studied, not as the battle-field
of good and evil, but as exhibiting certain irresistible
tendencies, which, whether good or bad, must have
their way.   Writers like Carlyle talk of 'eternal
truth;' but practically they take the personages whom
they choose for their heroes as the real canon of right
and wrong.   It is the fashion to be cosmopolite; but
in stripping himself of narrow local prejudices, the
cosmopolite too often casts away much that he ought

* The great distinction, which Bentham expressed with characteristic terseness, between regarding others as having a *personality* of their own, or as merely *things*, lies at the root, not
only of morality, but of the question between the believer in
Fate, and the believer in a God.

to cherish. The most popular periodicals are those whose line it is, while keeping higher questions of principle in the background, to insist mainly on what is convenient for the moment. The most popular novels are animated by the same spirit; and a clever novel more than anything else is a faithful mirror of the habits and feelings of the day. Thackeray's sympathies, for instance, were on the whole with what is right and good; and yet all his humour and pathos are instinct with the sentiment, though he owns it with a sigh, that human nature is as it is, must take its course, must have its fling. 'Adam Bede,' again, and ' The Mill on the Floss,' are exquisite photographs of life as it is; but they fail to remind us that it ought to be better than it is, and that our evil propensities may be and must be disciplined into subjection to the good. It is needless to accumulate instances. This practical deification of human nature, not as it should be, but as it is, is a characteristic danger of our time. Unchecked, it cannot but end in substituting for the

Self-reverence, self-knowledge, self-control,

of which our great poet sings, an utter selfishness disguised in the apotheosis of humanity at large.

How is the evil to be met ? The bane indicates the antidote. Every error is the perversion of a truth; and the perversion points to the truth by which it must be corrected. Side by side with this New Religion stands the great institution, unchanged amid the vicissitudes of ages, which deduces its origin from no speculations of man's finite intellect, but from the teaching of One who has proved Himself to be the Incarnation of Deity.*

The institution of which we speak does not, like Positivism, invite its votaries by a promise of omniscience, but it sheds light enough to guide them step by step from the cradle to the grave. It does not, like Positivism, proffer an Utopian felicity in this life, but, while showing how much even of temporal evil may be healed, and how the curse which remains may be converted into a blessing by endurance, it fixes its stedfast gaze on that great Hereafter, which Positivism shrinks from contemplating; and, while Positivism declaims and theorises, it is incessantly at work to ameliorate the lot of man. It does not, like Positivism, profess to be demonstrated like a theorem in Euclid, but it has in itself a concurrence of practical evidences, which is more than enough for those who do not close their hearts and minds against it. It does no like Positivism, profess to account for everything; but it does account, as nothing else can, for the strange inadequacies and incongruities of man's earthly career, by showing that it is only the rehearsal in time of the part which he must play in eternity. It does not, like Positivism, present to the superficial glance a perfect symmetry of outline and proportion; and yet, as in those old Gothic cathedrals which have been called the 'petrifaction' of our religion, there is a

---

* The positivist forgets how largely the atmosphere which he breathes is impregnated with Christianity, and that the very 'Altruism' on which he prides himself would have been, in its truest sense, simply inconceivable without that.

latent symmetry, a mutual interdependence of all its
parts, which grows on the beholder continually. It
is based, more truly than any merely human creed,
on those principles of induction which satisfy the philosopher; but it can approve itself practically to all,
learned and unlearned too. It is no system, for those
who crave for an artificial completeness and precision;
and yet it has seen system after system of human
manufacture crumble into dust as though they had
never been, and swept from the earth like castles
which children make with cards, while its own
weather-stained walls are proof against the storms of
ages, because they are built upon the Rock. It is
the Church which the hands of the Apostles have
reared on the divine Lord, who is its corner-stone.

But the evil must be met, as always, by careful and
patient discrimination. In every system, however
false, there is yet the utterance of needs, which the
truth only can satisfy; there are germs of good to be
fostered into a healthy maturity; they are tendencies
which, dangerous as they are, may be directed into
other channels. Positivism cannot be counteracted by
the unreasoning dogmatism, which is, in one sense, its
provocative and its cause: indeed Positivism is itself
another form of that yearning for infallible certitude,
which requires every letter of Holy Scripture to be
certified by divine authority. Every science has its
borderland, a region of twilight, where judgment must
be suspended, and theology more than other sciences,
because it lies on the very confines of knowledge
forbidden to man. The theologian must beware of

venturing too near the limits which divine Providence overruling the creeds of the Church, has marked out for him. He must not presume to define, on such subjects as that of inspiration, or of a future state, or of the immutability beyond this life of human ideas of morality, or on the mode of CHRIST'S presence in the Church, or, in short, on any mystery whatever, more than the HOLY SPIRIT has willed to reveal to man —in other words, more than is needful for him. There is a Christian sense as well as an anti-christian sense in the axiom of the Positivist, that we must take things as they are. They embody that spirit of resignation in which man must wait for more perfect knowledge until the day shall come ' for things to be revealed,' when he shall ' know even as he is known.' They remind us of that great truth, old as the Athenian philosophy, often neglected now, by positivists and by transcendentalists alike, that the highest knowledge possible for man in this life is only of things in their relation to ourselves, not in their essential being, of phenomena not of realities. With regard to things practically beyond his reach, the Christian must act, as the positivist unreasonably does with regard to things beyond his power of demonstrating; he must leave them on one side for the present.

The Catholic Church can alone satisfy those aspirations after an imaginary good, which have seduced to Positivism adherents worthy of a better cause. Here they may find that true comprehensiveness which would gather all sorts and conditions of men into its bosom; and which, though sometimes distorted by misinterpretation, can adapt itself to all the varying wants of humanity. Here they may find that reverence for whatever there is of good in the past or the distant, which gathers up and assimilates to itself 'that nothing be lost,' the scattered fragments of truth. Here they may find, if they will look through the idiosyncrasies of particular schools and mark well the beating of the great heart of the Church, that true philanthropy, that heroic abnegation of self, which they desire. The human messenger who delivers the message of the Gospel may sometimes degrade it into the language of mere self-preservation. But a deeper insight sees that the prudence which the Gospel inculcates is only the means to the end, a necessary step towards the fulfilment of yet higher duties. If the positivist longs for the full and free development of man's corporeal endowments, 'the sound mind in the sound body,' in Christianity, more emphatically than elsewhere, is recognised the dignity of the body as being a 'servant unto righteousness,' 'the temple of the HOLY GHOST,' the sharer in a glorified immortality. The Church, like its great Apostle, becomes ' all things to all men.' Unflinching in the assertion of the great doctrinal verities, which are the charter of its inheritance, it yet presents these doctrines in such manner as best to penetrate the heart. It is the divorce of practice from doctrine, of morality from theology, of reason from faith, which more than anything else hinders the universal reception of the truth. It is in the practical appeal which He makes so pleadingly to man through all which is dear to man in himself or in others, that the voice of the SAVIOUR pierces the heart. 'Apud philosophos,' says one himself foremost among philosophers, 'multa sunt acutè dicta et leniter calentia, sed in iis omnibus hoc non invenio; Venite ad Me omnes qui laboratis et onerati estis, et Ego vobis requiem præbebo.'

> There is no GOD, the foolish saith,
>   But none, there is no sorrow;
> And nature oft the cry of faith
>   In bitter need will borrow:
> Eyes which the preacher could not school
>   By wayside graves are raised,
> And lips say, 'God be pitiful!'
>   Which ne'er said, 'God be praised!'

E. BARRETT BROWNING.

LONDON

PRINTED BY SPOTTISWOODE AND CO.

NEW-STREET SQUARE

39 PATERNOSTER ROW, E.C.

LONDON, *April* 1875.

GENERAL LIST OF WORKS

PUBLISHED BY

MESSRS. LONGMANS, GREEN, AND CO.

HISTORY, POLITICS, HISTORICAL MEMOIRS, &c.

Journal of the Reigns of King George IV. and King William IV.

By the late C. C. F. Greville, Esq. Clerk of the Council to those Sovereigns.

Edited by H. Reeve, Registrar of the Privy Council.

Fourth Edition. 3 vols. 8vo. price 36s.

The Life of Napoleon III. derived from State Records, Unpublished Family Correspondence, and Personal Testimony.

By Blanchard Jerrold.

Four Vols. 8vo. with numerous Portraits and Facsimiles. VOLS. I. and II. price 18s. each.

*** *Vols. III. and IV. completing the work, will be published in the Autumn.*

A

Recollections and Suggestions, 1813–1873.
By *John Earl Russell, K.G.*
New Edition, revised and enlarged. 8vo. 16s.

Introductory Lectures on Modern History delivered in Lent Term 1842 ; *with the Inaugural Lecture delivered in December* 1841.
By *the late Rev. Thomas Arnold, D.D.*
8vo. price 7s. 6d.

On Parliamentary Government in England: its Origin, Development, and Practical Operation.
By *Alpheus Todd.*
2 vols. 8vo. £1. 17s.

The Constitutional History of England since the Accession of George III. 1760–1870.
By *Sir Thomas Erskine May, K.C.B.*
Fourth Edition. 3 vols. crown 8vo. 18s.

Democracy in Europe; a History.
By *Sir Thomas Erskine May, K.C.B.*
2 vols. 8vo.   [*In the press.*

The History of England from the Fall of Wolsey to the Defeat of the Spanish Armada.
By *J. A. Froude, M.A.*
CABINET EDITION, 12 vols. cr. 8vo. £3. 12s.
LIBRARY EDITION, 12 vols. 8vo. £8. 18s.

The English in Ireland in the Eighteenth Century.
By *J. A. Froude, M.A.*
3 vols. 8vo. £2. 8s.

The History of England from the Accession of James II.
By *Lord Macaulay.*
STUDENT'S EDITION, 2 vols. cr. 8vo. 12s.
PEOPLE'S EDITION, 4 vols. cr. 8vo. 16s. .
CABINET EDITION, 8 vols. post 8vo. 48s.
LIBRARY EDITION, 5 vols. 8vo. £4.

Critical and Historical Essays contributed to the Edinburgh Review.
By *the Right Hon. Lord Macaulay.*
Cheap Edition, authorised and complete, crown 8vo. 3s. 6d.
STUDENT'S EDITION, crown 8vo. 6s.
PEOPLE'S EDITION, 2 vols. crown 8vo. 8s.
CABINET EDITION, 4 vols. 24s.
LIBRARY EDITION, 3 vols. 8vo. 36s.

Lord Macaulay's Works. Complete and uniform Library Edition.
Edited by his Sister, Lady Trevelyan.
8 vols. 8vo. with Portrait, £5. 5s.

Lectures on the History of England from the Earliest Times to the Death of King Edward II.
By *W. Longman, F.S.A.*
Maps and Illustrations. 8vo. 15s.

The History of the Life and Times of Edward III.
By *W. Longman, F.S.A.*
With 9 Maps, 8 Plates, and 16 Woodcuts.
2 vols. 8vo. 28s.

History of England under the Duke of Buckingham and Charles the First, 1624–1628.
By S. Rawson Gardiner, late Student of Ch. Ch.
2 vols. 8vo. with two Maps,. 24s.

History of Civilization in England and France, Spain and Scotland.
By Henry Thomas Buckle.
3 vols. crown 8vo. 24s.

A Student's Manual of the History of India from the Earliest Period to the Present.
By Col. Meadows Taylor, M.R.A.S.
Second Thousand. Cr. 8vo. Maps, 7s. 6d.

A Sketch of the German Constitution, and of the Events in Germany from 1815 to 1871.
By A. Nicholson, Third Secretary in Her Britannic Majesty's Embassy at Berlin.
8vo. price 5s.

Studies from Genoese History.
By Colonel G. B. Malleson, C.S.I. Guardian to His Highness the Maharájá of Mysore.
Crown 8vo. 10s. 6d.

The History of India from the Earliest Period to the close of Lord Dalhousie's Administration.
By John Clark Marshman.
3 vols. crown 8vo. 22s. 6d.

Indian Polity; a View of the System of Administration in India.
By Lieut.-Colonel George Chesney.
Second Edition, revised, with Map. 8vo. 21s.

Waterloo Lectures; a Study of the Campaign of 1815.
By Colonel Charles C. Chesney, R.E.
Third Edition. 8vo. with Map, 10s. 6d.

Essays in Modern Military Biography.
By Colonel Charles C. Chesney, R.E.
8vo. 12s. 6d.

The Imperial and Colonial Constitutions of the Britannic Empire, including Indian Institutions.
By Sir E. Creasy, M.A.
With 6 Maps. 8vo. 15s.

The Oxford Reformers— John Colet, Erasmus, and Thomas More; being a History of their Fellow-Work.
By Frederic Seebohm.
Second Edition. 8vo. 14s.

The History of Persia and its present Political Situation; with Abstracts of all Treaties and Conventions between Persia and England.
By Clements R. Markham, C.B. F.R.S.
8vo. with Map, 21s.

The Mythology of the Aryan Nations.
By Geo. W. Cox, M.A. late Scholar of Trinity College, Oxford.
2 vols. 8vo. 28s.

A History of Greece.
By the Rev. Geo. W. Cox, M.A. late Scholar of Trinity College, Oxford.
Vols. I. and II. 8vo. Maps, 36s.

The History of Greece.
By C. Thirlwall, D.D. late Bp. of St. David's.
8 vols. fcp. 8vo. 28s.

The Tale of the Great Persian War, from the Histories of Herodotus.
By Rev. G. W. Cox, M.A.
Fcp. 8vo. 3s. 6d.

The History of the Peloponnesian War, by Thucydides.
Translated by Richd. Crawley, Fellow of Worcester College, Oxford.
8vo. 21s.

Greek History from Themistocles to Alexander, in a Series of Lives from Plutarch.
Revised and arranged by A. H. Clough.
Fcp. 8vo. Woodcuts, 6s.

History of the Romans under the Empire.
By the Very Rev. Charles Merivale, D.C.L. Dean of Ely.
8 vols. post 8vo. 48s.

The Fall of the Roman Republic; a Short History of the Last Century of the Commonwealth.
By Dean Merivale, D.C.L.
12mo. 7s. 6d.

The Sixth Oriental Monarchy; or the Geography, History, and Antiquities of Parthia. Collected and Illustrated from Ancient and Modern sources.
By Geo. Rawlinson, M.A.
With Maps and Illustrations. 8vo. 16s.

The Seventh Great Oriental Monarchy; or, a History of the Sassanians: with Notices Geographical and Antiquarian.
By Geo. Rawlinson, M.A.
8vo. with Maps and Illustrations.
[In the press.

Encyclopædia of Chronology, Historical and Biographical; comprising the Dates of all the Great Events of History, including Treaties, Alliances, Wars, Battles, &c. Incidents in the Lives of Eminent Men, Scientific and Geographical Discoveries, Mechanical Inventions, and Social, Domestic, and Economical Improvements.
By B. B. Woodward, B.A. and W. L. R. Cates.
8vo. 42s.

The History of Rome.
By Wilhelm Ihne.
Vols. I. and II. 8vo. 30s.   Vols. III. and IV. in preparation.

History of European Morals from Augustus to Charlemagne.
By W. E. H. Lecky, M.A.
2 vols. 8vo. 28s.

History of the Rise and Influence of the Spirit of Rationalism in Europe.
By W. E. H. Lecky, M.A.
Cabinet Edition, 2 vols. crown 8vo. 16s.

Introduction to the Science of Religion: Four Lectures delivered at the Royal Institution; with two Essays on False Analogies and the Philosophy of Mythology.
By F. Max Müller, M.A.
Crown 8vo. 10s. 6d.

The Stoics, Epicureans, and Sceptics.
Translated from the German of Dr. E. Zeller, by Oswald J. Reichel, M.A.
Crown 8vo. 14s.

Socrates and the Socratic Schools.
Translated from the German of Dr. E. Zeller, by the Rev. O. J. Reichel, M.A.
Crown 8vo. 8s. 6d.

The History of Philosophy, from Thales to Comte.
By George Henry Lewes.
Fourth Edition, 2 vols. 8vo. 32s.

Sketch of the History of the Church of England to the Revolution of 1688.
By T. V. Short, D.D. sometime Bishop of St. Asaph.
New Edition. Crown 8vo. 7s. 6d.

The Historical Geography of Europe.
By E. A. Freeman, D.C.L
8vo. Maps.   [In the press.

Essays on the History of the Christian Religion.
By John Earl Russell, K.G.
Fcp. 8vo. 3s. 6d.

History of the Reformation in Europe in the Time of Calvin.
By the Rev. J. H. Merle D'Aubigné, D.D.
Vols. I. to V. 8vo. £3. 12s. Vols. VI. & VII. completion.   [In the press.

**The Student's Manual
of Ancient History: con-
taining the Political History, Geographical Posi-
tion, and Social State of
the Principal Nations of
Antiquity.**
By W. Cooke Taylor, LL.D.
Crown 8vo. 7s. 6d.

**The Student's Manual of
Modern History: contain-
ing the Rise and Progress
of the Principal European
Nations, their Political
History, and the Changes
in their Social Condition.**
By W. Cooke Taylor, LL.D.
Crown 8vo. 7s. 6d.

The Crusades.
By the Rev. G. W. Cox,
M.A.
Fcp. 8vo. with Map, 2s. 6d.

**The Era of the Pro-
testant Revolution.**
By F. Seebohm, Author of
'The Oxford Reformers.'
With 4 Maps and 12 Diagrams. Fcp. 8vo.
2s. 6d.

**The Thirty Years' War,
1618–1648.**
By Samuel Rawson Gar-
diner.
Fcp. 8vo. with Maps, 2s. 6d.

**The Houses of Lancaster
and York; with the Con-
quest and Loss of France.**
By James Gairdner.
Fcp. 8vo. with Map, 2s. 6d.

Edward the Third.
By the Rev. W. Warburton,
M.A.
Fcp. 8vo. with Maps, 2s. 6d.

BIOGRAPHICAL WORKS.

Autobiography.
By John Stuart Mill.
8vo. 7s. 6d.

**Life and Correspondence
of Richard Whately, D.D.
late Archbishop of Dublin.**
By E. Jane Whately.
New Edition, with Additional Correspondence. Crown 8vo. with Portrait,
price 10s. 6d.

**Life and Letters of Gil-
bert Elliot, First Earl of
Minto, from 1751 to 1806,
when his Public Life in
Europe was closed by his
Appointment to the Vice-
Royalty of India.**
Edited by the Countess of
Minto.
3 vols. post 8vo. 31s. 6d.

Memoir of Thomas First Lord Denman, formerly Lord Chief Justice of England.
By Sir Joseph Arnould, B.A. K.B.
With two Portraits. 2 vols. 8vo. 32s.

The Life of Lloyd First Lord Kenyon.
By Hon. G. T. Kenyon, M.A.
With Portraits. 8vo. 14s.

Recollections of Past Life.
By Sir Henry Holland, Bart. M.D. F.R.S.
Third Edition. Post 8vo. 10s. 6d.

Isaac Casaubon, 1559-1614.
By Mark Pattison, Rector of Lincoln College, Oxford.
8vo. price 18s.

Life of Alexander von Humboldt.
Edited by Karl Bruhns, and translated by Jane and Caroline Lassell.
With 3 Portraits. 2 vols. 8vo. 36s.

Biographical and Critical Essays, reprinted from Reviews, with Additions and Corrections.
By A. Hayward, Q.C.
Second Series, 2 vols. 8vo. 28s. Third Series, 1 vol. 8vo. 14s.

The Life of Isambard Kingdom Brunel, Civil Engineer.
By I. Brunel, B.C.L.
With Portrait, Plates, and Woodcuts. 8vo. 21s.

Lord George Bentinck; a Political Biography.
By the Right Hon. B. Disraeli, M.P.
New Edition. Crown 8vo. 6s.

Memoir of George Edward Lynch Cotton, D.D. Bishop of Calcutta; with Selections from his Journals and Correspondence.
Edited by Mrs. Cotton.
Second Edition. Crown 8vo. 7s. 6d.

The Life and Letters of the Rev. Sydney Smith.
Edited by his Daughter, Lady Holland, and Mrs. Austin.
Crown 8vo. 2s. 6d. sewed; 3s. 6d. cloth.

Essays in Ecclesiastical Biography.
By the Right Hon. Sir J. Stephen, LL.D.
Cabinet Edition. Crown 8vo. 7s. 6d.

Leaders of Public Opinion in Ireland; Swift, Flood, Grattan, O'Connell.
By W. E. H. Lecky, M.A.
Crown 8vo. 7s. 6d.

Illustrations of the Life of Shakespeare, in a Series of Essays on a Variety of Subjects connected with his Personal and Literary History.
By James Orchard Halli-well, F.R.S.

Part I. with 16 Illustrations, Woodcuts, and Facsimiles of MSS. Folio, 42s.

Life of the Duke of Wellington.
By the Rev. G. R. Gleig, M.A.

Crown 8vo. with Portrait, 5s.

Felix Mendelssohn's Letters from Italy and Switzerland, and Letters from 1833 to 1847. Translated by Lady Wallace.

With Portrait. 2 vols. crown 8vo. 5s. each.

The Rise of Great Families; other Essays and Stories.
By Sir Bernard Burke, C.B. LL.D.

Crown 8vo. 12s. 6d.

Dictionary of General Biography; containing Concise Memoirs and Notices of the most Eminent Persons of all Ages and Countries.
Edited by W. L. R. Cates.

8vo. 21s.

Memoirs of Sir Henry Havelock, K.C.B.
By John Clark Marshman.
People's Edition. Crown 8vo. 3s. 6d.

Vicissitudes of Families.
By Sir Bernard Burke, C.B.

New Edition. 2 vols. crown 8vo. 21s.

MENTAL and POLITICAL PHILOSOPHY.

Comte's System of Positive Polity, or Treatise upon Sociology.
Translated from the Paris Edition of 1851–1854, and furnished with Analytical Tables of Contents. In Four Volumes, each forming in some degree an independent Treatise :—

Vol. I. The General View of Positivism and Introductory Principles. Translated

by J. H. Bridges, M.B. formerly Fellow of Oriel College, Oxford. 8vo. price 21s.

Vol. II. The Social Statics, or the Abstract Laws of Human Order. Translated by Frederic Harrison, M.A. [In May.

Vol. III. The Social Dynamics, or the General Laws of Human Progress (the Philosophy of History). Translated by E. S. Beesly, M.A. Professor of History in University College, London. 8vo. [In Sept.

Vol. IV. The Synthesis of the Future of Mankind. Translated by Richard Congreve, M.D., and an Appendix, containing the Author's Minor Treatises, translated by H. D. Hutton, M.A. Barrister-at-Law. 8vo. [Before Christmas.

Order and Progress:
Essays on Constitutional
Problems, *partly reprinted,
with Additions, from the
Fortnightly Review.*
By Frederic Harrison, of
Lincoln's Inn.

1 *vol. 8vo.* [*In the press.*

*Essays Critical & Narrative, partly original and
partly reprinted from Reviews.*
By W. Forsyth, Q.C. M.P.

8vo. 16s.

*Essays, Political, Social,
and Religious.*
By Richd. Congreve, M.A.

8vo. 18s.

*Essays on Freethinking
and Plainspeaking.*
By Leslie Stephen.

Crown 8vo. 10s. 6d.

*Essays, Critical and
Biographical, contributed
to the Edinburgh Review.*
By Henry Rogers.

New Edition. 2 vols. crown 8vo. 12s.

*Essays on some Theological Controversies of the
Time, contributed chiefly
to the Edinburgh Review.*
By Henry Rogers.

New Edition. Crown 8vo. 6s.

Democracy in America.
By Alexis de Tocqueville.
Translated by Henry
Reeve, C. B. D. C. L.

New Edition. 2 vols. post 8vo. [*In the press.*

On Representative Government.
By John Stuart Mill.

Fourth Edition, crown 8vo. 2s.

On Liberty.
By John Stuart Mill.

Post 8vo. 7s. 6d. crown 8vo. 1s. 4d.

*Principles of Political
Economy.*
By John Stuart Mill.

2 vols. 8vo. 30s. or 1 vol. crown 8vo. 5s.

*Essays on some Unsettled
Questions of Political Economy.*
By John Stuart Mill.

Second Edition. 8vo. 6s. 6d.

Utilitarianism.
By John Stuart Mill.

Fourth Edition. 8vo. 5s.

*A System of Logic,
Ratiocinative and Inductive.* By John Stuart Mill.

Eighth Edition. 2 vols. 8vo. 25s.

The Subjection of Women.
By John Stuart Mill.

New Edition. Post 8vo. 5s.

B

Examination of Sir William Hamilton's Philosophy, and of the principal Philosophical Questions discussed in his Writings.
By John Stuart Mill.

Fourth Edition. 8vo. 16s.

Dissertations and Discussions.
By John Stuart Mill.

Second Edition. 3 vols. 8vo. 36s. VOL. *IV.* (completion) in May.

Analysis of the Phenomena of the Human Mind.
By James Mill. New Edition, with Notes, Illustrative and Critical.

2 vols. 8vo. 28s.

A Systematic View of the Science of Jurisprudence.
By Sheldon Amos, M.A.

8vo. 18s.

A Primer of English Constitutional History.
By Sheldon Amos, M.A.

New Edition, revised. Post 8vo.
[Nearly ready.

Principles of Economical Philosophy.
By H. D. Macleod, M.A. Barrister-at-Law.

Second Edition, in 2 vols. Vol. *I.* 8vo. 15s.
Vol. *II.* Part I. price 12s.

The Institutes of Justinian; with English Introduction, Translation, and Notes.
By T. C. Sandars, M.A.

Fifth Edition. 8vo. 18s.

Lord Bacon's Works,
Collected and Edited by R. L. Ellis, M.A. J. Spedding, M.A. and D. D. Heath.

New and Cheaper Edition. 7 vols. 8vo. £3. 13s. 6d.

Letters and Life of Francis Bacon, including all his Occasional Works. Collected and edited, with a Commentary, by J. Spedding.

7 vols. 8vo. £4. 4s.

The Nicomachean Ethics of Aristotle. Newly translated into English.
By R. Williams, B.A.

8vo. 12s.

The Politics of Aristotle; Greek Text, with English Notes.
By Richard Congreve, M.A.

New Edition, revised. 8vo. 18s.

The Ethics of Aristotle; with Essays and Notes.
By Sir A. Grant, Bart. M.A. LL.D.

Third Edition. 2 vols. 8vo. price 32s.

Bacon's Essays, with Annotations.
By R. Whately, D.D.
New Edition. 8vo. 10s. 6d.

The Essays of Lord Bacon; with Critical and Illustrative Notes, and an Example with Answers of an Examination Paper.
By the Rev. John Hunter, M.A.
Crown 8vo. price 3s. 6d.

Picture Logic, or the Grave made Gay; an Attempt to Popularise the Science of Reasoning by the combination of Humorous Pictures with Examples of Reasoning taken from Daily Life.
By A. Swinbourne, B.A.
With Woodcut Illustrations from Drawings by the Author. Fcp. 8vo. price 5s.

Elements of Logic.
By R. Whately, D.D.
New Edition. 8vo. 10s. 6d. cr. 8vo. 4s. 6d.

Elements of Rhetoric.
By R. Whately, D.D.
New Edition. 8vo. 10s. 6d. cr. 8vo. 4s. 6d.

An Outline of the Necessary Laws of Thought: a Treatise on Pure and Applied Logic.
By the Most Rev. W. Thomson, D.D. Archbishop of York.
Ninth Thousand. Crown 8vo. 5s. 6d.

An Introduction to Mental Philosophy, on the Inductive Method.
By J. D. Morell, LL.D.
8vo. 12s.

Elements of Psychology, containing the Analysis of the Intellectual Powers.
By J. D. Morell, LL.D.
Post 8vo. 7s. 6d.

The Secret of Hegel: being the Hegelian System in Origin, Principle, Form, and Matter.
By J. H. Stirling, LL.D.
2 vols. 8vo. 28s.

Sir William Hamilton; being the Philosophy of Perception: an Analysis.
By J. H. Stirling, LL.D.
8vo. 5s.

Ueberweg's System of Logic, and History of Logical Doctrines.
Translated, with Notes and Appendices, by T. M. Lindsay, M.A. F.R.S.E.
8vo. 16s.

The Senses and the Intellect.
By A. Bain, LL.D. Prof. of Logic, Univ. Aberdeen.
8vo. 15s.

Mental and Moral Science; a Compendium of Psychology and Ethics.

By A. Bain, LL.D.

Third Edition. Crown 8vo. 10s. 6d. Or separately: Part I. Mental Science, 6s. 6d. Part II. Moral Science, 4s. 6d.

The Philosophy of Necessity; or, Natural Law as applicable to Mental, Moral, and Social Science.

By Charles Bray.

Second Edition. 8vo. 9s.

Hume's Treatise on Human Nature.

Edited, with Notes, &c. by T. H. Green, M.A. and the Rev. T. H. Grose, M.A.

2 vols. 8vo. 28s.

Hume's Essays Moral, Political, and Literary.

By the same Editors.

2 vols. 8vo. 28s.

*** The above form a complete and uniform Edition of HUME'S Philosophical Works.

MISCELLANEOUS & CRITICAL WORKS.

Miscellaneous and Posthumous Works of the late Henry Thomas Buckle. Edited, with a Biographical Notice, by Helen Taylor.

3 vols. 8vo. £2. 12s. 6d.

Short Studies on Great Subjects.
By J. A. Froude, M.A. formerly Fellow of Exeter College, Oxford.

CABINET EDITION, 2 vols. crown 8vo. 12s.
LIBRARY EDITION, 2 vols. 8vo. 24s.

Lord Macaulay's Miscellaneous Writings.

LIBRARY EDITION, 2 vols. 8vo. Portrait, 21s.
PEOPLE'S EDITION, 1 vol. cr. 8vo. 4s. 6d.

Lord Macaulay's Miscellaneous Writings and Speeches.

Students' Edition. Crown 8vo. 6s.

Speeches of the Right Hon. Lord Macaulay, corrected by Himself.

People's Edition. Crown 8vo. 3s. 6d.

Lord Macaulay's Speeches on Parliamentary Reform in 1831 and 1832.

16mo. 1s.

The Rev. Sydney Smith's Essays contributed to the Edinburgh Review.

Authorised Edition, complete in One Volume Crown 8vo. 2s. 6d. sewed, or 3s. 6d. cloth.

The Rev. Sydney Smith's Miscellaneous Works.

Crown 8vo. 6s.

The Wit and Wisdom of the Rev. Sydney Smith.

Crown 8vo. 3s. 6d.

The Miscellaneous Works of Thomas Arnold, D.D. Late Head Master of Rugby School and Regius Professor of Modern History in the Univ. of Oxford, collected and republished.
8vo. 7s. 6d.

Manual of English Literature, Historical and Critical.
By Thomas Arnold, M.A.
New Edition. Crown 8vo. 7s. 6d.

Realities of Irish Life.
By W. Steuart Trench.
Cr. 8vo. 2s. 6d. sewed, or 3s. 6d. cloth.

Lectures on the Science of Language.
By F. Max Müller, M.A. &c.
Seventh Edition. 2 vols. crown 8vo. 16s.

Chips from a German Workshop; being Essays on the Science of Religion, and on Mythology, Traditions, and Customs.
By F. Max Müller, M.A. &c.
3 vols. 8vo. £2.

Southey's Doctor, complete in One Volume.
Edited by Rev. J. W. Warter, B.D.
Square crown 8vo. 12s. 6d.

Families of Speech.
Four Lectures delivered at the Royal Institution.
By F. W. Farrar, D.D.
New Edition. Crown 8vo. 3s. 6d.

Chapters on Language.
By F. W. Farrar, D.D. F.R.S.
New Edition. Crown 8vo. 5s.

A Budget of Paradoxes.
By Augustus De Morgan, F.R.A.S.
Reprinted, with Author's Additions, from the Athenæum. 8vo. 15s.

Principles of Education, drawn from Nature and Revelation, and applied to Female Education in the Upper Classes.
By the Author of 'Amy Herbert.'
2 vols. fcp. 8vo. 12s. 6d

From January to December; a Book for Children.
Second Edition. 8vo. 3s. 6d.

The Election of Representatives, Parliamentary and Municipal; a Treatise.
By Thos. Hare, Barrister.
Fourth Edition. Post 8vo. 7s.

Miscellaneous Writings of John Conington, M.A. Edited by J. A. Symonds, M.A. With a Memoir by H. J. S. Smith, M.A.
2 vols. 8vo. 28s.

Recreations of a Country Parson.
By *A. K. H. B.*
Two Series, 3s. 6d. each.

Landscapes, Churches, and Moralities.
By *A. K. H. B.*
Crown 8vo. 3s. 6d.

Seaside Musings on Sundays and Weekdays.
By *A. K. H. B.*
Crown 8vo. 3s. 6d.

Changed Aspects of Unchanged Truths.
By *A. K. H. B.*
Crown 8vo. 3s. 6d.

Counsel and Comfort from a City Pulpit.
By *A. K. H. B.*
Crown 8vo. 3s. 6d.

Lessons of Middle Age.
By *A. K. H. B.*
Crown 8vo. 3s. 6d.

Leisure Hours in Town
By *A. K. H. B.*
Crown 8vo. 3s. 6d.

The Autumn Holidays of a Country Parson.
By *A. K. H. B.*
Crown 8vo. 3s. 6d.

Sunday Afternoons at the Parish Church of a Scottish University City.
By *A. K. H. B.*
Crown 8vo. 3s. 6d.

The Commonplace Philosopher in Town and Country.
By *A. K. H. B.*
Crown 8vo. 3s. 6d.

Present-Day Thoughts.
By *A. K. H. B.*
Crown 8vo. 3s. 6d.

Critical Essays of a Country Parson.
By *A. K. H. B.*
Crown 8vo. 3s. 6d.

The Graver Thoughts of a Country Parson.
By *A. K. H. B.*
Two Series, 3s. 6d. each.

DICTIONARIES and OTHER BOOKS of REFERENCE.

A Dictionary of the English Language.
By R. G. Latham, M.A. M.D. Founded on the Dictionary of Dr. S. Johnson, as edited by the Rev. H. J. Todd, with numerous Emendations and Additions.
4 vols. 4to. £7.

Thesaurus of English Words and Phrases, classified and arranged so as to facilitate the expression of Ideas, and assist in Literary Composition.
By P. M. Roget, M.D.
Crown 8vo. 10s. 6d.

English Synonymes.
By E. J. Whately. Edited by Archbishop Whately.
Fifth Edition. Fcp. 8vo. 3s.

A Practical Dictionary of the French and English Languages.
By Léon Contanseau, many years French Examiner for Military and Civil Appointments, &c.
Post 8vo. 10s. 6d.

Contanseau's Pocket Dictionary, French and English, abridged from the Practical Dictionary, by the Author.
Square 18mo. 3s. 6d.

New Practical Dictionary of the German Language; German - English and English-German.
By Rev. W. L. Blackley, M.A. and Dr. C. M. Friedländer.
Post 8vo. 7s. 6d.

A Dictionary of Roman and Greek Antiquities. With 2,000 Woodcuts from Ancient Originals, illustrative of the Arts and Life of the Greeks and Romans.
By Anthony Rich, B.A.
Third Edition. Crown 8vo. 7s. 6d.

The Mastery of Languages; or, the Art of Speaking Foreign Tongues Idiomatically.
By Thomas Prendergast.
Second Edition. 8vo. 6s.

A Practical English Dictionary.
By John T. White, D.D. Oxon. and T. C. Donkin, M.A.
1 vol. post 8vo. uniform with Contanseau's Practical French Dictionary.
[In the press.

A Latin-English Dictionary.
By John T. White, D.D. Oxon. and J. E. Riddle, M.A. Oxon.
Third Edition, revised. 2 vols. 4to. 42s.

White's College Latin-English Dictionary; abridged from the Parent Work for the use of University Students.
Medium 8vo. 18s.

A Latin-English Dictionary adapted for the use of Middle-Class Schools, By John T. White, D.D. Oxon.
Square fcp. 8vo. 3s.

White's Junior Student's Complete Latin-English and English-Latin Dictionary.
Square 12mo. 12s.
Separately { ENGLISH-LATIN, 5s. 6d.
{ LATIN-ENGLISH, 7s. 6d.

A Greek-English Lexicon.
By H. G. Liddell, D.D. Dean of Christchurch, and R. Scott, D.D. Dean of Rochester.
Sixth Edition. *Crown 4to.* 36s.

A Lexicon, Greek and English, abridged for Schools from Liddell and Scott's Greek-English Lexicon.
Fourteenth Edition. *Square 12mo.* 7s. 6d.

An English-Greek Lexicon, containing all the Greek Words used by Writers of good authority.
By C. D. Yonge, B.A.
New Edition. 4to. 21s.

Mr. Yonge's New Lexicon, English and Greek, abridged from his larger Lexicon.
Square 12mo. 8s. 6d.

M'Culloch's Dictionary, Practical, Theoretical, and Historical, of Commerce and Commercial Navigation.
Edited by H. G. Reid.
8vo. 63s.

The Post Office Gazetteer of the United Kingdom: a Complete Dictionary of all Cities, Towns, Villages, Hamlets, Unions, Registrars' Districts, Territorial Divisions, &c; and of Gentlemen's Seats, Railway Stations, Natural Features, and Objects of Note in Great Britain and Ireland; including several thousands of Extra Names of Places, supplied by permission of the Postal Authorities: the whole adapted to the Postal, Railway, and Telegraphic Systems, and to the Sheets of the Ordnance Survey.
By J. A. Sharp; assisted (in the Postal Information) by R. F. Pitt, of the General Post Office.
8vo. pp. circa 2,000, *price* 42s.
[*In May.*

A General Dictionary of Geography, Descriptive, Physical, Statistical, and Historical; forming a complete Gazetteer of the World. By A. Keith Johnston, F.R.S.E.

New Edition, thoroughly revised.

[*In the press.*

The Public Schools Manual of Modern Geography Forming a Companion to ' The Public Schools Atlas of Modern Geography.' By Rev. G. Butler, M.A.

[*In the press.*

The Public Schools Atlas of Modern Geography. In 31 Maps, exhibiting clearly the more important Physical Features of the Countries delineated. Edited, with Introduction, by Rev. G. Butler, M.A.

Imperial quarto, 3s. 6d. sewed ; 5s. cloth.

The Public Schools Atlas of Ancient Geography. Edited, with an Introduction on the Study of Ancient Geography, by the Rev. G. Butler, M.A.

Imperial Quarto. [*In the press.*

ASTRONOMY and METEOROLOGY.

The Universe and the Coming Transits; Researches into and New Views respecting the Constitution of the Heavens. By R. A. Proctor, B.A.

With 22 Charts and 22 Diagrams. 8vo. 16s.

The Transits of Venus; A Popular Account of Past and Coming Transits, from the first observed by Horrocks A.D. 1639 to the Transit of A.D. 2012. By R. A. Proctor, B.A.

With 20 Plates (12 Coloured) and 27 Woodcuts. Crown 8vo. 8s. 6d.

Saturn and its System. By R. A. Proctor, B.A.

8vo. with 14 Plates, 14s.

Essays on Astronomy. A Series of Papers on Planets and Meteors, the Sun and Sun-surrounding Space, Stars and Star Cloudlets. By R. A. Proctor, B.A.

With 10 Plates and 24 Woodcuts. 8vo. 12s.

The Moon; her Motions, Aspect, Scenery, and Physical Condition. By R. A. Proctor, B.A.

With Plates, Charts, Woodcuts, and Lunar Photographs. Crown 8vo. 15s.

The Sun; Ruler, Light, Fire, and Life of the Planetary System. By R. A. Proctor, B.A.

Second Edition. Plates and Woodcuts. Cr. 8vo. 14s.

C

The Orbs Around Us; a Series of Familiar Essays on the Moon and Planets, Meteors and Comets, the Sun and Coloured Pairs of Suns.
By R. A. Proctor, B.A.
Second Edition, with Chart and 4 Diagrams. Crown 8vo. 7s. 6d.

Other Worlds than Ours; The Plurality of Worlds Studied under the Light of Recent Scientific Researches.
By R. A. Proctor, B.A.
Third Edition, with 14 Illustrations. Cr. 8vo. 10s. 6d.

Brinkley's Astronomy. Revised and partly re-written, with Additional Chapters, and an Appendix of Questions for Examination.
By John W. Stubbs, D.D. and F. Brunnow, Ph.D.
With 49 Diagrams. Crown 8vo. 6s.

Outlines of Astronomy.
By Sir J. F. W. Herschel, Bart. M.A.
Latest Edition, with Plates and Diagrams. Square crown 8vo. 12s.

A New Star Atlas, for the Library, the School, and the Observatory, in 12 Circular Maps (with 2 Index Plates).
By R. A. Proctor, B.A.
Crown 8vo. 5s.

Celestial Objects for Common Telescopes.
By T. W. Webb, M.A. F.R.A.S.
New Edition, with Map of the Moon and Woodcuts. Crown 8vo. 7s. 6d.

Larger Star Atlas, for the Library, in Twelve Circular Maps, photolithographed by A. Brothers, F.R.A.S. With 2 Index Plates and a Letterpress Introduction.
By R. A. Proctor, BA.
Second Edition. Small folio, 25s.

Magnetism and Deviation of the Compass. For the use of Students in Navigation and Science Schools.
By J. Merrifield, LL.D.
18mo. 1s. 6d.

Dove's Law of Storms, considered in connexion with the ordinary Movements of the Atmosphere.
Translated by R. H. Scott, M.A.
8vo. 10s. 6d.

Air and Rain; the Beginnings of a Chemical Climatology.
By R. A. Smith, F.R.S.
8vo. 24s.

Nautical Surveying, an Introduction to the Practical and Theoretical Study of.
By J. K. Laughton, M.A.
Small 8vo. 6s.

Schellen's Spectrum Analysis, in its Application to Terrestrial Substances and the Physical Constitution of the Heavenly Bodies.
Translated by Jane and C. Lassell; edited, with Notes, by W. Huggins, LL.D. F.R.S.
With 13 Plates and 223 Woodcuts. 8vo. 28s.

Air and its Relations to Life: 1774–1874. *Being, with some Additions, a Course of Lectures delivered at the Royal Institution of Great Britain in the Summer of* 1874.
By Walter Noel Hartley, F.C.S.
1 vol. small 8vo. with Illustrations.

NATURAL HISTORY and PHYSICAL SCIENCE.

The Correlation of Physical Forces.
By the Hon. Sir W. R. Grove, F.R.S. &c.
Sixth Edition, with other Contributions to Science. 8vo. 15s.

Professor Helmholtz' Popular Lectures on Scientific Subjects.
Translated by E. Atkinson, F.C.S.
With many Illustrative Wood Engravings. 8vo. 12s. 6d.

Ganot's Natural Philosophy for General Readers and Young Persons; a Course of Physics divested of Mathematical Formulæ and expressed in the language of daily life.
Translated by E. Atkinson, F.C.S.
Cr. 8vo. with 404 Woodcuts, 7s. 6d.

Ganot's Elementary Treatise on Physics, Experimental and Applied, for the use of Colleges and Schools.
Translated and edited by E. Atkinson, F.C.S.
New Edition, with a Coloured Plate and 726 Woodcuts. Post 8vo. 15s.

Weinhold's Introduction to Experimental Physics, Theoretical and Practical; including Directions for Constructing Physical Apparatus and for Making Experiments.
Translated by B. Loewy, F.R.A.S. With a Preface by G. C. Foster, F.R.S.
With 3 Coloured Plates and 404 Woodcuts. 8vo. price 31s. 6d.

Principles of Animal Mechanics.
By the Rev. S. Haughton, F.R.S.

Second Edition. 8vo. 21s.

Text-Books of Science, Mechanical and Physical, adapted for the use of Artisans and of Students in Public and other Schools. (The first Ten edited by T. M. Goodeve, M.A. Lecturer on Applied Science at the Royal School of Mines; the remainder edited by C. W. Merrifield, F.R.S. an Examiner in the Department of Public Education.)

Small 8vo. Woodcuts.

Edited by T. M. Goodeve, M.A.

Anderson's *Strength of Materials*, 3s. 6d.
Bloxam's *Metals*, 3s. 6d.
Goodeve's *Mechanics*, 3s. 6d.
——— *Mechanism*, 3s. 6d.
Griffin's *Algebra & Trigonometry*, 3s. 6d.
  Notes on the same, with Solutions, 3s. 6d.
Jenkin's *Electricity & Magnetism*, 3s. 6d.
Maxwell's *Theory of Heat*, 3s. 6d.
Merrifield's *Technical Arithmetic*, 3s. 6d.
  Key, 3s. 6d.
Miller's *Inorganic Chemistry*, 3s. 6d.
Shelley's *Workshop Appliances*, 3s. 6d.
Watson's *Plane & Solid Geometry*, 3s. 6d.

Edited by C. W. Merrifield, F.R.S.

Armstrong's *Organic Chemistry*, 3s. 6d.
Thorpe's *Quantitative Analysis*, 4s. 6d.
Thorpe and Muir's *Qualitative Analysis*, 3s. 6d.

Fragments of Science.
By John Tyndall, F.R.S.

Third Edition. 8vo. 14s.

Address delivered before the British Association assembled at Belfast.
By John Tyndall, F.R.S. President.

8th Thousand, with New Preface and the Manchester Address. 8vo. price 4s. 6d.

Heat a Mode of Motion.
By John Tyndall, F.R.S.

[New Edition, nearly ready.

Sound; a Course of Eight Lectures delivered at the Royal Institution of Great Britain.
By John Tyndall, F.R.S.

[New Edition, nearly ready.

Researches on Diamagnetism and Magne-Crystallic Action; including the Question of Diamagnetic Polarity.
By John Tyndall, F.R.S.

With 6 Plates and many Woodcuts. 8vo. 14s.

Contributions to Molecular Physics in the domain of Radiant Heat.
By John Tyndall, F.R.S.

With 2 Plates and 31 Woodcuts. 8vo. 16s.

Lectures on Light, delivered in the United States of America in 1872 and 1873.
By J. Tyndall, F.R.S.

Crown 8vo. 7s. 6d.

Notes of a Course of Seven Lectures on Electrical Phenomena and Theories, delivered at the Royal Institution.
By *J. Tyndall, F.R.S.*
Crown 8vo. 1s. sewed, or 1s. 6d. cloth.

Notes of a Course of Nine Lectures on Light, delivered at the Royal Institution.
By *J. Tyndall, F.R.S.*
Crown 8vo. 1s. sewed, or 1s. 6d. cloth.

A Treatise on Magnetism, General and Terrestrial.
By *Humphrey Lloyd, D.D. D.C.L. Provost of Trinity College, Dublin.*
8vo. price 10s. 6d.

Elementary Treatise on the Wave-Theory of Light.
By *H. Lloyd, D.D. D.C.L.*
Third Edition. 8vo. 10s. 6d.

An Elementary Exposition of the Doctrine of Energy.
By *D. D. Heath, M.A. formerly Fellow of Trinity College, Cambridge.*
Post 8vo. 4s. 6d.

Professor Owen's Lectures on the Comparative Anatomy and Physiology of Invertebrate Animals.
2nd Edition, with 235 Woodcuts. 8vo. 21s.

The Comparative Anatomy and Physiology of the Vertebrate Animals.
By *Richard Owen, F.R.S.*
With 1,472 Woodcuts. 3 vols. 8vo. £3. 13s. 6d.

Fragmentary Papers on Science and other subjects.
By the late Sir *H. Holland, Bart. Edited by his Son, the Rev. J. Holland.*
8vo. price 14s.

Light Science for Leisure Hours; a Series of Familiar Essays on Scientific Subjects, Natural Phenomena, &c.
By *R. A. Proctor, B.A.*
First and Second Series. 2 vols. crown 8vo. 7s. 6d. each.

Kirby and Spence's Introduction to Entomology, or Elements of the Natural History of Insects.
Crown 8vo. 5s.

Strange Dwellings; a Description of the Habitations of Animals, abridged from 'Homes without Hands.'
By *Rev. J. G. Wood, M.A.*
With Frontispiece and 60 Woodcuts. Crown 8vo. 7s. 6d.

Homes without Hands; a Description of the Habitations of Animals, classed according to their Principle of Construction.
By *Rev. J. G. Wood, M.A.*
With about 140 Vignettes on Wood. 8vo. 21s.

Out of Doors ; a Selection of Original Articles on Practical Natural History.
By Rev. J. G. Wood, M.A.
With 6 Illustrations from Original Designs engraved on Wood. Crown 8vo. 7s. 6d.

The Polar World : a Popular Description of Man and Nature in the Arctic and Antarctic Regions of the Globe.
By Dr. G. Hartwig.
With Chromoxylographs, Maps, and Woodcuts. 8vo. 10s. 6d.

The Sea and its Living Wonders.
By Dr. G. Hartwig.
Fourth Edition, enlarged. 8vo. with many Illustrations, 10s. 6d.

The Tropical World.
By Dr. G. Hartwig.
With about 200 Illustrations. 8vo. 10s. 6d.

The Subterranean World.
By Dr. G. Hartwig.
With Maps and many Woodcuts. 8vo. 21s.

The Aerial World; a Popular Account of the Phenomena and Life of the Atmosphere.
By Dr. George Hartwig.
With Map, 8 Chromoxylographs, and 60 Woodcuts. 8vo. price 21s.

A Familiar History of Birds.
By E. Stanley, D.D. late Ld. Bishop of Norwich.
Fcp. 8vo. with Woodcuts, 3s. 6d.

Insects at Home; a Popular Account of British Insects, their Structure Habits, and Transformations.
By Rev. J. G. Wood, M.A.
With upwards of 700 Woodcuts. 8vo. 21s.

Insects Abroad ; being a Popular Account of Foreign Insects, their Structure, Habits, and Transformations.
By Rev. J. G. Wood, M.A.
With upwards of 700 Woodcuts. 8vo. 21s.

Rocks Classified and Described.
By B. Von Cotta.
English Edition, by P. H. LAWRENCE (with English, German, and French Synonymes), revised by the Author. Post 8vo. 14s.

Primæval World of Switzerland.
By Professor Oswald Heer.
Translated by W. S. Dallas, F.L.S. and edited by James Heywood, M.A. F.R.S.
2 vols. 8vo. with numerous Illustrations.
[In the press.

The Origin of Civilisation, and the Primitive Condition of Man; Mental and Social Condition of Savages.
By Sir J. Lubbock, Bart. M.P. F.R.S.
Third Edition, with 25 Woodcuts. 8vo. 18s.

The Native Races of the Pacific States of North America.
By Hubert Howe Bancroft.

Vol. I. *Wild Tribes, their Manners and Customs*; with 6 Maps. 8vo. 25s.

₊ To be completed in the course of the present year, in Four more Volumes—

Vol. II. *Civilized Nations of Mexico and Central America.*
Vol. III. *Mythology and Languages of both Savage and Civilized Nations.*
Vol. IV. *Antiquities and Architectural Remains.*
Vol. V. *Aboriginal History and Migrations; Index to the Entire Work.*

A Manual of Anthropology, or Science of Man, based on Modern Research.
By Charles Bray.

Crown 8vo. 5s.

A Phrenologist amongst the Todas, or the Study of a Primitive Tribe in South India; History, Character, Customs, Religion, Infanticide, Polyandry, Language.
By W. E. Marshall, Lieut.-Col. Bengal Staff Corps.

With 26 Illustrations. 8vo. 21s.

The Ancient Stone Implements, Weapons, and Ornaments of Great Britain.
By John Evans, F.R.S.

With 2 Plates and 476 Woodcuts. 8vo. 28s.

The Elements of Botany for Families and Schools.
Eleventh Edition, revised by Thomas Moore, F.L.S.

Fcp. 8vo. with 154 Woodcuts, 2s. 6d.

Bible Animals; a Description of every Living Creature mentioned in the Scriptures, from the Ape to the Coral.
By Rev. J. G. Wood, M.A.

With about 100 Vignettes on Wood. 8vo. 21s.

The Rose Amateur's Guide.
By Thomas Rivers.

Tenth Edition. Fcp. 8vo. 4s.

A Dictionary of Science, Literature, and Art.
Fourth Edition, re-edited by the late W. T. Brande (the Author) and Rev. G. W. Cox, M.A.

3 vols. medium 8vo. 63s.

On the Sensations of Tone, as a Physiological Basis for the Theory of Music.
By H. Helmholtz, Professor of Physiology in the University of Berlin.
Translated by A. J. Ellis, F.R.S.

[Nearly ready.

The Treasury of Botany, or Popular Dictionary of the Vegetable Kingdom; with which is incorporated a Glossary of Botanical Terms.
Edited by J. Lindley, F.R.S. and T. Moore, F.L.S.

With 274 Woodcuts and 20 Steel Plates. Two Parts, fcp. 8vo. 12s.

Handbook of Hardy Trees, Shrubs, and Herbaceous Plants; containing Descriptions &c. of the Best Species in Cultivation; with Cultural Details, Comparative Hardiness, suitability for particular positions, &c. Based on the French Work of Decaisne and Naudin, and including the 720 Original Woodcut Illustrations. By W. B. Hemsley.

Medium 8vo. 21s.

Loudon's Encyclopædia of Plants; comprising the Specific Character, Description, Culture, History, &c. of all the Plants found in Great Britain.

With upwards of 12,000 Woodcuts. 8vo. 42s.

A General System of Descriptive and Analytical Botany. Translated from the French of Le Maout and Decaisne, by Mrs. Hooker. Edited and arranged according to the English Botanical System, by J. D. Hooker, M.D. &c. Director of the Royal Botanic Gardens, Kew.

With 5,500 Woodcuts. Imperial 8vo. 52s. 6d.

Forest Trees and Woodland Scenery, as described in Ancient and Modern Poets. By William Menzies, Deputy Surveyor of Windsor Forest and Parks, &c.

In One Volume, imperial 4to. with Twenty Plates, Coloured in facsimile of the original drawings, price £5. 5s.
[Preparing for publication.

CHEMISTRY and PHYSIOLOGY.

Miller's Elements of Chemistry, Theoretical and Practical. Re-edited, with Additions, by H. Macleod, F.C.S. 3 vols. 8vo. £3.

PART   I. CHEMICAL PHYSICS, 15s.
PART II. INORGANIC CHEMISTRY, 21s.
PART III. ORGANIC CHEMISTRY, 24s.

Select Methods in Chemical Analysis, chiefly Inorganic. By Wm. Crookes, F.R.S.

With 22 Woodcuts.   Crown 8vo. 12s. 6d.

A Dictionary of Chemistry and the Allied Branches of other Sciences. By Henry Watts, F.C.S. assisted by eminent Scientific and Practical Chemists.

6 vols. medium 8vo. £8. 14s. 6d.

Second Supplement completing the Record of Discovery to the end of 1872.

8vo. price 42s.   In May.

Todd and Bowman's Physiological Anatomy, and Physiology of Man.

Vol. II. with numerous Illustrations, 25s.

Vol. I. New Edition by Dr. LIONEL S. BEALE, F.R.S. *in course of publication, with numerous Illustrations. Parts I. and II. in 8vo. price 7s. 6d. each.*

Elementary Lessons on Structure of Man and Animals, with especial reference to the Principles

affecting Health, Food, and Cooking, and the Duties of Man to Animal Creation. By Mrs. Buckton.

With Illustrations engraved on Wood. 1 vol. small 8vo.

Outlines of Physiology, Human and Comparative. By J. Marshall, F.R.C.S. Surgeon to the University College Hospital.

2 vols. cr. 8vo. with 122 Woodcuts, 32s.

The FINE ARTS and ILLUSTRATED EDITIONS.

Poems. By William B. Scott.

I. Ballads and Tales. II. Studies from Nature. III. Sonnets &c. Illustrated by Seventeen Etchings by L. Alma Tadema *and* William B. Scott. *Crown 8vo.* [*Nearly ready.*

Half-hour Lectures on the History and Practice of the Fine and Ornamental Arts. By W. B. Scott, Assistant Inspector in Art, Department of Science and Art.

Third Edition, with 50 Woodcuts. Crown 8vo. 8s. 6d.

Albert Durer, his Life and Works; including Autobiographical Papers and Complete Catalogues. By William B. Scott.

With 6 Etchings by the Author and other Illustrations. 8vo. 16s.

In Fairyland; Pictures from the Elf-World. By Richard Doyle. With a Poem by W. Allingham.

With 16 coloured Plates, containing 36 Designs. Second Edition, folio, 15s.

A Dictionary of Artists of the English School: Painters, Sculptors, Architects, Engravers, and Ornamentists; with Notices of their Lives and Works. By Samuel Redgrave.

8vo. 16s.

The New Testament, illustrated with Wood Engravings after the Early Masters, chiefly of the Italian School.

Crown 4to. 63s.

D

Moore's Lalla Rookh,
Tenniel's Edition, with 68
Wood Engravings.
Fcp. 4to. 21s.

Moore's Irish Melodies,
Maclise's Edition, with 161
Steel Plates.
Super royal 8vo. 31s. 6d.

Lyra Germanica; the
Christian Year and the
Christian Life. Trans-
lated by Miss Winkworth.
With about 325 Woodcut Illustrations by J.
Leighton, F.S.A. and other Artists.
2 vols. 4to. price 42s.

Lord Macaulay's Lays
of Ancient Rome. With
90 Illustrations on Wood
from Drawings by G.
Scharf.
Fcp. 4to. 21s.

Miniature Edition, with
Scharf's 90 Illustrations
reduced in Lithography.
Imp. 16mo. 10s. 6d.

Sacred and Legendary
Art.
By Mrs. Jameson.
6 vols. square crown 8vo. price £5. 15s. 6d.
as follows:—

Legends of the Saints
and Martyrs.
New Edition, with 19 Etchings and 187
Woodcuts. 2 vols. 31s. 6d.

Legends of the Monastic
Orders.
New Edition, with 11 Etchings and 88
Woodcuts. 1 vol. 21s.

Legends of the Madonna.
New Edition, with 27 Etchings and 165
Woodcuts. 1 vol. 21s.

The History of Our Lord,
with that of his Types and
Precursors.
Completed by Lady East-
lake.
Revised Edition, with 13 Etchings and 281
Woodcuts. 2 vols. 42s.

The USEFUL ARTS, MANUFACTURES, &c.

A Manual of Architec-
ture: being a Concise His-
tory and Explanation of the
Principal Styles of Euro-
pean Architecture, Ancient,
Mediæval, and Renaissance;
with a Glossary.

By Thomas Mitchell.

With 150 Woodcuts.   Crown 8vo. 10s. 6d.

History of the Gothic
Revival; an Attempt to
shew how far the taste for
Mediæval Architecture was
retained in England during
the last two centuries, and
has been re-developed in the
present.
By Charles L. Eastlake,
Architect.

With 48 Illustrations.   Imp. 8vo. 31s. 6d.

Industrial Chemistry; a Manual for Manufacturers and for Colleges or Technical Schools. Being a Translation of Professors Stohmann and Engler's German Edition of Payen's 'Précis de Chimie Industrielle,' by Dr. J. D. Barry. Edited, and supplemented with Chapters on the Chemistry of the Metals, by B. H. Paul, Ph.D.
8vo. with Plates and Woodcuts.
[In the press.

Gwilt's Encyclopædia of Architecture, with above 1,600 Woodcuts. Fifth Edition, with Alterations and Additions, by Wyatt Papworth.
8vo. 52s. 6d.

The Three Cathedrals dedicated to St. Paul in London; their History from the Foundation of the First Building in the Sixth Century to the Proposals for the Adornment of the Present Cathedral. By W. Longman, F.S.A.
With numerous Illustrations. Square crown 8vo. 21s.

Hints on Household Taste in Furniture, Upholstery, and other Details. By Charles L. Eastlake, Architect.
New Edition, with about 90 Illustrations. Square crown 8vo. 14s.

Lathes and Turning, Simple, Mechanical, and Ornamental. By W. Henry Northcott.
With 240 Illustrations. 8vo. 18s.

Handbook of Practical Telegraphy. By R. S. Culley, Memb. Inst. C.E. Engineer-in-Chief of Telegraphs to the Post-Office.
Sixth Edition, Plates & Woodcuts. 8vo. 16s.

Principles of Mechanism, for the use of Students in the Universities, and for Engineering Students. By R. Willis, M.A. F.R.S. Professor in the University of Cambridge.
Second Edition, with 374 Woodcuts. 8vo. 18s.

Perspective; or, the Art of Drawing what one Sees: for the Use of those Sketching from Nature. By Lieut. W. H. Collins, R.E. F.R.A.S.
With 37 Woodcuts. Crown 8vo. 5s.

Encyclopædia of Civil Engineering, Historical, Theoretical, and Practical. By E. Cresy, C.E.
With above 3,000 Woodcuts. 8vo. 42s.

A Treatise on the Steam Engine, in its various applications to Mines, Mills, Steam Navigation, Railways and Agriculture.
By *J. Bourne, C.E.*

With Portrait, 37 Plates, and 546 Woodcuts. 4to. 42s.

Catechism of the Steam Engine, in its various Applications.
By *John Bourne, C.E.*

New Edition, with 89 Woodcuts. Fcp. 8vo. 6s.

Handbook of the Steam Engine.
By *J. Bourne, C.E. forming a KEY to the Author's Catechism of the Steam Engine.*

With 67 Woodcuts. Fcp. 8vo. 9s.

Recent Improvements in the Steam Engine.
By *J. Bourne, C.E.*

With 124 Woodcuts. Fcp. 8vo. 6s.

Lowndes's Engineer's Handbook; explaining the Principles which should guide the Young Engineer in the Construction of Machinery.

Post 8vo. 5s.

Guns and Steel; Miscellaneous Papers on Mechanical Subjects.
By *Sir J. Whitworth, C.E. F.R.S.*

With Illustrations. Royal 8vo. 7s. 6d.

Ure's Dictionary of Arts, Manufactures, and Mines. Seventh Edition, re-written and greatly enlarged by R. Hunt, F.R.S. assisted by numerous Contributors.

With 2,000 Woodcuts. 3 vols. medium 8vo. price £5. 5s.   [In April.

Handbook to the Mineralogy of Cornwall and Devon; with Instructions for their Discrimination, and copious Tables of Locality.
By *J. H. Collins, F.G.S.*

With 10 Plates, 8vo. 6s.

Practical Treatise on Metallurgy,
Adapted from the last German Edition of Professor Kerl's Metallurgy by W. Crookes, F.R.S. &c. and E. Röhrig, Ph.D.

3 vols. 8vo. with 625 Woodcuts. £4. 19s.

Treatise on Mills and Millwork.
By *Sir W. Fairbairn, Bt.*

With 18 Plates and 322 Woodcuts. 2 vols. 8vo. 32s.

Useful Information for Engineers.
By *Sir W. Fairbairn, Bt.*

With many Plates and Woodcuts. 3 vols. crown 8vo. 31s. 6d.

The Application of Cast and Wrought Iron to Building Purposes.
By Sir W. Fairbairn, Bt.
With 6 Plates and 118 Woodcuts. 8vo. 16s.

Practical Handbook of Dyeing and Calico-Printing.
By W. Crookes, F.R.S. &c.
With numerous Illustrations and Specimens of Dyed Textile Fabrics. 8vo. 42s.

Occasional Papers on Subjects connected with Civil Engineering, Gunnery, and Naval Architecture.
By Michael Scott, Memb. Inst. C.E. & of Inst. N.A.
2 vols. 8vo. with Plates, 42s.

Mitchell's Manual of Practical Assaying.
Fourth Edition, revised, with the Recent Discoveries incorporated, by W. Crookes, F.R.S.
8vo. Woodcuts, 31s. 6d.

Loudon's Encyclopædia of Gardening : comprising the Theory and Practice of Horticulture, Floriculture, Arboriculture, and Landscape Gardening.
With 1,000 Woodcuts. 8vo. 21s.

Loudon's Encyclopædia of Agriculture: comprising the Laying-out, Improvement, and Management of Landed Property, and the Cultivation and Economy of the Productions of Agriculture.
With 1,100 Woodcuts. 8vo. 21s.

RELIGIOUS and MORAL WORKS.

An Exposition of the 39 Articles, Historical and Doctrinal.
By E. H. Browne, D.D. Bishop of Winchester.
New Edition. 8vo. 16s.

Historical Lectures on the Life of Our Lord Jesus Christ.
By C. J. Ellicott, D.D.
Fifth Edition. 8vo. 12s.

An Introduction to the Theology of the Church of England, in an Exposition of the 39 Articles. By Rev. T. P. Boultbee, LL.D.
Fcp. 8vo. 6s.

Sermons for the Times preached in St. Paul's Cathedral and elsewhere.
By Rev. T. Griffith, M.A.
Crown 8vo. 6s.

Sermons; including Two Sermons on the Interpretation of Prophecy, and an Essay on the Right Interpretation and Understanding of the Scriptures.
By the late Rev. Thomas Arnold, D.D.
3 vols. 8vo. price 24s.

Christian Life, its Course, its Hindrances, and its Helps; Sermons preached mostly in the Chapel of Rugby School.
By the late Rev. Thomas Arnold, D.D.
8vo. 7s. 6d.

Christian Life, its Hopes, its Fears, and its Close; Sermons preached mostly in the Chapel of Rugby School.
By the late Rev. Thomas Arnold, D.D.
8vo. 7s. 6d.

Sermons Chiefly on the Interpretation of Scripture.
By the late Rev. Thomas Arnold, D.D.
8vo. price 7s. 6d.

Sermons preached in the Chapel of Rugby School; with an Address before Confirmation.
By the late Rev. Thomas Arnold, D.D.
Fcp. 8vo. price 3s. 6d.

Three Essays on Religion: Nature; the Utility of Religion; Theism.
By John Stuart Mill.
Second Edition. 8vo. price 10s. 6d.

Synonyms of the Old Testament, their Bearing on Christian Faith and Practice.
By Rev. R. B. Girdlestone.
8vo. 15s.

Reasons of Faith; or, the Order of the Christian Argument Developed and Explained.
By Rev. G. S. Drew, M.A.
Second Edition. Fcp. 8vo. 6s.

The Eclipse of Faith: or a Visit to a Religious Sceptic.
By Henry Rogers.
Latest Edition. Fcp. 8vo. 5s.

Defence of the Eclipse of Faith.
By Henry Rogers.
Latest Edition. Fcp. 8vo. 3s. 6d.

A Critical and Grammatical Commentary on St. Paul's Epistles.
By C. J. Ellicott, D.D.
8vo. Galatians, 8s. 6d. Ephesians, 8s. 6d. Pastoral Epistles, 10s. 6d. Philippians, Colossians, & Philemon, 10s. 6d. Thessalonians, 7s. 6d.

The Life and Epistles of St. Paul.

By Rev. W. J. Conybeare, M.A. and Very Rev. J. S. Howson, D.D.

LIBRARY EDITION, *with all the Original Illustrations, Maps, Landscapes on Steel, Woodcuts, &c.* 2 *vols.* 4*to.* 48*s.*

INTERMEDIATE EDITION, *with a Selection of Maps, Plates, and Woodcuts.* 2 *vols. square crown* 8*vo.* 21*s.*

STUDENT'S EDITION, *revised and condensed, with* 46 *Illustrations and Maps.* 1 *vol. crown* 8*vo.* 9*s.*

Fasting Communion, how Binding in England by the Canons. With the testimony of the Early Fathers. An Historical Essay.

By the Rev. H. T. Kingdon, M.A. Assistant-Curate, S. Andrew's, Wells Street; late Vice-Principal of Salisbury Theological College.

Second Edition. 8*vo.* 10*s.* 6*d.*

An Examination into the Doctrine and Practice of Confession.

By the Rev. W. E. Jelf, B.D. sometime Censor of Ch. Ch. Bampton Lecturer 1857; Whitehall Preacher 1846; Author of 'Quousque' &c.

8*vo. price* 7*s.* 6*d.*

Evidence of the Truth of the Christian Religion derived from the Literal Fulfilment of Prophecy.

By Alexander Keith, D.D.

40*th Edition, with numerous Plates. Square* 8*vo.* 12*s.* 6*d. or in post* 8*vo. with* 5 *Plates,* 6*s.*

Historical and Critical Commentary on the Old Testament; with a New Translation.

By M. M. Kalisch, Ph.D.

Vol. I. Genesis, 8*vo.* 18*s. or adapted for the General Reader,* 12*s. Vol. II.* Exodus, 15*s. or adapted for the General Reader,* 12*s. Vol. III.* Leviticus, *Part I.* 15*s. or adapted for the General Reader,* 8*s. Vol. IV.* Leviticus, *Part II.* 15*s. or adapted for the General Reader,* 8*s.*

The History and Literature of the Israelites, according to the Old Testament and the Apocrypha.

By C. De Rothschild and A. De Rothschild.

Second Edition. 2 *vols. crown* 8*vo.* 12*s.* 6*d. Abridged Edition, in* 1 *vol. fcp.* 8*vo.* 3*s.* 6*d.*

Ewald's History of Israel.

Translated from the German by J. E. Carpenter, M.A. with Preface by R. Martineau, M.A.

5 *vols.* 8*vo.* 63*s.*

Commentary on Epistle to the Romans.

By Rev. W. A. O'Conor.

Crown 8*vo.* 3*s.* 6*d.*

A Commentary on the Gospel of St. John.
By Rev. W. A. O'Conor.
Crown 8vo. 10s. 6d.

The Epistle to the Hebrews; with Analytical Introduction and Notes.
By Rev. W. A. O'Conor.
Crown 8vo. 4s. 6d.

Thoughts for the Age.
By Elizabeth M. Sewell.
New Edition. Fcp. 8vo. 3s. 6d.

Passing Thoughts on Religion.
By Elizabeth M. Sewell.
Fcp. 8vo. 3s. 6d.

Preparation for the Holy Communion; the Devotions chiefly from the works of Jeremy Taylor.
By Elizabeth M. Sewell.
32mo. 3s.

Bishop Jeremy Taylor's Entire Works; with Life by Bishop Heber.
Revised and corrected by the Rev. C. P. Eden.
10 vols. £5. 5s.

Hymns of Praise and Prayer.
Collected and edited by Rev. J. Martineau, LL.D.
Crown 8vo. 4s. 6d.

The Book of Psalms of David the King and Prophet, disposed according to the Rhythmical Structure of the Original; with Three Essays,
1. The Psalms of David restored to David; 2. The External Form of Hebrew Poetry; 3. The Zion of David restored to David. By E. F. Crown 8vo. with Map and Illustrations, 8s. 6d.

Spiritual Songs for the Sundays and Holidays throughout the Year.
By J. S. B. Monsell, LL.D.
Fourth Edition. Fcp. 8vo. 4s. 6d.

Lyra Germanica; Hymns translated from the German by Miss C. Winkworth.
2 series, fcp. 8vo. 3s. 6d. each.

Endeavours after the Christian Life; Discourses.
By Rev. J. Martineau, LL.D.
Fifth Edition. Crown 8vo. 7s. 6d.

An Introduction to the Study of the New Testament, Critical, Exegetical, and Theological.
By Rev. S. Davidson, D.D.
2 vols. 8vo. 30s.

Lectures on the Pentateuch & the Moabite Stone; with Appendices.
By J. W. Colenso, D.D. Bishop of Natal.
8vo. 12s.

Supernatural Religion; an Inquiry into the Reality of Divine Revelation.
New Edition. 2 vols. 8vo. 24s.

The Pentateuch and Book of Joshua Critically Examined.
By J. W. Colenso, D.D. Bishop of Natal.
Crown 8vo. 6s.

The New Bible Commentary, by Bishops and other Clergy of the Anglican Church, critically examined by the Rt. Rev. J. W. Colenso, D.D. Bishop of Natal.
8vo. 25s.

TRAVELS, VOYAGES, &c.

Italian Alps; Sketches from the Mountains of Ticino, Lombardy, the Trentino, and Venetia.
By Douglas W. Freshfield, Editor of 'The Alpine Journal.'
Crown 8vo. with Map and Illustrations. [In April.

Here and There in the Alps.
By the Hon. Frederica Plunket.
With Vignette-title. Post 8vo. 6s. 6d.

The Valleys of Tirol; their Traditions and Customs, and How to Visit them.
By Miss R. H. Busk, Author of 'The Folk-Lore of Rome,' &c.
With Frontispiece and 3 Maps. Crown 8vo. 12s. 6d.

Spain; Art-Remains and Art-Realities; Painters, Priests, and Princes: being Notes of Things seen and of Opinions formed during nearly Three Years' Residence and Travels in that Country.
By H. W. Baxley, M.D.
2 vols. crown 8vo. 21s.

Eight Years in Ceylon.
By Sir Samuel W. Baker, M.A. F.R.G.S.
New Edition, with Illustrations engraved on Wood by G. Pearson. Crown 8vo. Price 7s. 6d.

The Rifle and the Hound in Ceylon.
By Sir Samuel W. Baker, M.A. F.R.G.S.
New Edition, with Illustrations engraved on Wood by G. Pearson. Crown 8vo. Price 7s. 6d.

E

Meeting the Sun; a Journey all round the World through Egypt, China, Japan, and California.
By William Simpson, F.R.G.S.
With Heliotypes and Woodcuts. 8vo. 24s.

The Rural Life of England.
By William Howitt.
Woodcuts, 8vo. 12s. 6d.

The Dolomite Mountains. Excursions through Tyrol, Carinthia, Carniola, and Friuli.
By J. Gilbert and G. C. Churchill, F.R.G.S.
With Illustrations. Sq. cr. 8vo. 21s.

The Alpine Club Map of the Chain of Mont Blanc, from an actual Survey in 1863–1864.
By A. Adams-Reilly, F.R.G.S. M.A.C.
In Chromolithography, on extra stout drawing paper 10s. or mounted on canvas in a folding case, 12s. 6d.

The Alpine Club Map of the Valpelline, the Val Tournanche, and the Southern Valleys of the Chain of Monte Rosa, from actual Survey.
By A. Adams-Reilly, F.R.G.S. M.A.C.
Price 6s. on extra Stout Drawing Paper, or 7s. 6d. mounted in a Folding Case.

Untrodden Peaks and Unfrequented Valleys; a Midsummer Ramble among the Dolomites.
By Amelia B. Edwards.
With numerous Illustrations. 8vo. 21s.

The Alpine Club Map of Switzerland, with parts of the Neighbouring Countries, on the scale of four miles to an Inch.
Edited by R. C. Nichols, F.S.A. F.R.G.S.
In Four Sheets, in Portfolio, 42s. or mounted in a Case, 52s. 6d. Each Sheet may be had separately, price 12s. or mounted in a Case, 15s.

The Alpine Guide.
By John Ball, M.R.I.A. late President of the Alpine Club.
Post 8vo. with Maps and other Illustrations.

Eastern Alps.
Price 10s. 6d.

Central Alps, including all the Oberland District.
Price 7s. 6d.

Western Alps, including Mont Blanc, Monte Rosa, Zermatt, &c.
Price 6s. 6d.

Introduction on Alpine Travelling in general, and on the Geology of the Alps.
Price 1s. Either of the Three Volumes or Parts of the 'Alpine Guide' may be had with this Introduction prefixed, 1s. extra.

Guide to the Pyrenees, for the use of Mountaineers.
By Charles Packe.

Second Edition, with Maps &c. and Appendix. Crown 8vo. 7s. 6d.

How to See Norway; embodying the Experience of Six Summer Tours in that Country, with Hints on the Choice of Routes and the Localities of the best Scenery.
By J. R. Campbell.

With Map and 5 Woodcuts, fcp. 8vo. 5s.

Visits to Remarkable Places, and Scenes illustrative of striking Passages in English History and Poetry.
By William Howitt.

2 vols. 8vo. Woodcuts, 25s.

Forty Years of American Life.
By T. L. Nichols, M.D. Author of 'Human Physiology,' 'Esoteric Anthropology,' &c.

New Edition, revised and condensed. Crown 8vo. 10s. 6d.

WORKS of FICTION.

Whispers from Fairyland.
By the Rt. Hon. E. H. Knatchbull - Hugessen, M.P. Author of 'Stories for my Children,' &c.

With 9 Illustrations from Original Designs engraved on Wood by G. Pearson. Crown 8vo. price 6s.

Lady Willoughby's Diary during the Reign of Charles the First, the Protectorate, and the Restoration.

Crown 8vo. 7s. 6d.

Centulle, a Tale of Pau.
By Denys Shyne Lawlor.

Crown 8vo. 10s. 6d.

The Folk-Lore of Rome, collected by Word of Mouth from the People.
By R. H. Busk.

Crown 8vo. 12s. 6d.

Cyllene; or, The Fall of Paganism.
By Henry Sneyd, M.A.

2 vols. post 8vo. 14s.

Becker's Gallus; or Roman Scenes of the Time of Augustus.

Post 8vo. 7s. 6d.

Becker's Charicles: Illustrative of Private Life of the Ancient Greeks.

Post 8vo. 7s. 6d.

Tales of the Teutonic Lands.
By Rev. G. W. Cox, M.A.
and E. H. Jones.
Crown 8vo. 10s. 6d.

Tales of Ancient Greece.
By the Rev. G. W. Cox,
M.A.
Crown 8vo. 6s. 6d.

The Modern Novelist's Library.
Atherstone Priory, 2s. boards; 2s. 6d. cloth.
The Burgomaster's Family, 2s. boards;
2s. 6d. cloth.
MELVILLE'S Digby Grand, 2s. and 2s. 6d.
———— Gladiators, 2s. and 2s.6d.
———— Good for Nothing,2s. & 2s. 6d.
———— Holmby House, 2s. and 2s. 6d.
———— Interpreter, 2s. and 2s. 6d.
———— Kate Coventry, 2s. and 2s. 6d.
———— Queen's Maries, 2s. and 2s. 6d.
———— General Bounce, 2s. and 2s. 6d.
TROLLOPE'S Warden, 1s. 6d. and 2s.
———— Barchester Towers, 2s. and
2s. 6d.
BRAMLEY-MOORE'S Six Sisters of the Valleys, 2s. boards; 2s. 6d. cloth.

Novels and Tales.
By the Right Hon. Benjamin Disraeli, M.P.
Cabinet Editions, complete in Ten Volumes,
crown 8vo. 6s. each, as follows :—

Lothair, 6s.	Venetia, 6s.
Coningsby, 6s.	Alroy, Ixion, &c. 6s.
Sybil, 6s.	Young Duke, &c. 6s.
Tancred, 6s.	Vivian Grey, 6s.
Henrietta Temple, 6s.	
Contarini Fleming, &c. 6s.	

Stories and Tales.
By Elizabeth M. Sewell,
Author of ' The Child's
First History of
Rome,' 'Principles
of Education,' &c.
Cabinet Edition, in Ten
Volumes :—

Amy Herbert, 2s. 6d.	Ivors, 2s. 6d.
Gertrude, 2s. 6d.	Katharine Ashton,
Earl's Daughter,	2s. 6d.
2s. 6d.	Margaret Percival,
Experience of Life,	3s. 6d.
2s. 6a.	Laneton Parsonage,
Cleve Hall, 2s. 6d.	3s. 6d.
Ursula, 3s. 6d.	

POETRY and THE DRAMA.

Ballads and Lyrics of Old France; with other Poems.
By A. Lang.
Square fcp. 8vo. 5s.

Moore's Lalla Rookh,
Tenniel's Edition, with 68
Wood Engravings.
Fcp. 4to. 21s.

Moore's Irish Melodies,
Maclise's Edition, with 161
Steel Plates.
Super-royal 8vo. 31s. 6d.

Miniature Edition of Moore's Irish Melodies, with Maclise's 161 *Illustrations reduced in Lithography.*
Imp. 16mo. 10s. 6d.

Milton's Lycidas and Epitaphium Damonis.
Edited, with Notes and
Introduction, by C. S.
Jerram, M.A.
Crown 8vo. 2s. 6d.

Lays of Ancient Rome; with Ivry and the Armada.
By the Right Hon. Lord Macaulay.
16mo. 3s. 6d.

Lord Macaulay's Lays of Ancient Rome. With 90 Illustrations on Wood from Drawings by G. Scharf.
Fcp. 4to. 21s.

Miniature Edition of Lord Macaulay's Lays of Ancient Rome, with Scharf's 90 Illustrations reduced in Lithography.
Imp. 16mo. 10s. 6d.

Horatii Opera, Library Edition, with English Notes, Marginal References and various Readings.
Edited by Rev. J. E. Yonge.
8vo. 21s.

Southey's Poetical Works with the Author's last Corrections and Additions.
Medium 8vo. with Portrait, 14s.

Bowdler's Family Shakspeare, cheaper Genuine Edition.
Complete in 1 vol. medium 8vo. large type, with 36 Woodcut Illustrations, 14s. or in 6 vols. fcp. 8vo. price 21s.

The Æneid of Virgil Translated into English Verse.
By J. Conington, M.A.
Crown 8vo. 9s.

Poems by Jean Ingelow.
2 vols. Fcp. 8vo. 10s.
FIRST SERIES, containing 'Divided,' 'The Star's Monument,' &c. 16th Thousand. Fcp. 8vo. 5s.
SECOND SERIES, 'A Story of Doom,' 'Gladys and her Island,' &c. 5th Thousand. Fcp. 8vo. 5s.

Poems by Jean Ingelow. First Series, with nearly 100 Woodcut Illustrations.
Fcp. 4to. 21s.

RURAL SPORTS, HORSE and CATTLE MANAGEMENT, &c.

Down the Road; or, Reminiscences of a Gentleman Coachman.
By C. T. S. Birch Reynardson.
With Twelve Chromolithographic Illustrations from Original Paintings by H. Alken. Medium 8vo. price 21s.

Blaine's Encyclopædia of Rural Sports; Complete Accounts, Historical, Practical, and Descriptive, of Hunting, Shooting, Fishing, Racing, &c.
With above 600 Woodcuts (20 from Designs by JOHN LEECH). 8vo. 21s.

A Book on Angling:
a Treatise on the Art of
Angling in every branch,
including full Illustrated
Lists of Salmon Flies.
By Francis Francis.
Post 8vo. Portrait and Plates, 15s.

Wilcocks's Sea-Fisher-
man: comprising the Chief
Methods of Hook and Line
Fishing, a glance at Nets,
and remarks on Boats and
Boating.
New Edition, with 80 Woodcuts.
Post 8vo. 12s. 6d.

The Ox, his Diseases and
their Treatment; with an
Essay on Parturition in the
Cow.
By J. R. Dobson, Memb.
R.C.V.S.
Crown 8vo. with Illustrations 7s. 6d.

A Treatise on Horse-
Shoeing and Lameness.
By J. Gamgee, Vet. Surg.
8vo. with 55 Woodcuts, 10s. 6d.

Youatt on the Horse.
Revised and enlarged by W.
Watson, M.R.C.V.S.
8vo. Woodcuts, 12s. 6d.

Youatt's Work on the
Dog, revised and enlarged.
8vo. Woodcuts, 6s.

Horses and Stables.
By Colonel F. Fitzwygram,
XV. the King's Hussars.
With 24 Plates of Illustrations. 8vo. 10s. 6d.

The Dog in Health and
Disease.
By Stonehenge.
With 73 Wood Engravings. Square crown
8vo. 7s. 6d.

The Greyhound.
By Stonehenge.
Revised Edition, with 25 Portraits of Grey-
hounds, &c. Square crown 8vo. 15s.

Stables and Stable Fit-
tings.
By W. Miles, Esq.
Imp. 8vo. with 13 Plates, 15s.

The Horse's Foot, and
how to keep it Sound.
By W. Miles, Esq.
Ninth Edition. Imp. 8vo. Woodcuts, 12s. 6d.

A Plain Treatise on
Horse-shoeing.
By W. Miles, Esq.
Sixth Edition. Post 8vo. Woodcuts, 2s. 6d.

Remarks on Horses'
Teeth, addressed to Pur-
chasers.
By W. Miles, Esq.
Post 8vo. 1s. 6d.

The Fly-Fisher's Ento-
mology.
By Alfred Ronalds.
With 20 coloured Plates. 8vo. 14s.

The Dead Shot, or Sports-
man's Complete Guide.
By Marksman.
Fcp. 8vo. with Plates, 5s.

WORKS of UTILITY and GENERAL INFORMATION.

Maunder's Treasury of Knowledge and Library of Reference; comprising an English Dictionary and Grammar, Universal Gazetteer, Classical Dictionary, Chronology, Law Dictionary, Synopsis of the Peerage, Useful Tables,&c.
Fcp. 8vo. 6s.

Maunder's Biographical Treasury.
Latest Edition, reconstructed and partly rewritten, with about 1,000 additional Memoirs, by *W. L. R. Cates.*
Fcp. 8vo. 6s.

Maunder's Scientific and Literary Treasury; a Popular Encyclopædia of Science, Literature, and Art.
New Edition, in part rewritten, with above 1,000 new articles, by *J. Y. Johnson.*
Fcp. 8vo. 6s.

Maunder's Treasury of Geography, Physical, Historical, Descriptive, and Political.
Edited by *W. Hughes, F.R.G.S.*
With 7 Maps and 16 Plates. Fcp. 8vo. 6s.

Maunder's Historical Treasury; General Introductory Outlines of Universal History, and a Series of Separate Histories.
Revised by the Rev. *G. W. Cox, M.A.*
Fcp. 8vo. 6s.

Maunder's Treasury of Natural History; or Popular Dictionary of Zoology.
Revised and corrected Edition. Fcp. 8vo. with 900 Woodcuts, 6s.

The Treasury of Bible Knowledge; being a Dictionary of the Books, Persons, Places, Events, and other Matters of which mention is made in Holy Scripture.
By Rev. *J. Ayre, M.A.*
With Maps, 15 Plates, and numerous Woodcuts. Fcp. 8vo. 6s.

Collieries and Colliers: a Handbook of the Law and Leading Cases relating thereto.
By *J. C. Fowler.*
Third Edition. Fcp. 8vo. 7s. 6d.

The Theory and Practice of Banking.
By *H. D. Macleod, M.A.*
Second Edition. 2 vols. 8vo. 30s.

Modern Cookery for Private Families, reduced to a System of Easy Practice in a Series of carefully-tested Receipts.

By Eliza Acton.

With 8 Plates & 150 Woodcuts. Fcp. 8vo. 6s.

A Practical Treatise on Brewing; with Formulæ for Public Brewers, and Instructions for Private Families.

By W. Black.

Fifth Edition. 8vo. 10s. 6d.

Three Hundred Original Chess Problems and Studies.

By Jas. Pierce, M.A. and W. T. Pierce.

With many Diagrams. Sq. fcp. 8vo. 7s. 6d. Supplement, price 3s.

The Theory of the Modern Scientific Game of Whist.

By W. Pole, F.R.S.

Seventh Edition. Fcp. 8vo. 2s. 6d.

The Cabinet Lawyer; a Popular Digest of the Laws of England, Civil, Criminal, and Constitutional.

Twenty-fourth Edition, corrected and extended. Fcp. 8vo. 9s.

Chess Openings.

By F. W. Longman, Balliol College, Oxford.

Second Edition, revised. Fcp. 8vo. 2s. 6d.

Pewtner's Comprehensive Specifier; a Guide to the Practical Specification of every kind of Building-Artificer's Work.

Edited by W. Young.

Crown 8vo. 6s.

Protection from Fire and Thieves. Including the Construction of Locks, Safes, Strong-Room, and Fire-proof Buildings; Burglary, and the Means of Preventing it; Fire, its Detection, Prevention, and Extinction; &c.

By G. H. Chubb, Assoc. Inst. C.E.

With 32 Woodcuts. Cr. 8vo. 5s.

Hints to Mothers on the Management of their Health during the Period of Pregnancy and in the Lying-in Room.

By Thomas Bull, M.D.

Fcp. 8vo. 5s.

The Maternal Management of Children in Health and Disease.

By Thomas Bull, M.D.

Fcp. 8vo. 5s.

INDEX.

Spottiswoode & Co , Printers, New-street Square, London